"*The Forgotten Ways* is a compelling challenge to awaken the church's innate entrepreneurial instinct and propel it into the fringes of our emerging culture. I recommend it highly, especially to those endowed with the boldness to align the church's operating system with the missional heart of God."

—**Andrew Jones,** www.tallskinnykiwi.com

"There are few books that one can describe as markers in the field of mission—this is one such book. It is essential reading for all those who are grappling with the key issue of what the church can and must become."

—**Martin Robinson,** author of *Planting Mission-Shaped Churches Today*

"This is a provocative and insightful contribution to the discovery of effective missional engagement with post-Christendom Western culture. Grounded in Alan's own experience as a missionary pastor and illustrated by examples from various places, *The Forgotten Ways* challenges and equips both inherited and emerging churches to recover the dynamic of a missional movement."

—**Stuart Murray Williams,** author of *Church after Christendom* and *Changing Mission: Learning from the Newer Churches*

"It is AD 30 all over again. While many church leaders are trying desperately to retrofit institutional expressions of Christianity in hopes of achieving better results, Al Hirsch helps us understand the necessity for us to reengage the movement in its primal missional form."

—**Reggie McNeal,** author of *Practicing Greatness: 7 Disciplines of Extraordinary Spiritual Leaders* and *The Present Future: Six Tough Questions for the Church*

"With a scholar's attention to detail and the critical lessons of history, as well as a first-century missionary's creative passion, Alan Hirsch recalls us to a faith life that is flexible, fast-moving, and unbound. He rescues the term 'missional' from the mass grave of church buzzwords in the process."

—**Greg Paul,** author of *God in the Alley: Being and Seeing Jesus in a Broken World*; founder and director of Sanctuary Ministries in Toronto

"Alan has been shattering paradigms and challenging ideas for years. Now, in *The Forgotten Ways*, Alan describes missional movements and challenges us to reorder the church around its mission, all filtered through his deeply personal experience. You will be provoked, challenged, and motivated to embrace the missional DNA and incarnational impulse of the early church in your own life and ministry."

—**Ed Stetzer,** author of *Breaking the Missional Code* and
Planting Missional Churches

"The age of Christendom is over, but a renewed age of true Christian movements and discipleship is dawning. Churches and leaders who don't pay attention to the analysis presented here are liable to be deceived into a Christianity that is either locked in the passing Christendom mode or, conversely, lost in mere emerging fads. The biblically based and Jesus-centered focus of this book makes it stand out above dozens of other books on similar themes. It must be read and pondered. Alan Hirsch's analysis is on target historically, biblically, and theologically."

—**Howard A. Snyder,** author of *Radical Renewal,*
The Community of the King, and *Models of the Kingdom*

THE FORGOTTEN WAYS

+reactivating the missional church

ALAN HIRSCH

Brazos Press
Grand Rapids, Michigan

© 2006 by Alan Hirsch

Published by Brazos Press
a division of Baker Publishing Group
P.O. Box 6287, Grand Rapids, MI 49516-6287
www.brazospress.com

Published in Australia and New Zealand by Strand Publishing, P.O. Box 5067, Erina Fair NSW 2250, Australia

Sixth printing, March 2008

Printed in the United States of America

Library of Congress Cataloging-in-Publication Data
Hirsch, Alan, 1959-
    The forgotten ways : reactivating the missional church / Alan Hirsch.
        p.   cm.
    Includes bibliographical references and index.
    ISBN 10: 1-58743-164-5 (pbk.)
    ISBN 978-1-58743-164-7 (pbk.)
    1. Church. 2. Missions. 3. Postmodernism-Religious aspects-Christianity. I. Title.
BV600.3.H57 2006
266-dc22   2006015904

This book is dedicated to the loving memory of my wonderful *Jewish Mama*, Elaine, rescued by the Messiah in the fullness of time. She lives on, not only in God, but in the life of her grateful and adoring son. Thanks, Mom!

So teach us to number our days, that we may apply *our* hearts unto wisdom.

Psalm 90:12

Special thanks . . .

To my beloved Debra, who has patiently loved a sometimes unlovable man and has shown me what it means to generously serve the poor.

To Pat Kavanagh—you will always be my pastor.

To the South Melbourne Restoration Community for giving me such a wonderful experience of communally expressed grace and forgiveness.

To my many colleagues in the various expressions of the Churches of Christ for always giving me enough rope to hang myself. Especially to Don Smith for believing in me and making space for an alien.

To my comrades in the Forge Mission Training Network, a very special thanks. I consider this work my legacy and contribution to the evolving DNA of our wonderful little movement. When I am sharing with you in this special work, I feel God's great pleasure.

To Dean Phelan, Paul Steele, and Andy Barker for generously sponsoring and helping develop the missional fitness tests and APEPT profiling system on the Web site.

contents

Foreword by Leonard Sweet   11

Section One: The Making of a Missionary
Introduction   15
A Journey of a Thousand Miles Begins with a Single Question
A Sneak Preview
Method in the Madness

1. Setting the Scene, Part 1: Confessions of a Frustrated Missionary   27
"South"
Phase 1: From Death to Chaos
Phase 2: Becoming a Church-Planting Church
Phase 3: From a Church to an Organic Movement

2. Setting the Scene, Part 2: Denominational and Translocal
Perspectives   49
A View from the Chopper
Christendom-schmissendom
A Missionary's Take
We've Always Done It This Way . . . er . . . Haven't We?
"It's Church, Jim, but Not as We Know It"
Who Put the M in the EMC?

Section Two: A Journey to the Heart of Apostolic Genius

Introduction   75

3. The Heart of It All: Jesus Is Lord   83
   Distilling the Message
   Hear, O Israel
   Jesus Is Lord
   The Heart of Things
   How Far Is Too Far?

4. Disciple Making   101
   "Little Jesus" in Disneyland
   The Conspiracy of "Little Jesus"
   Embodiment and Transmission
   Inspirational Leadership
   Leadership as an Extension of Discipleship
   Hitting the Road with Jesus

5. Missional-Incarnational Impulse   127
   Theological Roots
   Missional-Incarnational
   Missional Ecclesiology or . . . Putting First Things First

6. Apostolic Environment   149
   If You Want Missional Church, Then . . .
   An Apostolic Job Description
   Field of Dreams
   Creating Webs of Meaning
   A Stroke of (Apostolic) Genius
   The Final Word

7. Organic Systems   179
   Get a Life: The Church as a Living System
   The Problem of Institutions
   A Movement Ethos
   Networked Structures
   Viruslike Growth
   Let's Talk about Sex
   Finally

8. *Communitas,* Not Community   217
   "The Community for me"? or "Me for the Community"?
   Liminality and Communitas
   The Bible and Communitas

It's Everywhere! It's Everywhere!
The Mythos of Communitas
Artificial Environments and the Church
The Future and the Shaping of Things to Come
Mission as Organizing Principle
Beyond the Either-Or Church
So, Follow the Yellow Brick Road

Conclusion   243

Addendum and Glossary: A Crash Course in Chaos   247
We Just Got a New Set of Spectacles
Changing the Story
Survival Is Not Enough
How, Then, Shall We Live?
Come Forth! A Case Study in Emergent Structures

Glossary of Key Terms   273

Bibliography   287

Index   293

foreword

Have You Defragged Recently?

Sometimes our hard drives need defragmenting. Data entered on our hard drive isn't always done neatly. The more files you have, and the more programs you download, the more your hard drive gets scrambled by confusing, scattered, random inputs that get sprayed over lots of space. Computer crashes, power outages, and stalled programs just add to the fragmentation.

The harder your hard drive has to work to retrieve the original information, the slower it becomes, the more blurred the pictures are, and the more resistant everything is. As a serial procrastinator, I tend to put off my defragging until the computer almost grinds to a halt. Defragging requires I dedicate the computer to doing nothing but cleaning up the confusion my messes and misses have caused. This housecleaning can take hours. But once I go through the defragging process, my hard drive recovers its speed, and my images once again snap, crackle, and pop with clarity and conviction.

Christianity has undergone untold crashes and clashes in the past two thousand years. In the last five hundred years its original hard drive has wiped out so many times, especially in the West, that it has almost ground to a halt. In *The Forgotten Ways*, a voice from the place that gets to the future first has provided twenty-first-century Christianity with the best disk defragger available. Not only does Alan Hirsch bring a freshness to subjects that have been treated so often they feel used up and worn down, but he also gives us a vocabulary and vision that can help restore Christianity's original hard drive to its Apostolic Genius, which is the net result of the convergence of the six organic elements of mDNA (where m=missional). "What DNA does for biological systems," Hirsch writes, "mDNA does for ecclesial ones."

But first we will need to stop doing what we're doing and let this defrag-ger do its work on our minds and ministries. Hirsch has some unsettling things to say about leadership, consumerism, middle-class culture, Al Qaeda, community, seminaries, and the mega-church. He forces us to takes seri-ously the missional situation we're in, and in the process he cleans up the phrase "missional church" from frequent mishandling. We will also need to give up singing songs like "Shelter in the Time of Storm"; to stop pining after balance, safety, and stillness; and to stop being afraid to mix it up in the cultural zeitgeist or to be in the thick of things. It is one thing to create a countercultural community or a Christian subculture, but it is a much more difficult thing to live as an "incarnational-missional *communitas*" in the midst of a culture and not be bound by its dictates and decrees: to be "in" it, not "of" it, but not "out of it" either. When you open the windows to the world, as Pope John XXIII did, maybe we aren't letting the zeitgeist in so much as letting the Holy Spirit out to blow where it wills.

The church we will get back when Hirsch's defragger is done, however, is a church that engages the world while safeguarding the tradition. He calls it the EMC or Emerging Missional Church. I'll be referring to this book using the same letters, but with an addition annotation.

Like Einstein, whom he likes to quote, Hirsch has discovered the formula that unlocks the secrets of the ecclesial universe like Einstein's simple three letters and one number formula ($E=mc^2$) unlocked the secrets of the phys-ical universe. There are some books good enough to read to the end. There are only a few books good enough to read to the end of time. *The Forgotten Ways* is one of them.

Leonard Sweet

THE MAKING OF A MISSIONARY

introduction

A church which pitches its tents without constantly looking out for new ho-
rizons, which does not continually strike camp, is being untrue to its calling.
. . . [We must] play down our longing for certainty, accept what is risky, and
live by improvisation and experiment.

Hans Küng, *The Church as the People of God*

After a time of decay comes the turning point. The powerful light that has
been banished returns. There is movement, but it is not brought about by
force. . . . The movement is natural, arising spontaneously. The old is discarded
and the new is introduced. Both measures accord with the time; therefore no
harm results.

Ancient Chinese Saying

Imagine there was a power that lies hidden at the very heart of God's people.
Suppose this power was built into the initiating "stem cell" of the church
by the Holy Spirit but was somehow buried and lost through centuries of
neglect and disuse. Imagine that if rediscovered, this hidden power could
unleash remarkable energies that could propel Christianity well into the
twenty-second century—a missional equivalent to unlocking the power
of the atom. Is this not something that we who love God, his people, and
his cause would give just about anything to recover? I now believe that the
idea of latent inbuilt missional potencies is not a mere fantasy; in fact there
are primal forces that lie latent in every Jesus community and in every true
believer. Not only does such a thing exist, but it is a clearly identifiable phenomenon that has energized history's most outstanding Jesus movements,
perhaps the *most* remarkable expression of which is very much with us
today. This extraordinary power is being recovered in certain expressions

of Western Christianity, but not without significant challenge to, and resistance from, the current way in which we do things.

The fact that you have started reading this book will mean not only that you are interested in the search for a more authentic expression of *ecclesia* (the NT word for *church*), but you are in some sense aware of the dramatic changes in worldview that have been taking place in general culture over the last fifty years or so. Whatever one may call it, this shift from the modern to the postmodern, or from solid modernity to liquid modernity, has generally been difficult for the church to accept. We find ourselves lost in a perplexing global jungle where our well-used cultural and theological maps don't seem to work anymore. It seems as if we have woken up to find ourselves in contact with a strange and unexpected reality that seems to defy our usual ways of dealing with issues of the church and its mission. All this amounts to a kind of ecclesial future shock, where we are left wandering in a world we can't recognize anymore. In the struggle to grasp our new reality, churches and church leaders have become painfully aware that our inherited concepts, our language, and indeed our whole way of thinking are inadequate to describe what is going on both in and around us. The problems raised in such a situation are not merely intellectual but together amount to an intense spiritual, emotional, and existential crisis.

The truth is that the twenty-first century is turning out to be a highly complex phenomenon where terrorism, paradigmatic technological innovation, an unsustainable environment, rampant consumerism, discontinuous change, and perilous ideologies confront us at every point. In the face of this, even the most confident among us would have to admit, in our more honest moments, that the church as we know it faces a very significant adaptive challenge. The overwhelming majority of church leaders today report that they feel it is getting much harder for their communities to negotiate the increasing complexities in which they find themselves. As a result, the church is on massive, long-trended decline in the West. In this situation, we have to ask ourselves probing questions: "Will more of the same do the trick? Do we have the inherited resources to deal with this situation? Can we simply rework the tried and true Christendom understanding of church that we so love and understand, and finally, in an ultimate tweak of the system, come up with the winning formula?"[1]

I have to confess that I do not think that the inherited formulas will work anymore. And what is more, I know I am not alone in this view. There is a massive roaming of the mind going on in our day as the search for alternatives heats up. However, most of the new thinking as it relates to the future of Christianity in the West only highlights our dilemma and

---

1. For a definition of Christendom, see the glossary. The nature, history, and structure of Christendom are more fully explored in chapter 2.

generally proposes solutions that are little more than revisions of past approaches and techniques. Even much of the thinking about the so-called emerging church leaves the prevailing assumptions of church and mission intact and simply focuses on the issue of theology and spirituality in a postmodern setting. This amounts to a reworking of the theological "software" while ignoring the "hardware" as well as "operating system" of the church. In my opinion, this will not be enough to get us through. As we anxiously gaze into the future and delve back into our history and traditions to retrieve missiological tools from the Christendom toolbox, many of us are left with the sinking feeling that this is simply not going to work. The tools and techniques that fitted previous eras of Western history simply don't seem to work any longer. What we need now is a new set of tools. A new "paradigm"—a new vision of reality: a fundamental change in our thoughts, perceptions, and values, especially as they relate to our view of the church and mission.

And it's not that reaching into our past is not part of the solution. It is. The issue is simply that we generally don't go back far enough; or rather, that we don't delve *deep* enough for our answers. Every now and again we do get glimpses of an answer, but because of the radical and disturbing nature of the remedy we retreat to the safety of the familiar and the controllable. The *real* answers, if we have the courage to search for and apply them, are usually more radical than we are normally given to think, and because of this they undermine our sense of place in the world, with its status quo—not something that the Western church has generally been too comfortable with. But we are now living in a time when only a solution that goes to the very roots of what it means to be Jesus's people will do.

The conditions facing us in the twenty-first century not only pose a threat to our existence but also present us with an extraordinary opportunity to discover ourselves in a way that orients us to this complex challenge in ways that are resonant with an ancient energy. This energy not only links us with the powerful impulses of the original church, but also gives us wings with which to fly. The book in your hands now is one that could be labeled under the somewhat technical, and seemingly boring, category of *missional ecclesiology*, because it explores the nature of the Christian movements, and therefore the church as it is shaped by Jesus and his mission. But don't be fooled by the drab terminology—missional ecclesiology is dynamite. Mainly because the church (the *ecclesia*), when true to its real calling, when it is on about what God is on about, is by far and away the most potent force for transformational change the world has ever seen. It has been that before, is that now, and will be that again. This book is written in the hope that the church in the West can, by the power of the Holy Spirit, arouse and reengage that amazing power that lies within us.

A Journey of a Thousand Miles Begins with a Single Question

About four years ago I attended a seminar on missional church where the speaker asked a question. "How many Christians do you think there were in the year AD 100?" He then asked, "How many Christians do you think there were just before Constantine came on the scene, say, AD 310?"[2] Here is the somewhat surprising answer.

| AD 100 | as few as 25,000 Christians |
| AD 310 | up to 20,000,000 Christians |

He then asked the question that has haunted me to this day: "How did they do this? How did they grow from being a small movement to the most significant religious force in the Roman Empire in two centuries?" Now *that's* a question to initiate a journey! And delving into this question drove me to the discovery of what I will call Apostolic Genius (the built-in life force and guiding mechanism of God's people) and the living components or elements that make it up.[3] These components I have tagged missional DNA, or mDNA, for short.

So let me ask *you* the question—how *did* the early Christians do it? And before you respond, here are some qualifications you must factor into your answer.

- *They were an illegal religion throughout this period.* At best, they were tolerated; at the very worst they were very severely persecuted.
- *They didn't have any church buildings as we know them.* While archaeologists have discovered chapels dating from this period, they were definitely exceptions to the rule, and they tended to be very small converted houses.
- *They didn't even have the scriptures as we know them.* They were putting the canon together during this period.
- *They didn't have an institution or the professional form of leadership normally associated with it.* At times of relative calm, prototypical elements of institution did appear, but by what we consider institutional, these were at best pre-institutional.

2. Rodney Stark is considered to be the authority on these issues, and in his book called *The Rise of Christianity* he suggests an array of possible answers ranging from conservative to broad estimates. I have tried to average these estimates (according to Stark between 40 and 50 percent, exponentially per decade) and compare this with other sources. These are my findings. See R. Stark, *The Rise of Christianity: How the Obscure, Marginal, Jesus Movement Became the Dominant Religious Force in the Western World in a Few Centuries* (San Francisco: HarperCollins: 1996), 6–13.

3. See glossary.

- *They didn't have seeker-sensitive services, youth groups, worship bands, seminaries, commentaries, etc.*
- *They actually made it hard to join the church.* By the late second century, aspiring converts had to undergo a significant initiation period to prove they were worthy.

In fact they had none of the things we would ordinarily employ to solve the problems of the church, and yet they grew from 25,000 to 20 million in 200 years! *So,* how *did* the early church do it? In answering that question, we can perhaps find the answer to the question for the church and mission in our day and in our context. For herein lies the powerful mystery of church in its most authentic form.

But before the example of the early Christian movement can be dismissed as a freak of history, there is another, perhaps even more astounding manifestation of Apostolic Genius, that unique and explosive power inherent in all of God's people, in our own time—namely, the underground church in China. Theirs is a truly remarkable story: About the time when Mao Tse-tung took power and initiated the systemic purge of religion from society, the church in China, which was well established and largely modeled on Western forms due to colonization, was estimated to number about 2 million adherents. As part of this systematic persecution, Mao banished all foreign missionaries and ministers, nationalized all church property, killed all the senior leaders, either killed or imprisoned all second- and third-level leaders, banned all public meetings of Christians with the threat of death or torture, and then proceeded to perpetrate one of the cruelest persecutions of Christians on historical record.

The explicit aim of the Cultural Revolution was to obliterate Christianity (and all religion) from China. At the end of the reign of Mao and his system in the late seventies, and the subsequent lifting of the so-called Bamboo Curtain in the early eighties, foreign missionaries and church officials were allowed back into the country, albeit under strict supervision. They expected to find the church decimated and the disciples a weak and battered people. On the contrary, they discovered that Christianity had flourished beyond all imagination. The estimates *then* were about 60 million Christians in China, and counting! And it has grown significantly since then. David Aikman, former Beijing bureau chief for *Time* magazine, suggests in his book *Jesus in Beijing* that Christians may number as many as 80 million.[4] If anything, in the Chinese phenomenon we are witnessing the most significant transformational Christian movement in the history of the church. And remember, not unlike the early church, these people had very few Bibles (at times they shared only one page to a house church and then swapped that page with

4. Philip Yancey, "Discreet and Dynamic: Why, with No Apparent Resources, Chinese Churches Thrive," *Christianity Today*, July 2004, 72.

another house group). They had no professional clergy, no official leadership structures, no central organization, no mass meetings, and yet they grew like mad. How is this possible? How did they do it?[5]

But we can observe similar growth patterns in other historical movements. Steve Addison notes that by the end of John Wesley's lifetime one in thirty English men and women had become Methodists.[6] In 1776 fewer than 2 percent of Americans were Methodists. By 1850, the movement claimed the allegiance of 34 percent of the population. How did they do it? The twentieth century saw the rise of Pentecostalism as one of the most rapidly growing missionary movements in the history of the church. The movement has grown from humble beginnings in the early 1900s to 400 million by the end of the twentieth century. It is estimated that by 2050 Pentecostalism will have one billion adherents worldwide.[7] How did they do it?

These are dangerous stories, because they subvert us into a journey that will call us to a more radical expression of Christianity than the one we currently experience. It is the central task of this book to try and give a name to these phenomena and to try to identify the elements that constitute it. The phenomenon present in these dangerous stories I call Apostolic Genius, and the elements that make it up I have named mDNA; I will define these more fully later. The object of this book is to explore Apostolic Genius and to try to interpret it for our own missional context and situation in the West. These two key examples (the early church and the Chinese church) have been chosen not only because they are truly remarkable movements, but also because one is ancient and the other contemporary, so we can observe Apostolic Genius in two radically different contexts. I have also chosen them because both movements faced significant threats to their survival; in both cases this took the form of systematic persecution. This is significant because, as will explained later, the church in the West faces its own form of adaptive challenge as we negotiate the complexities of the twenty-first century—one that threatens our very survival.

Persecution drove both the early Christian movement and the Chinese church to discover their truest nature as an apostolic people. Persecution forced them away from any possible reliance on any form of centralized religious institution and caused them to live closer to, and more consistently

5. Another remarkable movement, one that changed the destiny of Europe and beyond, was the Celtic movement. While it is outside the scope of this book to explore the nature of the Irish mission to the West, there are many similarities to that of the early church and of the Chinese church.

6. Stephen Addison, "Movement Dynamics, Keys to the Expansion and Renewal of the Church in Mission," unpublished manuscript, 2003, 5.

7. Grant McClung, "Pentecostals: The Sequel" in *Christianity Today*, April 2006 (http://www.christianitytoday.com/ct/2006/004/7.30.html); see also, Walter J. Hollenwager, "From Azusa Street to the Toronto Phenomena: Historical Roots of the Pentecostal Movement, Concilium 3, ed. Jürgen Moltmann and Karl-Josef Kuschel (London: SCM, 1996): 3, quoted in Veli-Matti Karkkainen, "Pentecostal Missiology in Ecumenical Perspective: Contributions, Challenges, Controversies" in *International Review of Mission* (88), July 1999, 207.

with, their primal message, namely the gospel. We have to assume that if one is willing to die for being a follower of Jesus, then in all likelihood that person is a real believer. This persecution, under the sovereignty of God, acted as a means to keep these movements true to their faith and reliant on God—it purified them from the dross and any unnecessary churchly paraphernalia. It was by *being true to* the gospel that they unleashed the power of Apostolic Genius. And this is a huge lesson for us: as we face our own challenges, we will need to be sure about our faith and in whom it is we trust, or else risk the eventual demise of Christianity as a religious force in Western history—witness Europe in the last hundred years.

In pursuit of the answer to *that question*, the question of how these phenomenal Jesus movements actually did it, I have become convinced that the power that manifested itself in the dangerous stories of these two remarkable movements is available to us as well. And the awakening of that dormant potential has something to do with the strange mixture of the passionate love of God, prayer, and incarnational practice. Add to this mix the following: appropriate modes of leadership (as expressed in Ephesians 4), the recovery of radical discipleship, relevant forms of organization and structures, and the appropriate conditions for these to be able to catalyze. When these factors come together, the situation is ripe for something remarkable to take place.

To perhaps nail down this rather elusive concept of dormant (or latent) potentials, recall the story of *The Wizard of Oz*. The central character in this well-loved movie is Dorothy, who was transported in a big tornado from Kansas to the magical Land of Oz. Wanting to return home, she gets guidance from Glinda, the Good Witch of the North, who advises her to walk to the Emerald City and there consult the Wizard. On the yellow brick road she acquires three companions: the Scarecrow, who hopes the Wizard will be able to give him some brains; the Tin Woodsman, who wants the Wizard to give him a heart; and the Cowardly Lion, who hopes to acquire some courage. After surviving some dangerous encounters with the Wicked Witch of the West and numerous other nasty creatures, they eventually make it to see the Wizard, only to find out he is a hoax. They leave the Emerald City brokenhearted. But the Wicked Witch, perceiving the magic in Dorothy's ruby slippers, won't leave them alone. After a final encounter with the Wicked Witch and her minions, they overcome the source of evil and thereby liberate Oz. But through all their ordeals and in their final victory they discover that in fact they already have what they were looking for—in fact they had it all along. The Scarecrow is very clever, the Tinman has real heart, and the Lion turns out to be very brave and courageous after all. They didn't need the Wizard after all; what they needed was a situation that forced them to discover (or to activate) that which was already in them. They had what they were all looking for, only they didn't realize it. To cap it off, Dorothy had her answer to her wish all along; she had the capacity to return home to Kansas all along . . . in her ruby slippers. By clicking them together three times, she is transported back to her home in Kansas.

This story highlights the central assumption in this book and gives a hint to why it has been called *The Forgotten Ways*: namely, that all God's people carry within themselves the same potencies that energized the early Christian movement and that are currently manifest in the underground Chinese church. Apostolic Genius (the primal missional potencies of the gospel and of God's people) lies dormant in you, me, and every local church that seeks to follow Jesus faithfully in any time. We have quite simply forgotten how to access and trigger it. This book is written to help us identify its constituent elements and to help us to (re)activate it so that we might once again truly be a truly transformative Jesus movement in the West.

A Sneak Preview

There is a glossary of terms at the back of the book to assist the reader with definitions and technical terms that are found throughout. There is also an addendum (appropriately called "A Crash Course in Chaos"), which, although not essential in the flow of the text, nonetheless incorporates material that informs much of the present work. We can learn an astonishing amount about life, living systems, adaptation, and organizations from the study of nature and organic systems, and therefore I strongly suggest the reader tussle with it. But put on your helmets . . . it *is* a crash course, after all.

As will become clear throughout this book, I am committed to the idea of translating best practices in mission developed over the last century in the two-thirds world into that of the first world. This has aptly been called *missions-to-the-first-world* approach, and you will find that I am an ardent believer. Although this book is primarily about the mission of the whole people of God, mission is not limited to the corporate mission of the local church or denomination. Mission must take place in and through every aspect of life. And this is done by all Christians everywhere. Both forms of mission—the apostolic mission of the community—as well as the individual expression of mission by God's people must be activated if we are to become a truly missional church.

I have long been a student of the nature of movements both social and religious. I have tried to learn what exactly it is that makes movements tick, and what makes them so effective in the spreading of their message (as opposed to the more static institution). It is by recovering a genuine movement ethos that we can restore something of the dynamism of significant Jesus movements in history.[8] The reader will discern this fascination with movements all the way through the book.

8. I will use the term Jesus movements in a way that approximates what David Garrison calls church planting movements. He defines these as "a rapid mobilization of indigenous

Another feature of this work is the consistent critique of religious institutionalism. Because this could be unsettling to some, a word of clarification is needed to avoid unnecessary misunderstandings later on. I am critical of institutionalism not because I think it is a bad idea, but only because through my study of the phenomenal Jesus movements I have come to the unnerving conclusion that God's people are more potent by far when they have little of what we would recognize as church institution in their life together. For clarity, therefore, there needs to be a clear distinction between necessary organizational structure and institutionalism. As we shall see, structures *are* absolutely necessary for cooperative human action as well as for maintaining some form of coherent social patterns. However, it seems that over time the increasingly impersonal structures of the institution assume roles, responsibilities, and authority that legitimately belong to the whole people of God in their local and grassroots expressions. It is at this point that things tend to go awry.[9]

The material itself is structured in two sections.

Section 1

Section 1 sets the scene by referring to my own narrative to assist the reader in tracking some of the seminal ideas and experiences that have guided my thinking and fired my imagination. By narrating some of central themes in my own story, I hope to take the reader through what can be called a missional reading of the situation of the church in the West. This will be spread out over the first two chapters: Chapter 1 looks at the issue from the perspective of a local practitioner trying to guide a complex, inner-city church planting movement through the massive changes that were going on around about us. Chapter 2 explores the missional situation **in which we find ourselves** from the perspective of a strategic and translocal level. These two perspectives, one macro and one micro, are vital in coming to grips with the concepts of a missional-incarnational church.

churches planting churches that sweeps through a people group or population." See David Garrison, *Church Planting Movements* (Midlothian, VA: WIGTake, 2004), 21

9. We can observe from history that through the consolidation and centralization of power, institutions begin to claim an authority that they were not originally given and have no theological right to claim. It is at this point that the structures of *ecclesia* become somewhat politicized and therefore repressive of any activities that threaten the status quo inherent in it. This is institutional*ism* and historically it has almost always meant the effective expulsion of its more creative and disparate elements (e.g., Wesley and Booth). This is not to say that there does not appear to be some divine order (structure) given to the church. But it is to say that this order is almost always legitimized directly through the community's corporate affirmation of calling, personal character, charismatic empowerment, and spiritual authority. It always remains personal and never moves purely to the institutional. Our role model need be none less than our Founder. It seems that only he can wield significant power without eventually misusing it.

Section 2

Here is where the rubber hits the road. *This* is the heart of the book as it attempts to describe Apostolic Genius and the constituent elements of mDNA that make it blaze up.[10] Those who are impatient, time-restricted, or who feel they do not need to undertake a missional reading of this situation of the church in our current context can jump to this section because the real substance of the book is found in section two anyway. However, I believe that the reader will be amply rewarded by reading chapters one and two, so I strongly encourage it. Einstein said that when the solution is simple, God is speaking. Following this advice, I have tried to discern quintessential elements that combine to create Apostolic Genius and to simplify them to the absolutely irreducible components. There are six simple but interrelating elements of mDNA, forming a complex and living structure.[11] These present us with a powerful paradigm grid with which we will be able to assess our current understandings and experiences of church and mission. They are:

- **Jesus Is Lord:** At the center and circumference of every significant Jesus movement there exists a very simple confession. Simple, but one that fully vibrates with the primal energies of the scriptural faith, namely, that of the claim of the One God over every aspect of every life, and the response of his people to that claim (Deut. 6:4–6ff.). The way that this was expressed in the New Testament and later movements was simply "Jesus Is Lord!" With this simple confession they changed the world.[12]
- **Disciple Making:** Essentially, this involves the irreplaceable and life-long task of becoming like Jesus by embodying his message. This is perhaps where many of our efforts fail. Disciple making is an irreplaceable core task of the church and needs to be structured into every church's basic formula (chapter 4).

10. When we get to assessing the presence of Apostolic Genius in our own churches, I will introduce the idea of *missional fitness* or *missional agility*. I am currently trying to produce an online research tool that will help churches assess this for their own contexts. See the website www.theforgottenways.org for details.

11. The reader might be able to add more elements in a particular case of phenomenal movements, but I believe that this might not be common in other cases of similar phenomenal movements—hence, the idea of irreducibility and simplicity.

12. Chapter 3 deals with the spiritual center of all manifestations of Apostolic Genius. In trying to identify the essential theological and spiritual energies that motivate parabolic movements, it would be very easy to slip into theological reductionism. But as far as these remarkable Jesus movements go, there is a definite central core around which mDNA coalesces, and so it must be named. But in order to distill the core, explicit motifs in Jesus's teaching on the kingdom of God, the doctrine of the Incarnation, what has been called the *missio Dei* (the mission of God), and the church's response to these actions of God have been left out. However, these key themes are embedded in various sections throughout the book. I hope the reader will understand and forgive me for not addressing these more directly.

- **Missional-Incarnational Impulse:** Chapter 5 explores the twin impulses of remarkable missional movements, namely, the dynamic outward thrust and the related deepening impulse, which together *seed* and *embed* the gospel into different cultures and people groups.

- **Apostolic Environment:** Chapter 6 looks at another element of authentic mDNA—apostolic influence and the fertile environment that this creates in initiating and maintaining the phenomenal movements of God. This will relate to the type of leadership and ministry required to sustain metabolic growth and impact.

- **Organic Systems**: Chapter 7 explores the next element in mDNA, the idea of appropriate structures for metabolic growth. Phenomenal Jesus movements grow precisely because they do not have centralized institutions to block growth through control. Here we will find that remarkable Jesus movements have the feel of a movement, have structure as a network, and spread like viruses.

- *Communitas,* **Not Community:** The most vigorous forms of community are those that come together in the context of a shared ordeal or those that define themselves as a group with a mission that lies beyond themselves—thus initiating a risky journey. Too much concern with safety and security, combined with comfort and convenience, has lulled us out of our true calling and purpose. We all love an adventure. Or do we? This chapter aims at putting the adventure back into the venture.

And so the structure of Apostolic Genius will look something like this:

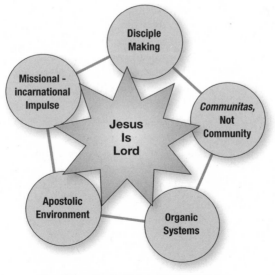

The Structure of Apostolic Genius

Method in the Madness

As indicated above, the task in this book is to try to identify the irreducible elements that constitute Apostolic Genius. And to do this I will be using both the early church and the twentieth-century Chinese church as my primary test cases.[13] Having discerned what appear to be distinctive patterns, I then tried to test the validity of my observations on other significant movements in the history of the church, and as far as my own expertise will allow, I have found them thoroughly consistent.

Furthermore, this book is written not from the perspective of an academic but rather from the perspective of a missionary and a strategist trying to help the church formulate a missional paradigm that can take us through the complexities of the twenty-first-century world in which we are called to be faithful. It is therefore painted in broad strokes and not in fine detail; this is consistent with my own personality and approach to issues, but it also ensures that we do get *precisely* the big picture. We are in need of a new paradigm, not a mere reworking of the existing one. It is therefore the whole that counts and not just the individual parts.

The book is therefore more prescriptive than it is merely descriptive. I have written largely with the missional practitioner in mind. This book would appeal most to those who are leading existing churches, to those who are initiating new forms of sustainable Christian community for the twenty-first century (what I will call the emerging missional church), and to those who are involved on the strategic level of ministry, namely that of leading movements, parachurches, and denominations.

Suffice to say here that in exploring these ideas I feel that I am peering into things that are very deep, things that, if recovered and applied, could have considerable ramifications for Western Christianity. I say this as someone who is not claiming something as my own. If anything, like all who receive a grace from God, I feel that I am the humble recipient of a revelation, an unearthing of something primal, in which I am privileged to participate. This book is a stumbling attempt to articulate that ever elusive revelation of the nature of Apostolic Genius—something that belongs to the gospel itself and therefore to the whole people who live by it. Albert Einstein said that when he was peering into the mysteries of the atom he felt he was peering over God's shoulder into things remarkable and wonderful. I must admit to feeling the same sense of awe as I look into these things.

---

13. I will refer to these variously as "apostolic movements," "phenomenal movements," or "Jesus movements," throughout this book.

setting the scene, part 1

+Confessions of a Frustrated Missionary

If you want to build a ship, don't summon people to buy wood, prepare tools, distribute jobs, and organize the work, rather teach people the yearning for the wide, boundless ocean.

Antoine de Saint-Exupéry

A great deal more failure is the result of an excess of caution than of bold experimentation with new ideas. The frontiers of the kingdom of God were never advanced by men and women of caution.

J. Oswald Sanders

In true biblical fashion, a reliable understanding of the nature of things comes out of a narrative—a *story* involving God's dealings with human beings in the rough and tumble of actual human history, including that of our own stories. A good friend of mine once said to me that our stories are vital because they are perhaps the only thing we can say with absolute authority—precisely because they are *our* stories. In setting out to explore the ideas of what makes up authentic missional DNA, I need to place this search in the context of my own story, because it is out of my own personal struggle in mission, and in ongoing efforts to lead the church into a genuine missional engagement, that I have come to the conclusions that I present in this book. I *can* speak authoritatively from my own story. All I ask you as the reader is to see if it can inform yours.

So if the reader will indulge me, I will tell you my story; it is a story brim-full with redemption. A story about God actively involved in the chaos of the people, communities, and organizations among whom I have had the privilege to minister for the last fifteen years. This account is not incidental to the ideas of this book, just as biblical narrative is not incidental to the ideas that underlie biblical truth but are its context and give it its historical meaning.

"South"

Possibly my most formative experience of ministry was my involvement in a remarkable inner-city church called South Melbourne Restoration Community (SMRC), of which I was privileged to serve as leader for about fifteen years. It's a little difficult to speak for much of the 140-year history of this church, because I was only an addition that came much later on—1989, to be exact. But for the purposes of this book, the important thing to note was that this church, originally called South Melbourne Church of Christ, had gone through the now familiar pattern of birth (in the late nineteenth century), growth (in the early part of the twentieth), and the rapid decline that has marked so many churches in the postwar period throughout the Western world. When my wife, Deb, and I were called there as rookie ministers in 1989, we were the last-ditch effort to turn it around. If we weren't success-ful, the church had decided to call it quits and close up shop. Because of the situation of relative desperation, this church was willing to become a place out of which a whole new community was to develop. And it is *this* story with which I most identify.

This particular story of redemption starts with a somewhat zany, wild-eyed Greek guy called George. George was a drug dealer and a "roadie" (a sound technician for bands), among other things. He had accumulated a number of parking fines that he was not disposed to pay. According to state law at the time, a person could "do time" in lieu of paying fines, and so George decided that this would be preferable from parting with his hard-earned drug dollars. He chose to go to jail for ten days rather than pay the fine. Now, George was a bit of a seeker (some called him a "tripper"), and he loved to philosophize about the nature of things. At the time he was explor-ing a wide variety of religious ideologies. At the time of his imprisonment, he had worked his way through a long list of religions, and it was time to come to grips with the Bible. And so he took his mom's big fat Greek family Bible with him to the jail. To his great surprise, while paging through it he encountered God (or rather God encountered him), and he found new life in Jesus right there in the prison cell.

On release, he hooked up with his brother John, an equally mad radical, and he too gave his life to Christ and became a follower. With characteristic zeal the two of them soon developed a list of all their friends, contacts, and people they sold drugs to and, armed with a big, black KJV Bible and a *Late Great Planet Earth* video (which they used more effectively than the Bible),[1] they met with all the people on their list. Within six months about fifty people had given their lives to the Lord! One of them was later to become my remarkable wife, Debra, and another was her sister Sharon. They were coming down from an LSD trip when they were exposed to the video and decided for Jesus. How could you not, watching *that* movie on acid?

It was an amazing thing, and I mention it here because it says so much about how God works at the fringes of society, in this case through the radical obedience of two slightly wacky Greek brothers called George and John. It was as if through George and John, God had scooped a people to himself from Melbourne's netherworld. In the group were gays, lesbians, Goths, drug addicts, prostitutes, and some relatively ordinary people, although all were rabid party animals. This untamed group of people, following their latent spiritual instincts, immediately began to cluster in houses and build a common life together. It was at this time, about six months after George's radical conversion, that I came into the picture. Although I had come from a similar background, I was then a first-year seminary student looking for something radical to do. Through a series of events, and much to my surprise, I was called to lead this crazy group. On reflection, this connection with the group was to become a defining motif in my life, and in my journey to becoming a missional leader.

That community rocked. And because the community would take in just about anyone who wanted a bed, the main house—thought to be previously used as a brothel—was crammed full of some really strange people. At times there were drug deals going on in the back rooms and Bible studies in the lounge that was filled to overflowing. John and George were arrested a few times for disturbing the peace while noisily trying to cast demons out of some unwitting victim in the backyard. And if this all sounds a bit shocking, let me say that for all the significant chaos and ambiguity in it all, there was something wonderfully *apostolic* about that group of people. They seemed to have a huge impact on everyone who came into contact with them. The Holy Spirit was almost tangibly present at times. It seems at least he was very willing to be present in the chaos. That experience also introduced us

---

1. For those of later generations, this movie was based on Hal Lindsay's apocalyptic vision of the late twentieth century. Based on a distinct vision of the end times, it was basically a way to scare people into accepting Jesus as Lord and Savior.

all to a model of radical ministry in the form of a remarkable pastor called Pat Kavanagh. Pat, an older man that came from a very different world, was a model of redemptive love in the midst of the mess, and it is largely because of him that the community survived and was transformed.

And because this is a book about missional dynamics, it is appropriate to make a comment about a significant characteristic of Jesus movements at this point. In the study of the history of missions, one can even be formulaic about asserting that *all great missionary movements begin at the fringes of the church*, among the poor and the marginalized, and seldom, if ever, at the center. It is vital that in pursuing missional modes of church, we get out of the stifling equilibrium of the center of our movements and denominations, move to the fringes, and engage in real mission there. But there's more to it than just mission; most great movements of mission have inspired significant and related movements of renewal in the life of the church. It seems that when the church engages at the fringes, it almost always brings life to the center. This says a whole lot about God and gospel, and the church will do well to heed it.

To cut a long story short, most of this group ended up joining us at South Melbourne Church of Christ when we were called there after completion of seminary training. It is here where the two histories, and in many ways the two alternate images of church—the one institutional and declining, and the other grassroots and vigorous—come into contact. And thus begins the remarkable story of which I was so privileged to partake. What is quite remarkable is that here, latent in this spontaneous, chaotic, and unchurched group of people, lay the seeds of an agile, evolving, missional movement, long before we even knew that such concepts existed. And while it did take us a bit of time, with lots of reflective experimentation, to get there, I believe that I can say that "South" has now all the elements of, and is in the process of becoming, a genuine missional movement in the city of Melbourne, Australia.

So what I propose to do with the rest of the chapter is to try to articulate the series of adaptations that had to take place for this fledgling phenomenon to become a genuine missional movement. I will embed some of the rationale for these various stages in the narrative so that the reader might be able to discern the evolution of a movement in the story of South. Three distinct stages in the life of this community can be discerned; they are as follows:

Phase 1: From Death to Chaos

This phase involved the reseeding of the established church with the new, and more missional, one. I have to say that nothing in my seminary training had prepared me for the experience of those years. Everything in my education was geared toward maintaining the established, more institutional forms of the church. The vast majority of the subjects on offer were theoretical and were taught by theoreticians, not practitioners. So we had to learn on the run, so to speak. On reflection, perhaps this is the only way we *really* learn, but certainly at the time this was the way that God chose to somehow make a missionary out of me.

Something about context: South Melbourne is located in the shadow of the central business district of Melbourne, and like many such locations across the Western world, it has become a mixture of yuppies, older working-class folk, subcultural groupings, a large gay population, and upper-class snobs. It was a challenge, to say the least. And I am not ashamed to admit that I had no real idea of what I was doing. There was very little in the way of functional denominational strategy or successful models to refer to for mission in these contexts. So, in terms of approach, we decided that all we would do was build an authentic Jesus community where all who came our way would experience love, acceptance, and forgiveness, no matter what—we *did* know a little about grace as we had all experienced it so convincingly ourselves. On this alone, on a real promise and experience of a grace-filled community, the church grew. We attracted just about every kind of freak in the neighborhood, and soon people began to cluster in communal houses. We had no real outreach programs per se. We simply "did community" and developed a certain ethos based on grace for the broken.

As the church grew and developed, the older folk who were part of the original history of the place began to struggle with all the mess and new life in the place. But to their credit, they did recognize that the future of the church lay in the newer image of church that God was birthing in their midst. And they did not actively resist to the point of ejecting the new, something that happens all too often in similar situations. In fact, one older woman, Isobel, who stayed with us faithfully through all the changes, did attempt at times to find another local church that was less chaotic, but she always returned, saying that no place she visited had the same "life" that we did. In the end, this new adaptation of the church became the predominant one, and thus begins the next phase.

Phase 2: Becoming a *Church-Planting Church*

From very early on, God had birthed into us a sense of missional obligation to those outside of the church. Again we had no real language for this, but we somehow intuited that we were "pregnant" with other churches that would reach unreached people groups in our city. We had a particular sense of calling to those people groups that made up the *subcultural* context in which we lived, the poor and the marginalized—people groups from which most of us had come, and people who would seldom, if ever, darken the door of the established church as we know it. Again, in doing this we were simply following the apostolic instincts that I have come to believe lie latent in the very gospel itself. In this case, these latent instincts expressed themselves in a desire to pass on the faith by creating new communities that were relevant to the subcultural context but faithful to ancient gospel.

Because of this drive to plant churches, it was at this time that we began to discern that fundamental change was going on in Western culture. It was the early nineties, and postmodernism as a cultural phenomenon was beginning to be felt at the level of popular culture—the great divide was taking place between the old modern and the new postmodern eras, resulting in the breakdown of culture into many different subcultures—what cultural theorists call microheterogenization, or simply subculturization.[2] So much for the grand cultural phenomena; on the ground in inner-city Melbourne, we had intuitively grasped that some form of neotribalization was taking place. There was a shift from people identifying with a large traditional grouping defined by overarching metanarratives (e.g., trade unionism, political ideology, national identities, religious groupings, etc.) to that of a myriad of smaller, emerging subcultural groups defined around anything from cultural interest to sexual preference. Looking around us from where we stood, it felt just like we were in a sort of subcultural Papua New Guinea, with its 900 language and tribal/ethnic groupings. And it quickly dawned on us that this must call into question our inherited way of engaging in the missional task. We realized that we needed to become missionaries and that the church needed to adopt a missionary stance in relation to its context. It also meant that the days of the one-size-fits-all approach to church were numbered. And so our missionary approach developed into that of targeting specific groupings in the newly tribalized urban milieu.

This phase was to last for about five years. Toward the end of this phase, we had begun to articulate something of the ideas that energized us, and we had developed something of a self-conscious "model." We felt that we had to become a church-planting church with a regional organization. Again we had intuited that the way to engage in mission across a region required a new form of organization. At this stage I began to study the nature of movements and how they organize. And so the embryonic movement called Restoration Community Network was born, and we renamed South Melbourne Church of Christ as South Melbourne Restoration Community (SMRC). This network subsequently birthed about six church plants in about seven years, some of which have been wonderful experiences of missional church, some of

2. Much has already been made of this, and the reader can get good overviews of this phenomenon from other books dedicated to the subject. See, for instance, Stanley Grenz, *A Primer on Postmodernism* (Grand Rapids: Eerdmans, 1996).

which have been glorious failures. There was a lot of struggle and pain in the failures, and feelings of great joy in the successes, but in it all we learned that if we wanted to get missional, we had to take significant risks.

The first church plant was in St. Kilda, Melbourne's red-light district, and was called Matthew's Party. This was a "street church" focused on reaching drug addicts and prostitutes. But with the subsequent sending out of our street-culture people, the sending church (SMRC) underwent a transformation. It morphed into what was then called a "Gen-X church," with the median age between twenty-five and thirty and a somewhat fluid community of up to 400 people, mainly singles, in its orbit. SMRC was fairly unique, possibly even in world context, in that up to 40 percent of the community came from the gay and lesbian subcultures. What made this more unique was that we did not take a politically correct, pro-gay stance, theologically speaking, but graciously called all people into a lifelong following of Jesus, which for some would involve lifelong celibacy; others whose desire and will were strong pursued heterosexual relationships. We still remained committed to ministry on the fringes, only now it was to alienated young adults and gay people.

Our second church-planting project was to Jewish people. I am Jewish, and my brother became a believer not long after my conversion to the Messiah. Both being held by the conviction that the gospel was to the Jew first (Rom. 1:16; 2:9–10), we started Celebrate Messiah Australia. This has been a remarkable story in itself, with hundreds of Jewish people coming to know their Messiah—unprecedented in Australian church history, at least. This has now become an independent agency that is flourishing in its own way. The fourth experiment was to the rave/dance scene. We found it very hard to build ongoing community in such a fluid and "trippy" environment, but it was a great experiment in cross-cultural mission—and we had lots of fun trying. We then experimented with house churches in the working-class western suburbs of Melbourne, but sadly, for various reasons, they did not sustain. I will reflect on some of this when I talk about embedding mDNA. Failures can be great teachers.

The last missional experiment of this phase was for me (and I believe for the church as well) a decisive one. Over the years up to this point two critical things had taken place. First, SMRC, the "mother ship," so to speak, had settled down somewhat from the more heady days of wild and chaotic community. And second, we had become known as a "cool church," and as a result lots of middle-class Christians, who for understandable reasons were alienated from the institutional church in various ways, had made their way into the community and settled down in it. So while maintaining its "groovy" and somewhat alternative vibe, South had inadvertently become safe and more self-consciously yuppie and, as a result, had lost something of its edge. Without anyone noticing, we had lost our original call and missional heart.

At the same time, and through my involvement in translocal ministries with Forge (a transdenominational mission training agency that I lead) and my denomination, my own formation and thinking as a missionary-to-the-West had developed. I had set about to seriously critique the Christendom *mode* of church and had begun to look beyond the *attractional* model of church to that of what I would later call a *missional-incarnational* (outward thrust and deepening seeding) one.[3] The missional-incarnational impulse forms one of the six elements of missional DNA that I articulate later in this book. Suffice to say at this point that I had become convinced that the inherited concept of church with its associated understanding of mission was birthed in a period when the church had ceased to operate as a missionary movement and had thereby become somewhat untrue to itself in the process. The Christendom mode of engagement, what I will later describe as *evangelistic-attractional*, was simply not up to the type of missionary challenge presented to us by our surrounding context: a context that required more of a cross-cultural missionary methodology than the "outreach and in-drag" model we had been using to that point.

And here I simply must insert some of our rationale by giving you something of a missional analysis. To illustrate, below you will see a pie chart that seeks to indicate the prevailing contemporary, evangelical-charismatic church's *appeal* to our general population in Australia. Based on my reading of significant research from all across the post-Christian West, I discovered that when surveyed, the average non-Christian population generally reported a high interest in God, spirituality, Jesus, and prayer that, taken together, indicated that a significant search for meaning was going on in our time. But the same surveys indicated that when asked what they thought about the church, the average non-Christian described a high degree of alienation. It seems that at present, most people report a "God? Yes! Church? No!" type of response. This will not be new to most readers; sensitive Christians would be aware of this response to the institutional church—but sadly not many have worked out the implications for the church in missional terms.

A combination of recent research in Australia indicates that about 10–15 percent of that population is attracted to what we can call the *contemporary church growth model*. In other words, this model has significant "market appeal" to about 12 percent of our population. The more successful forms of this model tend to be large, highly professionalized, and overwhelmingly middle-class, and express themselves culturally using contemporary, "seeker-friendly" language and middle-of-the-road music forms. They structure themselves around "family ministry" and therefore offer multigenera-

3. See my book, coauthored with Michael Frost, *The Shaping of Things to Come: Innovation and Mission for the 21st-Century Church* (Peabody, MA: Hendrickson, 2003) for this concept fleshed out in a more systematic way. I will refer to missional-incarnational impulse in one of the chapters of this book.

tional services. Demographically speaking, they tend to cater largely to what might be called the "family-values segment"—good, solid, well-educated citizens who don't abuse their kids, who pay their taxes, and who live, largely, what can be called a suburban lifestyle.

Not only is this type of church largely made up of Christian people who fit this profile, the research indicates that these churches can also be very effective in reaching *non-Christian* people fitting the same demographic description—the people within their cultural reach. That is, the church does not have to cross any *significant cultural barriers* in order to communicate the gospel meaningfully to that cultural context.[4] This situation looks something like this:

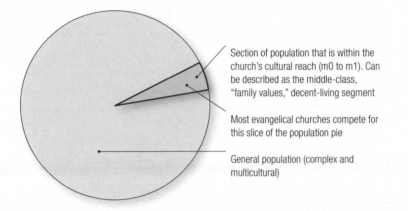

Section of population that is within the church's cultural reach (m0 to m1). Can be described as the middle-class, "family values," decent-living segment

Most evangelical churches compete for this slice of the population pie

General population (complex and multicultural)

"The votes are also in about how much Americans love church." Sally Morgenthaler reports the following statistics for the American scene. She says

> Despite what we print in our own press releases, the numbers don't look good. According to 2003 actual attendance counts, adult church-going is at 18 percent nationally and dropping. Evangelical attendance (again, actual seat-numbers, not telephone responses) accounts for 9% of the population, down from 9.2% in 1990. Mainline attendance accounts for 3.4% of the national population, down from 3.9% the previous decade. And Catholics are down a full percentage point in the same ten-year period: 6.2% from 7.2% in 1990. Of the 3,098 counties in the United States, 2,303 declined in church attendance.[5]

4. See glossary for a definition of "cultural distance." We will also explore it further in the next chapter

5. Sally Morgenthaler, "Windows in Caves and Other Things We Do with Perfectly Good Prisms," *Fuller Theological Seminary Theology News and Notes* (Spring 2005). Can be downloaded at http://www.easumbandy.com/resources/index.php?action=details&record=1386.

To intensify the problem we face in the new missional context we are finding ourselves in, George Barna predicts that "by 2025 the local church [as we know it now] will lose roughly half of its current 'market share' and . . . alternative forms of faith experience and expression will pick up the slack."[6] With these statistics in mind we can intuit that in America the current "market appeal" of the contemporary church growth model *might* be up to 35 percent (as opposed to 12 percent in Australia). But even if it is at this level of appeal, it is decreasing. It's time for a radical rethink taking into account both the strategic and the missional implications.

Strategic Issues

First, the strategic issues: the vast majority of evangelical churches, perhaps up to 95 percent, subscribe to the contemporary church growth approach in their attempts to grow the congregation, in spite of the fact that successful applications of this model remain relatively rare.[7] This is a strategic issue for us because various recombinations of contemporary church growth theory and practice seem to be the only solution we have to draw upon to try to halt the decline of Christianity. It seems to be the only arrow in our quiver—this can't be a good thing. Solutions based on church growth so dominate our imaginations that we can't seem to think outside of its frameworks or break out of its assumptions about the church and its mission. And that's tragic, because it doesn't seem to work for most of our churches and for the majority of our populations. In fact, it has become a source of frustration and guilt, because most churches do not have the combination of factors that make for a successful application of the model.

Missional Issues

Thus, in Australia we have the somewhat farcical situation of 95 percent of evangelical churches tussling with each other to reach 12 percent of the population. And *this* becomes a significant missional problem because it raises the question, "What about the vast majority of the population (in Australia's case, 85 percent; in the United States, about 65 percent) that

6. Press release on Barna's new book *Revolution*, from George Barna and Associates, at http://www.barna.org/FlexPage.aspx?Page=BarnaUpdateNarrow&BarnaUpdateID=201.

7. For the vast majority of churches, church growth techniques have not had any significant or lasting effect in halting their decline. Of the 480,000 or so churches in America, only a *very small* portion of them can be described as *successful* seeker-sensitive churches, and most of them have fewer than eighty members. What is more, the church in America is in decline in spite of having church growth theory and techniques predominating our thinking for the last forty or so years—for all its overt success in a few remarkable cases, it has failed to halt the decline of the church in America and the rest of the Western world.

report alienation from *precisely* that form of church?" How do they access the gospel if they reject this form of church? And what would church be like for them in their various settings? Because what is clear from the research in Australia, at least, is that when surveyed about what *they* think about the contemporary church growth expression of Christianity, the 85 percent range from being blasé ("good for them, but not for me") to total repulsion ("I would never go there"). At best, we can make inroads on the blasé; we can't hope to reach the rest of the population with this model—they are simply alienated from it and don't like it for a whole host of reasons.

What is becoming increasingly clear is that if we are going to meaningfully reach this majority of people, we are not going to be able to do it by simply doing more of the same. And yet it seems that when faced with our problems of decline, we automatically reach for the latest church growth package to solve the problem—we seem to have nowhere else to go. But simply pumping up the programs, improving the music and audiovisual effects, or jiggering the ministry mix won't solve our missional crisis. Something far more fundamental is needed.

A Test Case in Proximity Space

This combination of missional experience and reflection led the leadership of South to begin experimenting with significantly more incarnational modes of mission. We decided that in the context of Melbourne, a city obsessed with food and eating out, that we ought to try and see how we can engage our culture on its own turf (missional), rather than expecting them to come to ours (attractional). What drove us to this conclusion was asking *missionary questions,* namely, "What is good news for this people group?" and "What would the church look and feel like *among* this people group?" Both these questions assume that we don't fully know the answers *until* we ask them in the active context of mission. They require that we pay attention to the existential issues confronting a people *as they experience those issues.* And that we try to shape and form of communities of faith so that they can become an organic part of the cultural social fabric of the people group we are trying to reach. For Melbourne, where every third business has to do with food, and which has more cafés per capita than any other city in the world, we concluded that the missional church must seek to redeem the social pattern/rhythm of such spaces—reinvesting it with religious significance—and express what it means to be a people of God in a café-bar context. To this end, we purchased a large working restaurant in a busy café district and established it as a "proximity space."

A proximity space is not a church; rather, it involves the creation of places and/or events where Christians and not-yet-Christians can interact meaningfully with each other—effectively a missional space.[8] We called the café-bar Elevation. And for us it was a defining experience—both positively and negatively. Positively, because it was a marvelous way to do mission and relate our way into people's lives—and it was a significant learning experience. Negatively, because we were unable to sustain it financially and had to shut it down. We started out way too big, and September 11, 2001, along with some bad management decisions, knocked us out of business. However, I still believe that if we had been able to operate sustainably with our intended purpose and values, Elevation could have become a very effective form of mission in our city. The driving desire of the project was to engage people in a meaningful dialogue around Jesus and spirituality in a meaningful and organic way. To do this we ran art classes, interactive drama groups, philosophy discussion groups, guitar workshops, CD launches, book launches and discussions, and open mic nights (where people get to share poetry and music) as well as regular music nights. These are natural ways for people to engage organically in discussions of meaning, the essence of art, spirituality, etc. These were in addition to a regular offer of a large menu of good-value meals and hospitality, which formed the economic engine room of the project.

Our initial analysis estimated about 60,000 customers per annum at the café. Most of these people consumed sit-down meals and hung out in the lounge-bar. Through engaging advertising of our various interactive forums, we invited people into an organic dialogue, where we could get to know their names and at least start a relationship. It wasn't about overt evangelism in the first instance; that, we reckoned, would come later, through meaningful relationships.

Here's how the numbers work: of the 60,000 customers alone, half might express interest in the various forums on offer. Of those who express interest, half of these might make an effort to find out more. Of those who make an effort to find out more, only half might actually come along to a group. This means that around 4,000 people might well come to the groups, whether art, open mic, spirituality, or others. If we add those who might come for reasons other than a meal at Elevation, we would have a profitable, sustainable venue with its own vigorous cultural and spiritual life.

8. Michael and I report on such phenomena in our book: "Around the world Christians are developing cafés, nightclubs, art galleries, design studios, football teams etc., to facilitate such proximity and interaction. If the church service is the only space where we can meaningfully interact with unbelievers, we're in trouble. In Birmingham, England, Pip Piper, the founder of a design studio called One Small Barking Dog (great name!), runs a monthly gathering in a local café, the Medicine Bar. He has negotiated permission from the publican to deck the premises out as a 'spiritual space.' Using incense, projected images and ambient religious music, he designs a spiritual zone he calls Maji, and artists who would normally patronize the Medicine Bar as well as invited friends can hang out, experience the ambience and talk about faith, religion, spirituality." See *Shaping of Things to Come*, 24.

While we viewed Elevation as a proximity space, a genuine missional approach should aim at ultimately creating communities of faith around Jesus. This is how we modeled the project so that it formed faith communities.

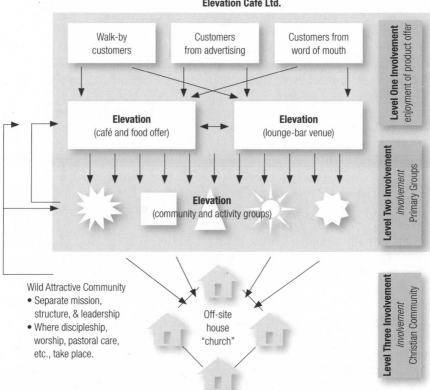

This is presented as something of a working rationale for such approaches to mission in the hope that it will inspire others to do the same. For SMRC, it represented a new mode of missional engagement. It was the logical next step of our approach to mission in this phase of our movement. It was a definite move away from the predominantly attractional mode into which

SMRC had comfortably settled. Its failure to sustain hit us all hard, but it drove me into something of a depression as well as a highly reflective process that probed the value of our work and the spiritual condition of SRMC specifically and the church generally.

When things were going bad for us, the directors of the café made a series of special appeals to the church community to get behind the project and make every effort to come along, bring a friend, and enjoy a meal, a drink or two, and some music together. What really unsettled us was that even after a number of these urgent appeals, the support for the project did not significantly increase. Possibly only about a third of the church really backed it, another third were mildly supportive, and the other third didn't even bother coming along. I have to say this really shook me up and made me reflect deeply on the impact of my own leadership and ministry at SMRC.

As the key leader I must, and do, take major responsibility for some bad decisions, and for not getting as much ownership as I ought, but once people were aware of what was at stake and yet did not respond as maturing disciples ought to, it deeply affected me. And it led me to ask what we had we really created over those last few years of ministry, in what by all external estimates was an effective and outstanding church. How does one assess the fruitfulness of fifteen years of ministry when it comes to this?

My reflections led me to investigate biblically how we really measure the effectiveness of a church and its missional impact. How *do* we know we are being fruitful? With what measures will we as God's people be weighed? How does God assess our effectiveness? (Is that not the inner meaning of judgment?) Because evidently he does (John 15:1–8, Revelation 1–3) and will (1 Pet. 4:17) judge his people. All this led me back to the questions about the nature of the church as the Bible defines it, and how we are to know that we are actually doing what we were meant to do in the first place. These are deep questions that led me, and in fact our whole leadership team, to a place of profound repentance and to new development and growth.

For us as the leadership team, the turning point was in asking the hard questions about how to determine the fruitfulness of the church. And this in turn drove us back to ask questions about the nature of the church and its innate purpose according to the scriptures. We had to go back to the essence of the church's function and purpose in the world. In order to do this we had to identify what comprised the essential components that together form a church. What are the irreducible minimums of a true expression of ecclesia? We came up with the following—a church is:

- *A covenanted community*: A church is formed people not by people just hanging out together, but ones bound together in a distinctive bond. There is a certain obligation toward one another formed around a covenant.

- *Centered on Jesus*: He is the new covenant with God and he thus forms as the true epicenter of an authentic *Christ*-ian faith. An *ecclesia* is not just a God-community—there are many such religious communities around. We are defined by our relationship to the Second Person of the Trinity, the Mediator, Jesus Christ. A covenant community centered around Jesus participates in the salvation that he brings. We receive the grace of God in him. But, more is required to truly constitute a church.

A true encounter with God in Jesus must result in

- *Worship*, defined as offering our lives back to God through Jesus.
- *Discipleship*, defined as following Jesus and becoming increasingly like him (Christlikeness).
- *Mission*, defined as extending the mission (the redemptive purposes) of God through the activities of his people.

It needs to be noted that practically as well as theologically these are profoundly interconnected, and each informs the other to create a complex phenomenon called "church." This definition is important because it distills the core aspects of what constitutes a faith *ecclesia*. Graphically represented it might look something like this:

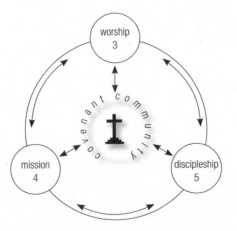

What's in a definition? Actually, the way we define church is crucial because it gives us a direct clue to the critical elements of authentic Christian community. It also highlights for us the major responses that constitute Christian spirituality, namely, worship, discipleship, and mission. We will be weighed up by God on the basis of the innate purpose of the church and thus our capacity to

1. Make disciples: people who are learning how, and what it means, to become Christlike,
2. Engage in his mission to the world, which is our mission (his purposes flow through *us*), and
3. Develop the authenticity, depth and breadth, of our worship.

If we were not fruitful in these areas, then we could not claim to be a faithful church *as God intended us to be.* And in this situation, just as in the seven churches of the Revelation (Revelation 1–3), we were in danger of having our lampstand removed. They too were judged and were called to repent. But for us, the central failure lay primarily in our inability to "make disciples." Our worship and mission were therefore enfeebled; they had no real foundations. I came to the horrifying conclusion that we had built much of SMRC on sand because we did not build it on discipleship (Matt. 7:26). What's the use of salt if it loses its saltiness (Matt. 5:13)?

Phase 3: From a Church to an Organic Movement

Our assessment as leaders of South at the time was that we as a community had lost our edge and our heart. When the chips came down, we could not draw upon the deeper resources of discipleship and an enduring sense of obligation and mission. It seemed to us as leaders that we did not really *value* God's, and therefore our, distinctive mission as a central function of the church. In fact, to our shame, at that point we had not seen any conversions to Jesus in the preceding two years! And this in what was possibly one of the most accepting and relevant churches in our city (you don't have 40 percent gay-lesbian attendance, many of them not-yet-Christians, without being accessible and open).

What was wrong? Our assessment: *we had not been successful at the task of making disciples, and therefore we were not fruitful in mission.* That in neglecting these two essential elements of *ecclesia,* we had become little more than a worship club for trendy people alienated from the broader expressions of church. The other two dimensions of fruitful *ecclesia* were almost completely missing. We were forced to the conclusion that all we had done was further cultivate a consumerist approach to Christianity. Like most churches in the modernist-Christendom mode, we had built the model of the church on a consumerist model and, in the end, paid the price.

Sound harsh? Didn't church-growth proponents explicitly teach us to mimic the shopping mall and apply it to the church? In this they were sincere, but they must have been unaware of the ramifications of this approach, because in the end the medium always becomes the message.[9] They were unaware of the latent virus in the model itself—that of consumerism and the sins of the middle class. Much of what can be tagged "consumerist middle-class" is built on the ideals of *comfort* and *convenience* (consumerism), and of *safety* and *security* (middle-class).

Winston Churchill once remarked that we shape our buildings, and then they shape us. How true. When we build our churches, the architecture and the shape say it all. See this:

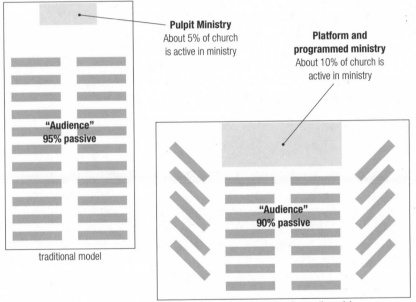

In the above figure, the vast majority of the church is *passive* in the equation. They are in a receptive mode and basically receive the services offered. That is, they are basically *consumptive*. They come to "get fed." But is this a faithful image of the church? Is the church really meant to be a "feeding trough" for otherwise capable middle-class people who are getting their careers on track? And to be honest, it is very easy for ministers to cater right into this: the prevailing understanding of leadership is that of the pastor-teacher. People gifted in this way love to teach and care for people, and the congregation in turn loves to outsource learning and to be cared for. I

9. See ibid., ch. 9, esp. 149ff.

have to admit that this now looks awfully codependent to me. Following the consumerist agenda, the church itself has become both a consumable and a service provider, a vendor of religious goods and services. But this "service-provision" approach is the very thing Jesus didn't do. He spoke in confusing riddles (parables) that evoked a spiritual search in the hearers. Nowhere does he give three-point devotional sermons that cover all the bases. His audience had to do all the hard work of filling in the blanks. In other words, they were not left passive but were activated in their spirits.

To be sure, at SMRC we had moved away from monological sermons to dialogical discussions. We experimented like mad in different forms of worship and connecting with God. We had developed a loungelike feel with couches in a semicircle and pop art all over the walls. We experimented in multisensory communication, and more. But in the end all we had succeeded in doing was making 20 percent of the community *active* in ministry, while leaving about 80 percent passive and consumptive.

Highly participatory, alternative worship.
About 20% of community is active in ministry

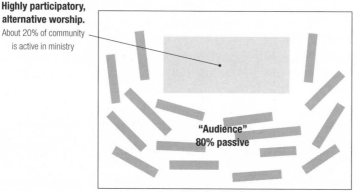

alternative church model

In fact, it seemed that we actually made matters worse for the participants, because all we did served to refine their already latent consumerism. Their "taste" in church had evolved. We discovered that if a community member left SMRC, for whatever reason, they found it much harder to go back to a "meat and potatoes" style of church, because they had acquired a taste for "spice and garlic," so to speak. We found that a lot of the people who left just wandered around and couldn't reconnect anywhere. This was very disturbing and it drove us to seriously ask, What was the end result of our engaging way of doing alternative church? Was it to make matters worse? My alarming answer is that I think so. Below is my reasoning . . .

God's gracious involvement aside, if you wish to grow a contemporary church following good church growth principles, there are several things you must do and constantly improve upon:

- Expand the building to allow for growth and redesign it along lines indicated in the diagram above (contemporary church-growth model).

- Ensure excellent preaching in contemporary style dealing with subjects that relate to the life of the hearers.

- Develop an inspiring worship experience (here limited to "praise and worship") by having an excellent band and positive worship leaders.

- Make certain you have excellent parking facilities, with car park attendants, to ensure minimum inconvenience in finding a parking space.

- Ensure excellent programs in the critical area of children's and youth ministry. Do so and people will put up with less elsewhere in the mix.

- Develop a good program of cell groups built around a Christian education model to ensure pastoral care and a sense of community.

- Make sure that next week is better than last week, to keep the people coming.

This is what church-growth practitioners call the "ministry mix." Improvement in one area benefits the whole, and constant attention to elements of the mix will ensure growth and maximize impact. The problem is that it caters right into consumerism. And the church with the best programs and the "sexiest" appeal tends to get more customers.

Let's test this: What do you think will happen if elements of the mix deteriorate or another new church with better programming locates itself within your region? Statistics right across the Western world where this model holds sway indicate that the *vast majority* of the church's growth comes from "switchers"—people who move from one church to another based on the perception and experience of the programming. There is precious little conversion growth. No one really gets to see the problem, because it "feels so right" and it "works for me." In fact, the church is on the decline right across the Western world, and we have had at least forty years of church-growth principles and practice.[10] We can't seem to make disciples based on a consumerist approach to the faith. We plainly *cannot consume our way into discipleship*. All of us must become much more active in the equation of becoming lifelong followers of Jesus. Consumption is detrimental to discipleship.[11]

10. In a dialogue between Michael Frost, many members of the faculty of Fuller's School of World Mission, and me, it was generally acknowledged by all there that church growth theory had, by and large, failed to reverse the church's decline in America and was therefore something of a failed experiment. The fact remains that more than four decades of church growth principles and practice has not halted the decline of the church in Western contexts.

11. This will be further explored in the chapter on discipleship as a key element in mDNA.

With all this in mind, we felt that we had to rebuild the church from the ground up around the key biblical functions of the church (Jesus, covenant community, discipleship, mission, and worship). For the whole leadership team it was this or resign en masse. Here are some of the philosophical foundations on which we proceeded to rebuild the church.[12]

1. We wanted to transform from a static, geographically located church to a dynamic movement across our city.
2. In order to ensure that we fulfilled the church's mandate to "make disciples," we simply had to reverse the ratio of active to passive (from 20:80 to 80:20) in order to move away from being a vendor of religious goods and services. We wanted the majority of community members to becoming active and directly involved in the journey of becoming like Jesus.
3. We wished to articulate and develop a fully reproducible system built on simple, easily embedded and transferable ideas (internalized DNA).
4. The movement had to be built on principles of organic multiplication, including operating as a network, not as a centralized organization.
5. Finally, mission (and not ministry) was to be the organizing principle of the movement

And here's what we came up with . . .

1. The basic ecclesial (church) unit was to become much smaller so as to transition from the active:passive ratio from 20:80 to 80:20. The larger unit simply cannot allow for maximum participation by all people present. In other words, we were moving to being a cell-based church. But not a cell church in precisely the same way as previously configured (à la Ralph Neighbor et al.), because to our thinking these groups were to become *the actual primary experience of church* rather than just being a program of the church. Each of these groups is a church in its own right. This is a big shift.
2. We would not develop a philosophy of ministry per se, but rather a covenant and some core practices. Behind this thinking was the belief that when we talk about core values, the appeal is to the head. I have yet to see a set of core values in any church's philosophy that I cannot agree with. They are, in some cases, little more than "motherhood statements" in confessional communities. What we wanted was to

12. These new, more distinctly missional foundations will represent an integration of the ideas in section 2 of this book. This is a working application of the reflections provided there. This is not an easily transferable model. It is my hope that by proposing what SMRC did to move from being a church to a movement, I can demonstrate how one church applied the concepts of mDNA.

covenant ourselves to a set of *practices that embodied* the core value and demonstrated it.[13]

3. Each group (and therefore the majority of the individual members of the group) had to be engaged in a healthy diet of spiritual disciplines—the only way to grow in Christlikeness that we were aware of. Being a slightly naughty church, we came up with what we called the TEMPT model.

	CORE PRACTICE	SPIRITUAL DISCIPLINE
T	*Together We Follow*	Community or togetherness
E	*Engagement with Scripture*	Integrating scripture into our lives
M	*Mission*	Mission (this is the central discipline that binds the others and integrates them)
P	*Passion for Jesus*	Worship and prayer
T	*Transformation*	Character development and accountability

Each group/church has to be engaged in all the practices each time it meets to be part of the movement. How they are to do these is entirely up to them and depends on the individual makeup, the leadership, and the missional context of the group. We encourage them to explore and develop new ways of practicing TEMPT. We call these smaller cellular churches TEMPT groups.

4. We would organize the movement in three basic rhythms: a weekly cycle featuring the TEMPT groups. There would be a monthly (tribal) meeting featuring all the TEMPT groups in a given region, and a biannual gathering of all the tribes in a movement-wide network. Each of these levels has a leadership structure appropriate to each level. Primary discipleship, worship, and mission would take place at the level of the TEMPT groups—the DNA of TEMPT would ensure that. Regional (tribal) coordination would ensure healthy leadership development and facilitate pastoral referrals and healthy networking. And the movement-wide leadership would facilitate the strategic level—and thus provide what will later will be called "apostolic environment."

5. In terms of DNA, other than movement-wide commitment to the practices of TEMPT, the only other requirement to belong to the movement is that each TEMPT group is covenanted to multiply itself as

---

13. We came up with the concept of practices because we felt that the word *discipline* would put off our Gen-Xers. But really, we had just given a new name to tried-and-true spiritual disciplines.

soon as it is organically feasible and possible. This ensures healthy multiplication and embeds an ongoing sense of mission.

All this was not done quickly and did not come easily. People accustomed to "being fed" are generally loath to move from passivity to activity. However, we did transition the church over a two-year period by using a healthy model of change where all were invited to give feedback and participate. South Melbourne Restoration Community (renamed The Red Network or simply Red[14]) now stands on new ground and faces a new future. When we go through the various aspects of mDNA in section 2 of this book, refer back to this story as a primary example of the application of missional church principles.

The strange thing is that after fifteen years in ministry and mission in this community, Deb and I have felt that after transitioning the church into new possibilities and repositioning it for organic mission in the twenty-first century, we have felt a calling to leave another missional project in order to explore elsewhere. And while this has been hard for us both, and has not always make a whole lot of sense, we believe that it has been absolutely right.

Clearly the problems of the church in our time can't be settled without some form of subjective involvement in the living issues of the day. It is not particularly useful to stand on dry land while trying to give swimming lessons. We need to be involved. Debra and I are still learning about mission from the local perspective, as we are deeply committed to local practice. In starting something new we get a chance to do it all again, hopefully not to repeat the same mistakes.

14. http://www.red.org.au/

$\nearrow^{2}$

setting the scene, part 2

+Denominational and Translocal Perspectives

Nothing is more difficult to carry out, nor more doubtful of success, nor more dangerous to handle, than achieving a new order of things.

Niccolò Machiavelli, *The Prince*

Strictly speaking one ought to say that the Church is always in a state of crisis and that its greatest shortcoming is that it is only occasionally aware of it. . . . This ought to be the case because of the abiding tension between the church's essential nature and its empirical condition. . . . That there were so many centuries of crisis-free existence for the Church was therefore an abnormality. . . . And if the atmosphere of crisislessness still lingers on in many parts of the West, this is simply the result of a dangerous delusion. Let us also know that to encounter crisis is to encounter the possibility of truly being the Church.

David Bosch, *Transforming Mission*

A View from the Chopper

The experience at SMRC, and the ensuing church planting movement to the subcultures and fringe dwellers that came out of it, gave me a perspective of missional church from a local church's viewpoint. This is where the rubber hits the road, where the gospel of Jesus Christ engages real people in real-life situations, and where the church needs to negotiate its way onto new ground. This is the real front line of the kingdom of God as it expresses itself through local communities of faith. But it is a somewhat narrow, micromission perspective. What was lacking was an overarching perspective that takes into account a more global and regional view of strategic issues relating to mission.

After a few years of various involvements at the denominational level, I was called to direct our Department of Mission, Education, and Development, effectively both the engine room and the strategic think tank of our denomination. At the same time I maintained my role as team leader in the emerging movement. Having two hefty roles like that just about killed me, but it was the best thing I could have done, because it put me in two critical places at the same time, affording me a strategic perspective of the church and Christianity. This highlighted the dilemma the church faces in the emerging global culture(s). Guiding a denomination while being engaged on the margins at the same time served to accentuate my increasing conviction that the church in the West had to change and adopt a missionary stance in relation to its cultural contexts or face increasing decline and possible extinction. It also created a lot of angst, and it was in this place of tension that I really transitioned from seeing myself primarily as a pastor to being a missionary to the West.

Christendom-schmissendom

Edward de Bono, no theologian but definitely the leading specialist in creative learning processes, remarks that if there is a known and successful cure for an illness, patients generally prefer the doctor to use the known cure rather than seek to design a better one. Yet there may be much better cures to be found. He rightly asks how we are ever to find a better cure if at each critical moment we always opt for the traditional treatment.[1] Think about this in relation to our usual ways of solving our problems. Do we not constantly default to previous patterns and ways of tackling issues of theology, spirituality, and church? To quote another Bono, this time from the

1. See Edward de Bono, *New Thinking for a New Millennium* (St. Ives, NSW, Aus.: Viking, 1999), ix.

band U2, it seems like we are "stuck in a moment and now [we] can't get out of it."[2] It is little wonder that our precommitments to the Christendom mode of church and thinking restrict us to past successes and give us no real solutions for the future. We always seem to default to its preconceived answers. Genuine learning and development is at best a risky process, but without journey and risk there can be no progress.

No one looking at the situation of the church today can say that over the last century or so things have not fundamentally changed. The reality we deal with is that after around 2,000 years of the gospel, we are on the decline in just about every Western cultural context. In fact, we are further away from getting the job done than we were at the end of the third century. Even America, for so long a bastion of a distinct and vigorous form of cultural Christendom, is now experiencing a society that is increasingly moving away from the church's sphere of influence and becoming genuinely neopagan. Much ink has been spilled in trying to analyze the situation. But seldom in these assessments do we hear a call for a radical rethink about the actual *mode* of the church's engagement—the way it perceives and shapes itself around its core tasks. Rarely do we hear a serious critique of the often hidden assumptions on which Christendom itself stands.[3] It seems that the template of this highly institutional version of Christianity is so deeply embedded in our collective psyche that we have inadvertently put it beyond the pale of prophetic critique. We have so divinized this mode of church through centuries of theologizing about it that we have actually confused it with the kingdom of God, an error that seems to have plagued Catholic thinking in particular throughout the ages.[4]

Most efforts at change in the church fail to deal with the very assumptions on which Christendom is built and maintains itself. The change of thinking needed in our day as far as the church and its mission are concerned must be radical indeed; that is, it must go to the roots of the problem. Perhaps a way of conceiving this is to reflect on how computers and software interrelate. Following the approach taken by the developers of Apple computers, if one seeks to constantly create a better computer product, systematic development has to take place on three levels, namely,

2. U2, "Stuck in a Moment," *All That You Can't Leave Behind*, 2000.

3. There are not many accessible books that critique Christendom from a missional perspective. However, two such books have appeared fairly recently. One is Stuart Murray's excellent book *Post-Christendom: Church and Mission in a Strange New World* (Carlisle: Paternoster, 2004), and the other is Douglas John Hall's *The End of Christendom and the Future of Christianity* (Harrisburg, PA: Trinity, 1997).

4. Theologically, we are right to say that the church is not the kingdom. It is but a sign, a symbol, and a foretaste of the kingdom of God. And while the kingdom expresses itself in and through the church in powerful ways, it is never the sole expression of it. The church is part of the kingdom, but the kingdom extends to God's rule everywhere.

those of machine language/hardware, operating system, and end-user programs.

---

programs:
interface with end user

---

operating system:
mediates between program and machine

---

machine language / hardware:
basic code of hardware

This illustration points out that it's no use developing great software when the operating system and the machine language, or hardware, won't or can't cope with it. Great user-programs are limited to the extent that the rest of the system remains undeveloped. There are underlying systemic issues that need to be addressed. To create a successful, world-leading product, development must be attentive to all three levels to be effective. Hence, Apple advances as an integrated whole.

This is a useful metaphor with which to analyze our approaches to change and reform. Many efforts to revitalize the church aim at simply adding or developing new programs or sharpening the theology and doctrinal base of the church. But seldom do we ever get to address the "hardware" or the "machine language" on which all this depends. This means that efforts to fundamentally reorient the church around its mission fail, because the foundational system, in this case the Christendom mode or understanding of church, cancels out what the "software" is requiring. Leadership must go deeper and develop the assumptions and configurations on which a more missional expression of *ecclesia* can be built.

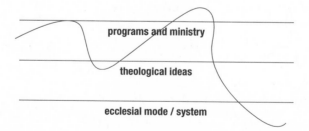

So we have to go to the issues of ecclesial mode, to the very way in which we configure the system from which we operate. This asks us to become aware of the (invisible) assumptions on which we build our experience of church and our purpose in the world.

Changing the Story

Although we hear about successful attempts to revitalize existing churches, the overall track record is actually very poor. Ministers report their attempts to revitalize the churches they lead do not yield the desired results. A lot of energy (and money) is put into the change programs, with all the usual communication exercises, consultations, workshops, and so on. In the beginning things seem to change, but gradually the novelty and impetus tend to wear off, and the organization ends up settling back into something of its previous template or configuration. So instead of managing new organizations, these leaders end up managing the unwanted side effects of their efforts. The reason for this is actually quite simple, though it is often overlooked: unless the paradigm at the heart of the culture is changed, there can be no lasting change.

Ivan Illich was once asked what he thought was the most radical way to change society; was it through violent revolution or gradual reform? He gave a careful answer. Neither. Rather, he suggested that if one wanted to change society, then one must tell an alternative story. Illich is right; we need to reframe our understandings though a different lens, an alternative story, if we wish to move beyond the captivity of the predominantly institutional paradigm that clearly dominates our current approach to leadership and church.

A paradigm, or systems story, "is the set of core beliefs which result from the multiplicity of conversations and which maintains the unity of the

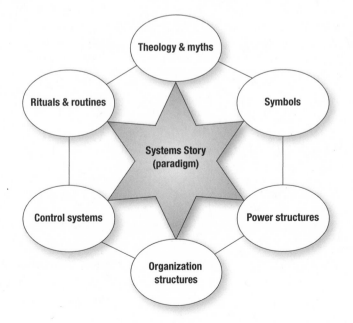

culture."[5] The "petals" in this diagram are "the manifestations of culture which result from the influence of the paradigm."[6] Most change programs concentrate on the petals; that is, they try to effect change by looking at structures, systems, and processes. Experience shows us that these initiatives usually have limited success. Church consultant Bill Easum is right when he notes that "following Jesus into the mission field is either impossible or extremely difficult for the vast majority of congregations in the Western world because of one thing: They have a systems story that will not allow them to take the first step out of the institution into the mission field, even though the mission field is just outside the door of the congregation."[7]

He goes on to note that every organization is built upon on "an underlying systems story." He points out that "this is not a belief system. It is the continually repeated life story that determines how an organization feels, thinks, and thus acts. This systems story determines the way an organization behaves, no matter how the organizational chart is drawn. It's the primary template that shapes all other things. Restructure the organization and leave the systems story in place, and nothing changes within the organization. It's futile trying to revitalize the church, or a denomination, without first changing the system."[8] Drilling down into this systems story—the paradigm, or mode of church—is, Easum suggests, one of the keys to change and constant innovation.

Easum notes that most theories about congregational life are flawed from the start, because they are based on an institutional and mechanical worldview.[9] Or what he calls the "Command and Control, Stifling Story." This view is particularly marked when you recognize how different the predominant forms of church are from the apostolic modes. The movement that Jesus initiated was an organic people movement; it was never meant to be a religious institution. We must allow this new-yet-ancient systems story to seep into our imaginations and reinform all our practices. Our organizations need to be re-evangelized. This is explored in a deeper way in the addendum entitled "A Crash Course in Chaos."

Yeah, but What Would the Bible Say?

Probing our ecclesial assumptions in this way ratchets up the level of discomfort because to do this we must explore, indeed critique, the inherited

5. Richard Seel, "Culture and Complexity: New Insights on Organisational Change," *Culture & Complexity—Organisations & People* 7.2 (2002): 2.

6. Ibid.

7. Bill Easum, *Unfreezing Moves: Following Jesus into the Mission Field* (Nashville: Abingdon, 2001), 31.

8. Ibid.

9. Ibid., 17.

institutional configuration of church from which the majority of us operate and from which we get our legitimacy. In doing this, are we are not doing something alien to our faith? Are we not are touching something sacred . . . inviolable? Not so. In scripture we discover that there is actually good theological substance in the consistent biblical critique of the religious institutions that so easily develop over time. From Yahweh's reluctant concession to the demand of the nation for a king like the other nations and the warning contained therein (1 Sam. 8:20–22) to the "anti-religion" of Jesus (Ellul) who had endless struggles with both the political and religious institutions of his day. In fact, both of these were directly responsible for his death. From the OT prophetic challenges to the often corrupt royalty and priesthood to the NT reappropriation of these offices into the very function and identity of the whole people of God (1 Pet. 2:9). Add Paul's insights into the nature of principalities and powers and impersonal evil abiding in structures and human ideologies (the *elemental principles* of Gal. 4:3–11 and Col. 2:8, 20–23), and we realize that the Bible sustains a thoroughly consistent warning against the centralization of power in a few individuals and concentration of it in inflexible and impersonal institutions.

Prophetic religion also warns against the ritualization of the relationship between God and his people as they seek to constantly remind Israel of the intensely personal nature of the covenant between God and his people. Martin Buber, a profound commentator on prophetic religion and religious movements, warns us about the dangers of religious institutionalism when he notes that "centralization and codification, undertaken in the interests of religion, are a danger to the core of religion." This is inevitably the case he says, unless there is a very vigorous life of faith embodied in the whole community, one that exerts an unrelenting pressure for renewal on the institution.[10] It was C. S. Lewis who observed that "there exists in every church something that sooner or later works against the very purpose for which it came into existence. So we must strive very hard, by the grace of God to keep the church focused on the mission that Christ originally gave to it."[11]

A prophetically consistent Christianity means that we must remain committed to a constant critique of the structures and rituals we set up and maintain. Perhaps rather than calling this anti-institutionalism, a rather negative frame of mind, we should rather understand it as a form of "holy rebellion" based on the loving critique of religious institution modeled by the original apostles and prophets[12]—"holy rebels" who constantly attempted

10. Martin Buber quoted in Maurice Friedman, Martin Buber, *The Life of Dialogue* (Harper & Row, 1960), 82.

11. C. S. Lewis, quoted in W. Vaus, *Mere Theology, A Guide to the Thought of C. S. Lewis* (Downers Grove, IL: InterVarsity, 2004), 167.

12. "That which we would change, we must first love." Ascribed to Martin Luther King Jr.

to throw off encumbering ideologies, structures, codes, and traditions that limited the freedom of God's people and restricted the gospel message that they are mandated to pass on. This is prophetic religion in practice, and it remains one of the essential elements of a true experience of Christianity. It is rebellion because it refuses to submit to the status quo. But because it is a *holy* rebellion, it directs us toward a greater experience of God than we currently have.

Paradoxically, while holy rebellion represents a real (and perceived) challenge to established forms of church, it is also the key to its renewal. New movements are the source of much of its ongoing vitality because they are the wellspring of new ways of experiencing God and participating in his mission, and because of this they contain the seeds of Christianity's ongoing renewal. This is so because new movements awaken the centrality of the core meanings of the gospel freed from the paraphernalia of inherited traditions and rituals. As we shall see, vital movements arise always in the context of rejection by the predominant institutions (e.g., Wesley and Booth). But because vigorous movements of mission almost always create movements of renewal, in the end they do go on to produce renewal in the life of the broader church (e.g., Pentecostalism).

The challenge for the established church and its leaders is to discern the will of God for our time addressed to it in the mouths of its holy rebels. Read this text with these qualifications in mind. And although it might sometimes cause you to react in a defensive way, try to discern the glimmers of truth it might contain. This is critical, because I am now convinced that one of the major blockages to unleashing Apostolic Genius is our adherence to an obsolete understanding of the church. We simply have to find a way to push past the pat historical answers that so easily suggest themselves to a people whose imagination of what it means to be God's people has been taken hostage to a less than biblical imagination of church.

A Missionary's Take

One of the most useful ways of reading our situation comes from a conceptual tool developed by the pioneering missiologist Ralph Winter.[13] The concept is that of *cultural distance*. This was developed to assess just how far a people group is from a *meaningful* engagement with the gospel.

13. Ralph D. Winter, "The Highest Priority: Cross-Cultural Evangelism," in *Let the Earth Hear His Voice*, ed. J. D. Douglas (Minneapolis: World-Wide Publications, 1975), 213–25. See also Ralph D. Winter and Bruce Koch, "Finishing the Task: The Unreached People's Challenge," in *Perspectives on the World Christian Movement*, 3rd ed., ed. Ralph D. Winter and Steven C. Hawthorne (Carlisle: Paternoster, 1999), 509–24.

In order to discern this, we have to see it on a scale that goes something like this:

```
 ├───────────┼───────────┼───────────┼───────────┤
 m0          m1          m2          m3          m4
```

Each numeral with the prefix *m* indicates *one significant cultural barrier to the meaningful communication of the gospel.* An obvious example of such a barrier would be language. If you have to reach across a language barrier, you have a problem. Others could be race, history, religion/worldview, culture, etc. For instance, in Islamic contexts, the gospel has struggled to make any significant inroads, because religion, race, and history make a meaningful engagement with the gospel very difficult indeed. Because of the crusades, the Christendom church seriously damaged the capacity for Muslim people to apprehend Christ. So we might put mission to Islamic people in an m3 to m4 situation (religion, history, language, race, and culture). The same is true for the Jewish people in the West. It is very hard to "speak meaningfully" in either of these situations. Granted, these are the more extreme examples we might face in our everyday lives, but it is not hard to see how all the people around us fit somewhere along this scale.

Let me bring it closer to home: most of us can evaluate the people around us in these terms. If you see yourself or your church standing on the m0, here is how we *might* interpret our contexts:

m0–m1	Those with some concept of Christianity who speak the same language, have similar interests, are probably of the same nationality, and are from a class grouping similar to yours or your church's. Most of your friends would probably fit into this bracket.
m1–m2	Here we go to the average non-Christian in our context: a person who has little real awareness of, or interest in, Christianity but is suspicious of the church (they have heard bad things). These people might be politically correct, socially aware, and open to spirituality. This category might also include those previously offended by a bad experience of church or Christians. Just go to the average local pub/bar or nightclub to encounter these people.
m2–m3	People in this group have absolutely no idea about Christianity. They might be part of an ethnic group with different religious impulses or some fringy subculture. This category might include people marginalized by WASPy Christianity, e.g., the gay community. But this group will definitely include people actively antagonistic toward Christianity as they understand it.
m3–m4	This group might be inhabited by ethnic and religious groupings like Muslims or Jews. The fact that they are in the West might ameliorate some of the distance, but just about everything else gets in the way of a meaningful dialogue. They are highly resistant to the gospel.

Those who have seen that poignant movie *The Mission* must remember the scene where Jeremy Irons appears as Father Gabriel, a Jesuit priest who enters the South American rain forest with the intention of building a Christian mission. His challenging task is the conversion of a small tribe of native Amazonian Indians who had previously killed a number of would-be missionaries to that point. When his first encounter with them takes place, each party is culturally very remote and wary of the other (i.e., they are "culturally distant" from each other). They are separated by many cultural obstacles: fear, language, culture, religion, history, etc. The Indians are just about to kill Father Gabriel when he takes out a flute and plays some lyrical tune. Through a universal love for music he establishes a very tentative bridge of communication across the cultural chasm. This was to be the fragile start of a learning process whereby, over time, Father Gabriel and his small group of Jesuits succeed in befriending the natives, learning about their culture, language, and folklore, eventually establishing an effective mission among them. That loving attentiveness to the *other* that was required in that situation is true for all effective mission across cultural barriers. And the time has come for us in the West to learn that all *our* attempts to communicate the gospel are now cross-cultural. We are not in a dissimilar situation, only one more subtle.

So how does the idea of cultural distance relate to Christendom and our situation now? Well, the transformation of the church from marginal movement to central institution started with the Edict of Milan (AD 313), whereby Constantine, the newly crowned emperor who had claimed a conversion to Christianity, declared Christianity to be the official state religion, thereby eventually delegitimizing all others.[14] But Constantine went beyond eventually proclaiming Christianity as the top-dog official religion: in order to bolster his political regime, he sought to bond church and state in a kind of sacred embrace, and so he brought all the Christian theologians together and demanded that they come up with a common theology that would unite the Christians in the empire and so secure the political link between church and state. Not surprisingly, he also instituted a centralized church organization based in Rome to "rule" the churches and to unite all Christians everywhere under one institution, with direct links to the state. And so, everything changed, and what was thereafter called "Christendom" was instituted.

14. The edict permanently established religious toleration for Christianity within the Roman Empire. It was the outcome of a political agreement concluded in Milan between the Roman emperors Constantine I and Licinius in February 313. The proclamation, made for the East by Licinius in June 313, granted all persons freedom to worship whatever deity they pleased, assured Christians of legal rights (including the right to organize churches), and directed the prompt return to Christians of confiscated property. Previous edicts of toleration had been as short-lived as the regimes that sanctioned them, but this time the edict effectively established religious toleration. But its net result in sociopolitical terms was to establish the Christian religious hegemony as Christianity became the only legitimate religion of the court, and henceforth, if one sought any form of political power, one had to be a baptized Christian.

The foundation of the Christendom system was a close, though sometimes fraught, partnership between church and state, the two main pillars of society. Through the centuries, power struggles between popes and emperors resulted in one or the other holding sway for a time. But the Christendom system assumed that the church was associated with a status quo that was understood as Christian and had vested interests in its maintenance. The church provided religious legitimation for state activities, and the state provided secular force to back up ecclesiastical decisions.[15]

What is clear is that a number of very significant shifts took place after Constantine's deal with the church. In order to see our own experience of Christendom in a clearer light, it is necessary to outline the major shifts that took place after its imposition. According to Stuart Murray,[16] the Christendom shift meant:

- The adoption of Christianity as the official religion of a city, state, or empire
- The movement of the church from the margins of society to its center
- The creation and progressive development of a Christian culture or civilization
- The assumption that all citizens (except for the Jews) were Christian by birth
- The development of the *corpus Christianum,* where there was no freedom of religion and where political power was regarded as divinely authenticated
- Infant baptism as the symbol of obligatory incorporation into this Christian society
- Sunday as an official day of rest and obligatory church attendance, with penalties for noncompliance
- The definition of "orthodoxy" as the common belief shared by all, which was determined by powerful church leaders supported by the state
- The imposition of a supposedly Christian morality on the entire society (although normally Old Testament moral standards were applied)
- A hierarchical ecclesiastical system, based on a diocesan and parish arrangement, which was analogous to the state hierarchy and was buttressed by state support

15. Research notes graciously provided by Dr. Stuart Murray in 2005.

16. Murray, *Post-Christendom: Church and Mission in a Strange New World* (Carlisle: Paternoster, 2004), 76–78.

- The construction of massive and ornate church buildings and the formation of huge congregations
- A generic distinction between clergy and laity, and the relegation of the laity to a largely passive role
- The increased wealth of the church and the imposition of obligatory tithes to fund this system
- The defense of Christianity by legal sanctions to restrain heresy, immorality, and schism
- The division of the globe into "Christendom" or "heathendom" and the waging of war in the name of Christ and the church
- The use of political and military force to impose the Christian faith
- The use of the Old Testament, rather than the New, to support and justify many of these changes

This shift to Christendom was thoroughly paradigmatic, and the implications were absolutely disastrous for the Jesus movement that was incrementally transforming the Roman world from the bottom up. Rodney Stark, widely considered to be the prevailing expert on the church in this period, summed it up in these dramatic terms.

> Far too long, historians have accepted the claim that the conversion of the Emperor Constantine (ca. 285–337) caused the triumph of Christianity. To the contrary, he destroyed its most attractive and dynamic aspects, turning a high-intensity, grassroots movement into an arrogant institution controlled by an elite who often managed to be both brutal and lax.[17]

The net result of these shifts in terms of cultural distance was to bring the general culture with its people groups into the cultural distance of the church and its message. This cultural proximity was to last as long as the church retained its religious dominance over the prevailing culture. This is called the Christendom period, and it meant the sometimes complete ascendancy of church over state and society. This dominance was weakened by the advent of the Renaissance and the Reformation (fourteenth through sixteenth century) and subsequently declined and eventually came to an end during the late Enlightenment, or modern, period (nineteenth to twentieth century).

The Enlightenment sought to establish reason over revelation through philosophy and science, eventually forcing a separation of the power of the church from that of the state (the French Revolution). The state, and the public sphere along with it, was thereby stripped of religious influ-

17. Rodney Stark, *For the Glory of God* (Princeton: Princeton University Press, 2003), 33.

ences; the secular state was born, with science as the mediator of truth and the market as the mediator of meaning. The result of the Enlightenment period, among many other things, was the secularization of society and the subsequent marginalization of the church and its message. We who have lived in the twentieth century know this experientially all too well. The problem we face is that while as a sociopolitical-cultural force Christendom is dead, and we now live in what has been aptly called the post-Christendom era, the *church still operates in exactly the same mode.* In terms of how we understand and "do" church, little has changed for seventeen centuries.

With the breakup of the modern period and the subsequent postmodern period, things have begun to radically change. For one, the power of hegemonic ideologies has come to an end, and with that, the breakdown of the power of the state (e.g., the Soviet Union) and other forms of "grand stories" that bind societies or groups together in a grand vision. The net effect of this has been the resultant flourishing of subcultures, and what sociologists call the *heterogenization,* or simply the *tribalization,* of Western culture. Just as we had intuited from the local level at SMRC, a new tribalism was born in the postmodern era.

People now identify themselves less by grand ideologies, national identities, or political allegiances, and by much less grand stories: those of interest groups, new religious movements (New Age), sexual identity (gays, lesbians, transsexuals, etc.), sports activities, competing ideologies (neo-Marxist, neofascist, eco-rats, etc.), class, conspicuous consumption (metrosexuals, urban grunge, etc.), work types (computer geeks, hackers, designers, etc.), and so forth. On one occasion some youth ministry specialists I work with identified in an hour fifty easily discernible youth *subcultures* alone (computer nerds, skaters, homies, surfies, punks, etc.). Each of them takes their subcultural identity with utmost seriousness, and hence any missional response to them must as well.

The point here is that of the comparison between the situation of the Christendom church and that of our own: that to reach beyond our own cultural reference (m0–m1) and beyond significant cultural barriers (m1 through m4) is an entirely different thing. The problem is that the average church in the Christendom mode tends to be reasonably effective only within its own cultural reference (m0–m1). The Christendom church was built for that—it's called *outreach and in-drag* (and I'm not making fun, its how we actually operate). The seeker-sensitive approach is a pumped-up model of this . . . and only in rare cases is it ever successful on a large scale.

Using this as a grid with which to analyze the cultural distance of the church in Western contexts over the last 2,000 years, it might look something like this:

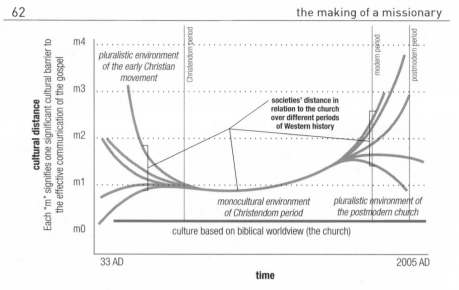

I fully recognize that this is an impossible simplification of the actual historical situation, but this diagram is designed to *distill* the essence of the changing situations of the church in terms of cultural distance. Note the differences in cultural distance during different periods of time. Note too the similarity between our situation and that of the early church. There are many cultural groups, some of which move toward us, with most moving away. Missionary approaches were/are required in both situations. But this was not the case during the Christendom period, because Christendom homogenized culture, and everyone born in its realm was considered to be Christian. And it is my contention that it was in this period that the church lost its primary missionary calling and shape, its movement ethos, and in doing so inadvertently suppressed its heritage of Apostolic Genius.

Now, in the postmodern period, the whole deal has shifted; *we are now back on genuinely missional ground.* In the contemporary situation, the vast majority of people around us (certainly in Australia, the United Kingdom, Europe, and increasingly the United States) range between m1 and m3 distant to where the church generally stands. In this situation the average church's attractional outreach is not going to cut it any more. Alpha (evangelistic groups), evangelistic services, and friendship evangelism will reach within our own cultural framework (m0–m1), but are seldom, if ever, effective beyond it. Remember Father Gabriel. To reach beyond significant cultural barriers we are going to have to adopt a missionary stance in relation to the culture. And partly that will mean adopting a *sending* approach rather than an *attractional* one,[18] and partly it will mean that we have to adopt best practices in cross-cultural mis-

18. I will dedicate a whole chapter to this when we look at an element of mDNA called the missional-incarnational impulse.

sion methodology. Whatever, it will necessitate a much more sophisticated approach than the ones generally in use at present and it will require that we readjust our paradigm of church to meet this challenge. It is time for the missional church to arise and for the sleeping giant to wake up.

Speaking of the Alpha course, this remarkable evangelistic tool has been used to bring many to the faith. I understand that up to 3 million people have participated in Alpha courses in the United Kingdom alone. The way it is generally used by churches is as an evangelistic tool to contribute to the church's numerical growth. The interesting thing is that in the United Kingdom, Alpha is most successful among what has been called the "*de*churched" rather than the genuinely unchurched—in other words, those who came within the m0–m1 framework. And in spite of its evangelistic power, viewed from a broader perspective it has not substantially added to church growth. There are certainly not 3 million new church members in the United Kingdom as a result of Alpha. In fact, the church there is still in serious decline. As such, Alpha, far from being an effective missionary tool, actually serves as a good example of how we don't reach very far beyond ourselves at all.

How can this be? A major part of the problem is that although largely dechurched people do come to faith in Jesus through Alpha, it seems that they still don't want to "go to church." It's that darn "*Jesus, yes. Church, no*" phenomenon again. People will come to faith in small, intimate communities of friends but generally don't want the organized-religion part of the deal. This swapping of agendas has sometimes been perceived as a "bait and switch" strategy, which is generally considered unethical in the commercial world. So we have now reached the vexing situation that the prevailing expression of church (Christendom) has become a major stumbling block to the spread of Christianity in the West. Applying the grid of Apostolic Genius, I find myself asking the question "What if instead of just being a church growth tool, Alpha became a church multiplication movement—a new church emerging out of the original Alpha group and reproducing itself from there?" My guess is that with a different paradigm driving it, it could really take off. It has so many elements of Apostolic Genius latent in its structure but is hindered by a more institutional understanding of church. Here we see the clash of the paradigms in stark form.

We've Always Done It This Way . . . er . . . Haven't We?

If you are feeling uncomfortable at this point, let me reiterate that Christendom in fact is *not* the original biblical mode of the early church, and so we do not need to feel too touchy about it. It's all right. . . . God's not going to strike us if we seek to find a better way to be faithful as well as missional. Progress is cool.

Think this is wrong? Then let's look at the essential *modes* of the church analyzed in three eras or epochs. I have constructed a distinctly sociological grid in order to view the issues in terms of social and organizational patterning, because it is useful to try to get a more objective look at our situation.[19] And while this table, like all comparative tables, is a simplification of the actual situation (real life is not that easily categorized), it does, I believe, *distill the essence* of each era. Take a look . . .

	APOSTOLIC AND POSTAPOSTOLIC MODE (AD 32 to 313)	CHRISTENDOM MODE (313 to current)	EMERGING MISSIONAL MODE (past 10 years)
Locus of gathering	Doesn't have dedicated sacral buildings; often underground and persecuted	Buildings become central to the notion, and experience, of church	Rejects the concern and need for dedicated "church" buildings
Leadership ethos	Leadership operating with at least a fivefold ministry-leadership ethos as in Eph 4. (apostle, prophet, evangelist, pastor, teacher)	Leadership by institutionally ordained clergy, thus creating a professional guild operating primarily in a pastor-teacher mode	Leadership embraces a pioneering-innovative mode including a fivefold ministry-leadership ethos. Noninstitutional by preference
Organizational structure(s)	Grassroots, decentralized, cellular, movement	Institutional-hierarchical and top-down notion of leadership and structure	Grassroots, decentralized, movements
Sacramental mode (means of grace)	Communion celebrated as a sacramentalized community meal; baptism by all	Increasing institutionalization of grace through the sacraments experienced only "in church"	Redeems, re-sacramentalizes, and ritualizes new symbols and events, including the meal
Position in society	Church is on the margins of society and underground	Church is perceived as central to society and surrounding culture	Church is once again on the fringes of society and culture
Missional-mode	Missionary, incarnational-sending church	Attractional (➚ "extractional" in missional settings beyond m1)	Missional; incarnational-sending; The church re-embraces a missional stance in relation to culture

The first era in this grid describes that exciting and definitive Jesus movement that spread across the Roman Empire and eventually subverted it. When analyzed, it is clear that this was very much a grassroots phenomenon, a people movement that lacked any easily definable institutions because in the context

19. This table has previously been used in Frost and Hirsch, *The Shaping of Things to Come*, 9.

of persecution it was unable to fully establish them. There was no HQ, and it spread by using the social rhythms and structures of the day. This movement dynamic basically continued in various forms until Constantine. When Constantine came on the scene, everything changed, absolutely everything.

Look down the middle column in the table (Christendom), and you will easily recognize to some degree all the elements of what we normally understand as "church." Is it not true that few can conceive of church without a special type of building with a special shape? We even call the buildings "churches," and we "go to church." Most leaders in the church get their authorization to minister from a centralized institution called a denomination. Most people who are ordained by the system are gifted in the modes of pastor-teacher, with accredited degrees. Gone are the other three types found in Ephesians 4. This is so because in a culture where all people are assumed to be Christian, the church needs only to care for them and teach the faith. In most denominations only ordained ministers are authorized to administer the sacraments, which is no longer a real living meal, but one of which the religious symbols and ideas are distilled and extracted from the experience of the physical meal and administered only within the confines of the church and its official ministry. In some quarters grace has even been perceived as a substance to be administered through the sacraments and only by priests. In effect, grace became a "possession" of the institutional church and not something easily experienced "outside" its direct sphere of control or influence.

And what of structure? The organizational structures of Christendom are in a real sense worlds away from that of the early church—something like comparing the United Nations to Al Qaeda (one being a thoroughgoing institution with centralized structures, policies, protocols, and the other being a reticulated network operating around a simple structure with a focused cause). In the Christendom era the church perceived itself as central to society and hence operated in the *attractional* mode. In this situation people *come to church* to hear the gospel, to be taught in the faith, and to partake of the sacraments.[20]

Please note here that I am *not* saying that God does not use, and has not used, this mode of church. Nor am I saying that the people within its structures are not sincere and genuine Christians. Most of us have found God in this mode. He has obviously used it and continues to be found in it today. What I'm saying is that because of the drastically changed conditions, this configuration of church is literally out*moded*. It will simply not be sufficient for the challenges of the twenty-first century—statistics and trends bear this out in every Western cultural context. It is no use simply rearranging

20. Later I will make the point that in missional settings, this *attractional* approach to church actually becomes *extractional*, because it severs the organic ties that the convert has with his or her host culture and creates something of a Christian cloister culturally distanced from its context. This is important enough a point to make here, because it goes to the issue of strategy and the nature of the missional church.

aspects of the same model without going to the roots of the paradigm. We must not abandon Christendom, for in it are God's people, but it needs a fundamental change, a conversion if you like, if it is to become genuinely missional. This change is possible, but not without major realignment of our current thinking and resources. And because Christendom is so deeply entrenched in our imaginations and practices, this shift will certainly not happen without significant political will to change. It will be resisted by those with the most significant vested interests in the current system.

"Now that the long Constantinian age has passed, we Christians find ourselves in a situation much more analogous to that of the New Testament Christians than to the Christendom for which some nostalgically long"[21]; Episcopalian theologian Robert Webber calls on evangelicals to return to a more pre-Constantinian understanding and experience of church.[22] To renew ourselves, we need to touch base with our deepest roots. To invoke and access the power of Apostolic Genius, we must be willing to take a journey of discovery and therefore be willing to walk away from what we think is secure and safe and take some risks. If it helps, the truly liberating thing to realize is that Christendom was *not* the original mode of the church, and hopefully it will not be the final one. It is high time for us to dethrone Constantine; as far as matters of church go, it seems he is *still* the emperor of our imaginations. The church now faces the challenge of discovering mission in a new paradigm while struggling to free itself from the Christendom mindset. Or in the words the ever insightful Loren Mead, "We are surrounded by the relics of the Christendom Paradigm, a paradigm that has largely ceased to work. [These] relics hold us hostage to the past and make it difficult to create a new paradigm that can be as compelling for the next age as the Christendom Paradigm has been for the past age."[23]

"It's Church, Jim, but Not as We Know It"

It is time to (re)discover a *new* story of the church and its mission. Enter the emerging missional church (EMC). This form of *ecclesia* is genuinely creative, because it does present a fundamentally alternative imagination

21. Rodney Clapp, quoted in R. E. Webber, *The Younger Evangelicals: Facing the Challenges of the New World* (Grand Rapids: Baker, 2002), 113–14.

22. Webber, *Younger Evangelicals.*

23. Loren Mead, *The Once and Future Church: Reinventing the Congregation for a New Mission Frontier* (Washington: Alban institute, 1991), 18. He says on p. 43, "The dilemma of the church in this transitional time is that the shells of the old structures still surround us even though many of them no longer work." He notes that some of these shells are institutions, some are roles, and some are mind-sets and expectations. Whatever, these need to be acknowledged, analyzed, and dealt with if we are to move on.

to the predominant one. And it is ancient, because, as we shall see, it looks, feels, and manifests itself as very similar to the original apostolic one. This is no accident, because as the thesis of this book will explore, the church is beginning to rediscover its Apostolic Genius and the associated mDNA (the central complex of guiding ideas, phenomena, structures, and experiences) that made the phenomenal Jesus movements genuinely dangerous stories and such remarkable and effective tools of God's redemptive mission to the world. And the good news is that every community of believers, itself the carrier of Apostolic Genius, can recover this lost identity *if* that community is willing to journey again. It's there . . . all we need to do is reach inside.

What is proposed here (in the "emerging missional" column of the table above) comes from significant personal research that has taken me across the world to various contexts. It also formed the basis of my work with Michael Frost in *The Shaping of Things to Come: Innovation and Mission for the 21ˢᵗ-Century Church*, so I will refer the reader there for some stories and more details.[24] However, a more current work on the emerging churches by Eddie Gibbs and Ryan Bolger includes an extensive analysis of forty-nine communities from both the United States and the United Kingdom.[25] This book is invaluable in getting a handle on some noteworthy aspects of this movement.

What follows is not a forced reading of the situation but describes the actual phenomenon of the emerging missional church that is taking place in our day—a phenomenon I have been very privileged to be a part of through my local work, but also through the marvelous vantage point of Forge Mission Training Network. Forge sees itself as a midwife to a new dream. It has a strategic focus on the EMC and is deeply involved.

What we are witnessing in our day is the emergence of new movements and communities, many of them as yet unformed and relatively disorganized. The remarkable thing in terms of structure is that there is no center, and no real circumference, and yet thanks largely to the Internet and new media, many are extensively connected across the globe. Most people in the EMC just seem to know one another. These communities and movements don't feel that God's people are irrevocably tied to certain types of buildings. Therefore, new forms of Christian community are emerging in dance clubs (e.g., Mosaic in Los Angeles, NGM in London), cafés (Allellon in Boise, Idaho, Jeebiz in Melbourne), riverbanks (Church on the Pine in Brisbane), theaters (The Green Room in Adelaide, Tribe of LA), pubs and bars (Holy Joes in London), sports clubs (Matthew's Party in Chicago), homes (House2House, Simple Church), businesses (Subterranean Shoe Room in San Francisco, In The Blood tattoo

24. See also Eddie Gibbs's *Church Next*, and Gerard Kelly's *RetroFuture*. Work by Brian McLaren and Leonard Sweet is also vital reading in this regard.

25. Eddie Gibbs and Ryan Bolger, *Emerging Churches: Creating Christian Community in Postmodern Cultures* (Grand Rapids: Baker Academic, 2006).

parlor in Pittsburgh), and church buildings (Three Nails in Pittsburgh, Moot in London). And yet they are real and authentic expressions of church if my definitions in the last chapter hold water. They are highly creative in resymbolizing the faith (called in various places the alternative worship movement). They are rich in conversations around spirituality, life, Jesus, God, faith, discipleship, and mission—conversations that try to include those outside the faith. The leadership emerging in them tends to be imbued with a creative and pioneering spirit. And few of them are ordained—this is a genuine grassroots *people movement*. There is a rediscovery of Christology and the person of Jesus as the center point of faith, rather than all the highly stylized dogmas and creeds that have defined the Christendom mode. On the whole it is very much a fringe movement—there is no sense that they have a central role in society at large—and yet it seems to be committed to faith in the public sphere. And what is exciting is that all these churches tend to have a missional heart, the desire to reach others with the message of redemption in Jesus.

Gibbs and Bolger list the following, more spirituality-focused, characteristics of the churches in the movement:

- Identifying primarily with Jesus
- Transforming secular space
- Living as community
- Welcoming the stranger
- Serving with generosity
- Participating as producers
- Creating as created beings
- Leading as a body
- Praying "Thy will be done"[26]

This search for new forms of church includes what many have called the "house church" or the "simple church" movement. Whereas most people continue to think of "going to church" as attending a service at one of the many church buildings located throughout their community, a new study from the Barna Group shows that millions of adults are trying out new forms of spiritual community and worship, with many abandoning the traditional forms altogether.

The new study, based on interviews with more than five thousand randomly selected adults from across the nation, found that 9% of adults attend a house church during a typical week. That is remarkable growth in the past decade, shooting up from just 1% to near double-digit involvement. In total, one out of

26. Ibid., table of contents.

five adults attends a house church at least once a month. Projecting these figures to the national population gives an estimate of more than 70 million adults who have at least experimented with house church participation. In a typical week roughly 20 million adults attend a house church gathering. Over the course of a typical month, that number doubles to about 43 million adults."[27]

This is remarkable. And while not all house churches are part of the larger emerging missional church phenomenon (some of them are quite reactionary, ingrown, conservative, and not at all innovative), they nonetheless constitute an active search for new and simpler forms of church that align closer to the rhythms of life.

As a total phenomenon, the massive search going on in our day, including as it does some of the house church and emerging church movements, contains the seeds of the future of the church in America and elsewhere. As Gerard Kelly, another important interpreter of this situation, observes,

> Experimental groups seeking to engage the Christian faith in a postmodern context will often lack the resources, profile or success record of the Boomer congregations. By definition, they are new, untried, relatively disorganized and fearful of self-promotion. They reject the corporate model of their Boomer forebears, and thus do not appear, according to existing paradigms, to be significant. But don't be fooled. Somewhere in the genesis and genius of these diverse groups is hidden the future of Western Christianity. To dismiss them is to throw away the seeds of our survival.[28]

Another quite remarkable feature is that by and large this phenomenon flies under the radar of most church observers, because they are looking for the familiar features of church as we know it through Christendom. As such it tends to be an underground movement. I have often had to field criticism of the EMC in the guise of pragmatic questions like "Where is it working?" or dismissed in phrases like "When I can see some success, I might consider it." But it *is* working. The answer is right there under our noses, but we can't seem to see it because we are looking for the wrong things. If we look for certain features obvious in the Christendom paradigm (like buildings, programs, overt leaders, church growth, organization, etc.), we will miss what is really happening

But it gets better: Dr. David B. Barrett and Todd M. Johnson, two of the editors of the standard statistical work on world trends called the *World Christian Encyclopedia,* published some amazing statistics in their 2001 annual report of Christian mission. According to them, there are 111 million Chris-

---

27. http://www.barna.org/FlexPage.aspx?Page=BarnaUpdateNarrowPreview&BarnaUpdateID=241

28. G. Kelly, *RetroFuture: Rediscovering Our Roots, Recharting Our Routes* (Downers Grove: InterVarsity, 1999).

tians without a local church.[29] A very significant figure, as these people came from us, are still trying to work out the Jesus factor, and are alienated from current expressions of church. Ministry to these churchless and somewhat dissatisfied sisters and brothers is critical in itself.[30] But more missional potential is packed into the unparalleled rise of the grouping that Barrett and Johnson call "independents," which according to them now number over 20,000 movements and networks, with a total of 394 million church members worldwide. Broadly defined, the movements in this phenomenon

- reject historical denominationalism and other restrictive centralized forms of authority and organization;
- gather in communities of various sizes;
- seek a life focused on Jesus (they definitely see themselves as Christians);
- seek a more effective missionary lifestyle and are one of the fastest-growing church movements in the world. In Barrett's estimation, they will have 581 million members in 2025. That is 120 million more than all Protestant movements together![31]

Now, this should make any Christian leader stop and take notice. Even though these stats report the world situation and, as such, include the Chi-

29. http://www.jesus.org.uk/dawn/2001/dawn07.html. One of the features of the EMC is that many of them have left the structures of the church. They no longer attend worship where things tend to be counted. Attendance at worship seems to be the measure of the Christendom and church growth modes of the church. But we would be unwise to dismiss those who have left as not being Christians. Many take their faith very seriously but struggle with the cultural expression of church. As someone who has been involved with young adults all my professional life, I venture to suggest that there are more people aged twenty to thirty-five who claim to be followers of Jesus who are outside the institution of the church than there are in the church at any given time.

30. A recent study by George Barna shows that traditionally church-bound Christianity, almost inconceivably, seems to hinder rather than encourage revival. The Barna Research Group's study report, entitled *The State of the Church: 2005* (Ventura, CA) discovered that the number of adults in the USA no longer attending church has almost doubled since 1991, from 39 million to 75 million. The adult population grew 15 percent over the same period. "It is mainly the men," says Barna, "who make up 55% of those who have left churches. Around half of churchgoers in the USA claim to have accepted Jesus Christ as Lord and Saviour," as do 12.5 million, or around 16%, of those who no longer attend church. Source: Barna Research Group (www.barna.org) and Andrew Strom's e-book (http://homepages.ihug.co.nz/~revival/00-Out-Of-Church.html). See also Alan Jameson, *A Churchless Faith* (Auckland: Philip Garside Publishing, 2001).

31. Source: http://www.jesus.org.uk/dawn/2001/dawn07.html. Their fuller findings are available at http://www.worldchristiandatabase.org/wcd/esweb.asp?WCI=Results&Query=289&PageSize=25&Page=172. Statistics are annually updated from Barrett's annual "Status of Global Mission" http://www.globalchristianity.org/resources.htm (see 2005 figures).

nese phenomenon, among others, even if only 10 percent (my guess) of the above figures relate to the West, we are dealing with something truly profound and remarkable. What Barrett and Johnson call the independent movement, I prefer to call the emerging missional church in Western contexts. But whatever terminology we use, it is very significant, because this is largely an unorganized Jesus movement-in-the-making. If are looking for real church growth, *here* it is. But sadly, if we continue to look at this through the increasingly obsolete lenses of the Christendom paradigm, we won't be able to see it and will simply miss it.

As indicated before, all this has led me to adopt a missionary identity and practice. The above analysis was part of my "conversion," and I present it here for your consideration. My own journey has led me to invest almost completely in making sure that the EMC establishes itself and begins to thrive. I really do believe, with Gerard Kelly, that the real future of Western Christianity resides in these fledgling groups and movements and that it is as worthy a cause as one can find. A few years ago there were fewer reasons to be optimistic about our situation. But today, I believe that we have passed some form of critical mass, and there is good reason for hope. But we must be willing to significantly realign resources, invest in the future, take a journey, and experiment like mad.[32]

Who Put the *M* in the EMC?

The independent/EMC phenomenon, along with my search to discover the crucial elements that make up Apostolic Genius, has given me a real sense of hope for the church in the West. The Spirit is moving in marvelous ways again. Movements are being sparked and the established church is just beginning to wake up to itself and its missional calling. But shedding Christendom is no easy task. The transition from Christendom modes to genuinely missional ones will not necessarily be an easy one for most churches and church leaders. And so the missionary analysis of our situation must not be avoided, because unless we see it for what it is, we will never move to becoming a more faithful and impacting expression of God's people.

The absolutely vital issue for newer emerging churches will be their capacity to become genuinely missional. If they fail to make this shift, then

32. The addendum entitled "A Crash Course in Chaos" will highlight the role of leadership in creating the conditions of this shift and why it is necessary. While it is not essential to the flow of this study of Apostolic Genius, I suggest that the reader grapple with the ideas presented in it, because the theories of chaos, complexity, and emergence are extremely rich in new metaphors and in new ways of thinking about people, organizations, and leadership. It is particularly profitable if one wants to get a real grasp of the idea of Apostolic Genius. I have found it to be quite profound and deeply enriching.

they too will be another readjustment of Christendom. A mere fad. As we will see throughout this book, new and emergent forms of church are the result of being missional, not the other way around. I therefore present the same challenge here to my brothers and sisters in the emerging church as I do to the established church: if you don't just want to be another church fad, don't just make the service and spirituality suit a postmodern audience, start at another place—put the M in the equation *first*, and *EC will* follow.

A JOURNEY
TO THE HEART
OF APOSTOLIC GENIUS

Introduction

In this section we come to the very heart of this book. The material here will have immediate relevance for ourselves and for the faith communities in which we serve as we try find that strangely *new yet ancient* way that has made God's people the most powerful transformative force in history. How we might apply this material will differ depending on our situations: for the established church or church leader wanting to evolve the church into a missional one, it will be critical to develop a healthy change process to help reorient the church into apostolic forms. It will mean really grappling with the missional situation that we face (as in chapters 1 and 2) as well as cultivating an active learning process in the context of chaos (see addendum). For the church planter/missionary it might mean embedding these ideas in the consciousness of the initial community (especially the leadership) *before* initiating the project, so that they form part of the fundamental consciousness of the church-planting team. For those still only contemplating all things missional, I hope that this section will help give some shape to those vital dreams.

Whatever the situation, I contend that the cultivation and development of each element of mDNA on its own will take the church closer to the nature of the church in its more phenomenal form (e.g., the early church and in China). It is a significant reflection of missional fitness to have various elements of the above mDNA active in the faith community. For instance, any church that adopts a missional-incarnational impulse has moved closer to being an authentic Jesus movement. Any church that focuses on disciple making is by definition going to be a more authentic church, and so forth. But my theory is that when *all six* elements are in place and mutually informing one another, infused by its spiritual instincts and center, and empowered by the Spirit, something fundamentally different is activated. It is at that point where, given the right conditions, metabolic growth and impact are catalyzed. A movement operating with Apostolic Genius is in my theory a distinctly higher and more authentic form of *ecclesia* than that which might have existed before.

Before trying to articulate the five critical elements of mDNA in this section, here are some fuller explanations and definitions of the ideas of Apostolic Genius, mDNA, and missional church.

mDNA

The *Encyclopedia Britannica* defines DNA as ". . . organic chemical of complex molecular structure that is found in all organic, living cells and in many viruses. DNA *codes genetic information for the transmission of inherited traits.*"[1] Its dictionary definition: "A *self-replicating* material which is *present in nearly all living organisms. . . .* It is the *carrier of genetic information.*" (emphases mine)[2] These will do for our purposes, because they get to the key areas:

- DNA is found in every living cell (except the most simplest of viruses).
- It codes genetic information for the transmission of inherited traits beyond that of the initiating organism.
- It is self-replicating.
- It carries vital information for healthy reproduction.

So what then is mDNA? The *m* is inserted purely to differentiate it from the biological version—it simply means *missional* DNA. So what DNA does for biological systems, mDNA does for ecclesial ones. And with this concept/metaphor I hope to explain why the presence of a simple, intrinsic, reproducible, central guiding mechanism is necessary for the reproduction and sustainability of genuine missional movements. As an organism holds together, and each cell understands its function in relation to its DNA, so the church finds its reference point in its built-in mDNA. As DNA carries the genetic coding, and therefore the life, of a particular organism, so too

---

1. *Encyclopedia Britannica, standard edition,* CD-ROM, *s.v.* "DNA."
2. Ibid.

mDNA codes Apostolic Genius (the life force that pulsated through the New Testament church and in other expressions of apostolic Jesus movements throughout history).

It is remarkable that in biological systems *each cell carries the full coding* of the whole organism. And even though one specific type of cell in an organism, say, a muscle or brain cell, usually only refers to a small portion of the genetic code for its own structure, it has the whole deal locked away inside it. The whole organism can be reproduced from one single cell. So I come to believe that every church, indeed every Christian, if truly birthed in Jesus Christ through the Holy Spirit, has the full coding of mDNA and therefore has direct access to the power of Apostolic Genius. It is *there,* only the more institutional forms have simply forgotten or suppressed it, because its primal and uncontrollable nature represents danger to the institution itself—it is so different and uncontainable. Institutional systems tend to try and organize through external hierarchical command and control; organic missional movements organize through healthy mDNA coding embedded in each cell and then let go. Cole highlights this difference by comparing the external (exoskeletal) structuring of the institutional with the internal (endoskeletal) structuring of organic systems.[3]

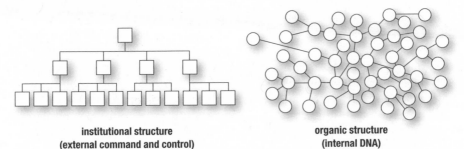

institutional structure   organic structure
(external command and control)   (internal DNA)

From my research on Jesus movements, we tend to access this powerful coding when we face a significant adaptive challenge (a threat to existence and/or a compelling opportunity). How else can we explain how the underground church in China activated Apostolic Genius? They *intuitively* seemed to know what to do when all external support structures and expressions were destroyed. How do we account for this? All their buildings were nationalized, all their thinkers were imprisoned, the entire existing leadership was killed, exiled, or imprisoned, and they were forbidden to gather on penalty of death and torture. How is it that in these conditions

3. Neil Cole, *The Organic Church: Growing Faith Where Life Happens* (San Francisco: Jossey-Bass, 2005), 126–27.

they just seemed to form themselves in a way almost totally identical to that of the early church? They had no access to material like this book to guide them—they didn't even have enough Bibles.

I have long pondered this mystery, and I can only suggest that they found it *in themselves*. Or more accurately, this potent coding is placed within them through the work of the Spirit and by the power of the gospel in the community. There is no other way of explaining this: it was already there, and the Spirit of Jesus activated it in the context of chaos and adaptive challenge. This is true in every situation where the church faces a serious threat or an overwhelming opportunity that compels it to the rediscovery of its true nature. Apostolic Genius, it seems, is coded into each and every community through latent mDNA; only for most of us it lies buried and forgotten.

Apostolic Genius

In coining this phrase I want to try to identify something that is very hard to "see" but that seems to be always present in the church when it is in its most phenomenal form. There is no current word or phrase to define this "spirit" that imbued the New Testament church and other expressions of apostolic forms of church.

Apostolic Genius is as hard for us to define as the idea of *life* is to biologists. Have you ever tried your hand at defining life?[4] Or electricity? In coining the phrase I hope to identify that primal energy, the spiritual current that seemed to thrust its way through those little communities of faith that transformed the world. Apostolic Genius, to my mind, is the total phenomenon resulting from a complex of multiform and real experiences of God, types of expression, organizational structures, leadership ethos, spiritual power, mode of belief, etc. And it is the active presence, or the lack of it, that makes all the difference to our experience of Jesus community, mission, and spiritual power.

Loaded into the term Apostolic Genius is the full aggregation of all the elements of mDNA that together form a constellation, as it were, each shedding light on the other. Diagrammatically, Apostolic Genius, composed as it is by the various elements of mDNA, looks something like this:

4. Try this for size: "Life is the state of a material complex or individual characterized by the capacity to perform certain functional activities, including metabolism, growth, reproduction, and some form of responsiveness and adaptation. Life is further characterized by the presence of complex transformations of organic molecules and by the organization of such molecules into the successively larger units of protoplasm, cells, organs, and organisms" (*Encyclopedia Britannica Standard Edition 2001 CD-ROM*, s.v. "life")—and that's only the start!

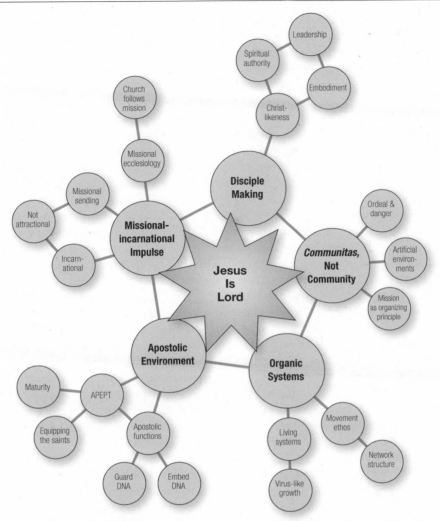

This rather strange diagram conveys in visual form the complex of phenomena, impulses, practices, structures, leadership modes, etc., that together form Apostolic Genius. It also presents a working outline of the entire structure of this section, where all will be explained. The six elements described here form the phenomenon called Apostolic Genius that in turn energizes and shapes all Jesus movements anywhere.

The rest of this book will be an attempt to describe these aspects of Apostolic Genius by identifying, defining, and translating each aspect of mDNA into our context in the West. Hopefully, by the end of the book, the reader will be provoked to pursue and recover these in the life of the church.

The main task remains to try to identify this elusive concept of Apostolic Genius, because in the recovery and activation of this potent inheritance in all of God's people lies the great renewal of the church in the West.

To ground this somewhat intangible idea in a contemporary Western example, I will refer throughout the book to the story of the Church Multiplication Associates (CMA). CMA is a movement that started in the United States but now has churches in sixteen countries around the world. Don't let this rather unsexy name obscure the profound treasure that has been discovered in this movement, which in six years grew to about 700+ churches. Neil Cole, the founder and leader of this movement, says that the story of CMA begins with his story of being a pastor in a successful, medium-sized, contemporary church.

This soft-spoken man has a real heart for the unevangelized, which leads him into some defining encounters with some fringy people. These experiences draw him deeper and deeper into thinking about more genuinely missional ways of doing church.[5] Imbued with an apostolic gifting, an innovator's audacity, and an uncanny ability to see things organically, he sets about planting a missional movement in Long Beach, California. The explicit ideas driving this church, and the resultant movement, are those of (1) simple, decentralized, reproducible, organic systems and (2) disciple making. These are the expressly stated organizing principles, but more goes on beneath the surface. These directly relate to two of the elements of mDNA, namely, disciple making (chapter 6) and organic systems (chapter 7). But even if the church and the movement do not use the terms, one doesn't have to look far to find the others: all six elements of mDNA are functioning in significant ways even though they are not explicitly named as such in this book.

- In CMA there is a definite missional-incarnational impulse—they are "doing church" in just about every conceivable social context—from car parks to cafés, pubs to houses. And they do not control through a central organization. They simply "let it go" and network each group through empowering relationships. We will study this in chapter 4.

- The observer will be able to discern the influence of a certain kind of leadership in Neil and others that can only be called *apostolic*. In fact, it is through Neil's apostolic influence that the core elements of mDNA were seeded in the first place. This linking of ancient gospel with authentic current expression is the true mark of apostolic ministry, as we will see in chapter 5.

5. Cole, "Organic Church"; and see his previous book, *Cultivating a Life for God: Multiplying Disciples through Life Transformation Groups* (St. Charles, IL: ChurchSmart, 1999) for a description of the CMA movement and dynamics.

- You will find mission-oriented communities that are fluid, adaptive, adventure-based, and formed in the context of a common purpose that lies outside of itself—what will be described as *communitas* in chapter 8.

Apostolic Genius is indeed alive and well in the movement. While CMA is a great example of it, it is by no means the only one. We will look at similar churches and movements all the way through the book in my attempt to translate into Western contexts the findings of Apostolic Genius in the postapostolic and Chinese movements. What is easily detectable in the CMA example is that the experience of church and following Jesus has become very simple and completely reproducible by just about any Christian. The systematic embedding of the mDNA of this movement squares with the purpose of DNA in all living systems: it codes its life and makes it transferable by all members of the group, not just some. This is the stuff that great movements are made of, because it contains and operates out of the Apostolic Genius that lies at the core of God's *ecclesia*.

In studying these phenomena, at a certain stage the revelation of God's marvelous design dawned on me: I came to see that Apostolic Genius is actually latent in all true Christians and is, I believe, one of the works of the Holy Spirit in us. In some mysterious way, when we are incorporated into God's family, we all seem to become "seeds" bearing the full potential of God's people within us. If you or I were blown like a seed into a different field, God could create a Jesus community out of both of us. This is the marvel of a true people movement. And where it is unleashed and cultivated, world transformation takes place.

Missional and *Missional Church*

The terms *missional* and *missional church* originated in the work of a group of North American practitioners, missiologists, and theorists called the Gospel and Our Culture Network (GOCN), who came together to try and work out some of the implications of the work of that remarkable missionary thinker Lesslie Newbigin. It was Newbigin who, after returning from a lifetime of work in India as a missionary, saw how pagan Western civilization really was. He began to articulate the view that we need to see the Western world as a mission field, and that we as God's people in this context needed to adopt a missionary stance in relation to our culture—just as we would in India, for instance.[6] His work captured

6. GOCN began to try build on Newbigin's insights and emphasized essentially that the work of mission involved what they called a "trialogue." Building on the concept of dialogue,

the imagination of a church in crisis and decline and shaped the thinking of generations.

However, the word *missional* has tended, over the years, to become very fluid, and it was quickly co-opted by those wishing to find new and trendy tags for what they were doing, be they missional or not. It is often used as a substitute for *seeker-sensitive, cell-group church,* or other church-growth concepts, thus obscuring its original meaning. So, do we dispose of it and come up with another term?[7] I think we need to keep it but reinvest it with deeper meaning. The word sums up precisely the emphasis of the radical Jesus movements that we need to rediscover today. But more than that, in my opinion it goes to the heart of the very nature and purpose of the church itself.

So a working definition of missional church is a community of God's people that defines itself, and organizes its life around, its real purpose of being an agent of God's mission to the world. In other words, the church's true and authentic organizing principle is mission. When the church is in mission, it is the true church. The church itself is not only a product of that mission but is obligated and destined to extend it by whatever means possible. The mission of God flows directly through every believer and every community of faith that adheres to Jesus. To obstruct this is to block God's purposes in and through his people.

If we can embed this inner meaning into our essential identity as God's people, we will be well on our way to becoming an adaptive organization. This mission can express itself in the myriad ways in which the kingdom of God expresses itself—highly varied and always redemptive.

---

in which there are two parties to a conversation, they maintained that mission essentially involved an active and ongoing conversation between three elements, namely, the gospel, the surrounding culture, and the church. They soon discovered that for the most part, two of the elements made for quite an active and relatively simple conversation; these were the dialogue between gospel and culture, and many were engaged in that discourse. However, the trialogue was not happening, because the church was seldom in the conversation. It had effectively taken itself out of the equation and had become a world unto itself. They sought to address this by trying to bring the church into the equation of mission and came up with the term *missional church.* Missional church in GOCN's perspective was a church that took the trialogue seriously and shaped itself around it. See Darrel Guder, ed., *Missional Church: A Vision for the Sending of the Church in North America* (Grand Rapids: Eerdmans, 1998).

7. I have long debated with myself about the word *mission* itself. It is so loaded with mixed history and tinged with colonialism, especially to the non-Christian mind. Do we get rid of that as well? Frankly, I can't get myself to do it. The idea of mission is so important, and I simply cannot come up with a better word. I think it is better to reload it with true meaning.

3 ↗

the heart of it all: Jesus is Lord

We know that an idol is nothing at all in the world and that there is no God but one. For even if there are so-called gods, whether in heaven or on earth ... yet for us there is but one God, the Father, from whom all things came and for whom we live; and there is but one Lord, Jesus Christ, through whom all things came and through whom we live.

1 Corinthians 8:4–6

The spontaneous expansion of the Church reduced to its elements is a very simple thing. It asks for no elaborate organization, no large finances, no great numbers of paid missionaries. In its beginning it may be the work of one man, and that a man neither learned in the things of this world, nor rich in the wealth of this world. . . . What is necessary is faith. What is needed is the kind of faith which uniting a man to Christ, sets him on fire.

Roland Allen, *The Compulsion of the Spirit*

When Paul completes his exploration into the mystery of God's involvement in our world, he soars into an ecstatic doxology, the substance of which takes us to the very essence of reality. He says, "Oh, the depth of the riches of the wisdom and knowledge of God! How unsearchable his judgments, and his paths beyond tracing out! 'Who has known the mind of the Lord? Or who has been his counselor?' 'Who has ever given to God, that God should repay him?' For from him and through him and to him are all things. To him be the glory forever! Amen" (Rom. 11:33–36). As is true of all moments of deep spiritual inspiration, the clarity of truth dawns upon Paul in utter simplicity, and in articulating these timeless words he points us to the very core of a Hebraic understanding of God: *"for from him and through him and to him are all things."* Here we touch the epicenter of the biblical consciousness of God. And to this spiritual core we must return if we are to renew the church in our day. This chapter will try to reinterpret our faith and following of Jesus in the light of the Hebraic understanding of life. And it all starts with Israel's basic confession, called the *Shema Yisrael* (Hear, O Israel) based on Deuteronomy 6:4.[1]

It is hard to determine where one inserts material that by its very nature is more than just an "element" of Apostolic Genius. All genuine Christian movements involve at their spiritual ground zero a living encounter with the One True God "through whom all things came and through whom we live" (1 Cor. 8:6). A God who in the very moment of redeeming us claims us as his own through Jesus our Savior. If we fail to apprehend this spiritual center and circumference of the Jesus movements, we can never fully understand them nor reinvoke the power that infused their lives and communities. Addison, in his exhaustive study of Christian movements, is right to conclude that they are maintained throughout by what he calls "white hot faith" brought about by a rediscovery of the place and importance of Jesus.[2]

1. For a more thorough exploration on Hebraic ideas and spirituality as they relate to missional church see *The Shaping of Things to Come*, chs. 7 and 8.
2. Addison, "Movement Dynamics," ch. 2.

While in some sense this is an element of Apostolic Genius, it is actually much more than that. This consciousness of God pervades the entire phenomenon. Please remember this as we begin to unpack the various mDNA elements of Apostolic Genius. It's all about God, after all.

Distilling the Message

Most people, when asked about how they think the early Christian movement (and the Chinese underground churches) grew so remarkably, answer that it was largely because they were true believers—that there was a real and abiding authenticity to their faith and that they therefore accessed the power of the Spirit that was available to them. Presumably, if one is willing to die for the faith, one has gone beyond easy believism into the realms of genuine faith and love for God. And such an assessment is right. Any study of the lives of these people cannot fail to inspire. Persecution drives the persecuted to live very close to their message—they simply cling to the gospel of Jesus and thus unlock its liberating power.

But there is more to it than that. One of the "gifts" that persecution seems to confer on the persecuted is that it enables them to distill the essence of the message and thus access it in a new way. Take the Chinese Jesus movement, for example. When all their external reference points are removed, when most of their leaders and theologians killed or imprisoned and all access to outside sources is cut off, they are somehow forced through sheer circumstance to unlock something truly potent and compelling in the message they carry as the people of God. The result is a Jesus movement unparalleled in history. What is going on here, and what can we in the West learn from this?

We know that persecuted Jesus movements are forced underground, usually adopt a more cell-like structure, and are forced to rely largely on relational networks in order to sustain themselves as self-conscious Christian communities. But in order to survive in the context of persecution, they also have to jettison all unnecessary impediments, including that of a predominantly institutional conception of *ecclesia*. But perhaps even more significantly, they have to condense and purify their core message that keeps them both faithful and hopeful. For an underground church, all the clutter of unnecessary traditional interpretations and theological paraphernalia is removed. It has neither the time nor the internal capacity to maintain weighty systematic theologies and churchly dogma. It must "travel light." Therefore all unnecessary complexities are extracted, and in the process a miracle happens—the people discover their true message, and the movement is born. Faith is once again linked in utter simplicity to Jesus, the author and completer of the faith. So at the heart of all great movements is a recovery of a simple Christology (essential conceptions of who Jesus is and what he does), one that accurately reflects the Jesus of New Testament faith—they are in a very literal sense *Jesus* movements.

But something else is unleashed in this recovery of simplicity, namely, the capacity to rapidly transfer the message along relational lines. Freed from the philosophical density of the academy and from dependence on the professional cleric, the gospel becomes profoundly "sneezable." This reference to sneezing is not just whimsical. We know from the study of ideas that they spread in patterns very similar to that of viral epidemics. We also know that in order to really take hold and become an "epidemic," they have to be easily transferred from one person to another. And to do this they need to be profound and yet simple—easily grasped by any person, and in many cases illiterate peasants.[3] In this sense, the gospel once again becomes a possession of the people and not purely of religious institutions that unwittingly make it hard for people to grasp and apply (Matthew 23). Given favorable social and religious conditions, and the right people relationships, easily transferable ideas can create powerful movements that can change societies (and in the case of economics, markets). This is clearly the situation of the gospel in the early church as well as the Chinese revolution. The desperate, prayer-soaked human clinging to Jesus, the reliance on his Spirit, and the distillation of the gospel message into the simple, uncluttered message of Jesus as Lord and Savior is what catalyzed the missional potencies inherent in the people of God.

This phenomenon of a movement identifying, distilling, and living (even dying) by its message is a massive clue as to the nature of Apostolic Genius and how we can recover it in the West. But in order to distill the message in our context, we need to once again appreciate its core, namely, that of the primary theme of the Bible: God's redemptive claim over our lives.

Hear, O Israel

As we have seen, the "gift" that persecution bestows on the people of God is the clarification of the central message of the church. This in turn raises the question, What is that message? What does it look and feel like when reduced to utter simplicity? This study of historical phenomenal Jesus movements has led me to conclude that the answer is found in the substance of a genuine biblical monotheism—an existential encounter with the One God who claims and saves us. As simple, and perhaps at first as uninspiring as this sounds, the belief that God is One lies at the heart of

---

3. This is precisely how Paul can plant a church in a week and then say that they have no need for any further instruction because they received the gospel in its fullness. (e.g., Acts 17:1–9; 1 and 2 Thess., Acts 16:11–40). The gospel was not so complex that people could not grasp it in a week with the apostle. In the Bible, it seems that it is not as complicated as we have often made it.

both the biblical faith and that of the remarkable Jesus movements of history. This irreducible affirmation lies at the heart of all authentic manifestations of Apostolic Genius. This chapter will try to reinterpret our faith and following of Jesus in the light of the Hebraic understanding of life. And it all starts with Israel's basic confession, called the *Shema Yisrael* (Hear, O Israel), based on Deuteronomy 6:4.

When the New Testament people of God confess that "Jesus is Lord and Savior," it is not just the simple confession that Jesus is our Master and we are his servants. It certainly is that, but given the Hebraic context of that confession, and the fact that Jesus is the fulfillment of the messianic promises to Israel, the confession wholly reverberates with beliefs that go back to Israel's primal confession that "Yahweh is Lord." As such, this confession touches upon the deepest possible currents in biblical revelation: themes that take us directly to the nature of God, his relation to his world, and to his claim over every aspect of our lives, both individual and communal. It also relates to the defining encounter, the redemptive experience that forms the covenant relationship between God and his people.

To truly appreciate the power and centrality of this claim we need to set it in its original religious context—that of religious pluralism or *polytheism*. People living in the ancient Near East were essentially a deeply spiritual people who recognized that life was filled with the sacred, the mystical, and the magical. There were numerous gods, demons, and angels who were seen as ruling over different spheres of life.[4] Life was profoundly spiritual, but it was ruled by innumerable deities, many of whom were not very pleasant characters.

So, for example, if you were a practicing polytheist living in that time and place and wanted to draw water down at the river, the trip would take you past the fields on which you depended, past the forest, and down to the river. The religious dilemma you would face in such a seemingly simple activity is that because there were different divinities ruling each of these aspects of life, this was no easy thing—it was fraught with spiritual danger. In order not to offend the *Baal* of the field that you would pass along the way, you would need to take a sacrificial offering and perform a religious ritual at the shrine of the

4. "Polytheism characterizes virtually all religions other than Judaism, Christianity, and Islam, which share a common tradition of monotheism, the belief in one God. Sometimes above the many gods a polytheistic religion will have a supreme creator and focus of devotion, as in certain phases of Hinduism (there is also the tendency to identify the many gods as so many aspects of the Supreme Being); sometimes the gods are considered as less important than some higher goal, state, or savior, as in Buddhism; sometimes one god will prove more dominant than the others without attaining overall supremacy, as Zeus in Greek religion. Typically, polytheistic cultures include belief in many demonic and ghostly forces in addition to the gods, and some supernatural beings will be malevolent; even in monotheistic religions there can be belief in many demons, as in New Testament Christianity." *Encyclopedia Britannica*, *standard edition*, CD-ROM, *s.v.* "polytheism."

field. Then you would have to pass that old foreboding tree. Imposing trees were often thought to contain nasty spirits called dryads, so you would have to be sure not to stir the dryad, and once again you would need to follow a prescribed ritual required to appease that particular dryad. Once again, your belief system would inform you that if the river goddess was offended, the river might dry up or flood, either way causing catastrophe and suffering. So once you reached the river, the goddess of the river, a particularly unpredictable deity, would also have to be placated with a sacrifice. Thus, the simple action of going to the river was actually quite a religiously complex process.

The polytheistic view extended way beyond rivers and fields. There were deities that presided over every possible sphere of life: the state (politics), the family, war, fertility, etc. Life as a polytheist is not only complex (each deity has to be encountered with the appropriate decorum) but is thoroughly superstitious (minor actions have massive spiritual consequences), and also dangerous (not all the gods are good; in fact, some are outright evil). This was the overwhelming religious context of Israel.

And into this context comes the *Shema* . . .

Hear, O Israel: The LORD *our God, the* LORD *is one. Love the* LORD *your God with all your heart and with all your soul and with all your strength.* These commandments that I give you today are to be upon your hearts. Impress them on your children. Talk about them when you sit at home and when you walk along the road, when you lie down and when you get up. Tie them as symbols on your hands and bind them on your foreheads. Write them on the doorframes of your houses and on your gates. (Deut. 6:4–9; emphasis mine)

The declaration in this religious context has direct and far-reaching implications: what this meant to the person(s) coming under this claim is that no longer could there be different gods for the different spheres of life, a god of the temple, another god of politics, a different god for fertility in the field, and yet another for the river, etc. Rather, Yahweh is the ONE God who rules over every aspect of life and the world. Yahweh is Lord of home, field, politics, work, etc., and the religious task was to honor this ONE God in and through all aspects of life. For *"from him and through him and to him are all things"* (Rom. 11:35). This is not only what constitutes the basis of worship, as we shall see later on, but also sets the agenda for the central religious task of discipleship. It is a call for the Israelite to live his or her life under the lordship of one God and not under the tyranny of the many gods. This is why the covenant between Israel and Yahweh begins with an absolute claim of Yahweh to all of Israel's life and a total ban on idols and false gods (Exod. 20:2–5). "When God invades man's consciousness, man's reliance on 'peace and security' vanishes from every nook of his existence. His life as a single whole becomes vulnerable. Broken down are the bulkheads between the chambers which confine explosions to one compartment. When God chooses man, He invests him with full responsibility for total obedience to an absolute demand."[5] Yahweh's lordship is at once complete and graceful salvation as well as total, unqualified demand. In biblical faith, salvation and lordship are inextricably linked.

So in the Hebraic perspective, monotheism is not so much a statement about God as eternal being in essential oneness, as it was for the Hellenist theologians, but rather an existential claim that there is only one God and he is Lord of every aspect of life. Again, here the concrete and practical nature of Hebraic thinking comes to the fore. Polytheists can compartmentalize life and distribute it among many powers. But as Maurice Friedman says, "the [person] of faith in the Israelite world . . . is not distinguished from the 'heathen' by a merely 'spiritual' view of the Godhead, but [rather] by the exclusiveness of his relationship to God, and by his reference of all things to him."[6] Monotheists (authentic *biblical* believers) have only *one* reference point for life and existence—namely God. The *Shema* is the first and original instance of this complete and systemic claim on our lives. It is thus a call to covenant loyalty, rather than being a statement of theological ontology (nature of being).[7] The implications are far-reaching, not just for theology, but for *worldview*—for orienting the believer toward life itself. This must influence how we conceive of life and faith itself.

Listen to theologian Paul Minear:

> The sole sovereignty of God is realized only by stern struggle with other gods, with all the forces that oppose his will. This is to say that, to the biblical writers themselves, monotheism begins, not as a stage of metaphysical speculation, not as a final step in the development out of polytheism, not as a merging of all gods into one (as in Hinduism), but when one God becomes the decisive reality for a particular man and thereby calls for the dethronement of all his other gods.
>
> This helps explain why early Christians found in the total obedience of Jesus a supreme and final manifestation of God. . . . It points to the reason why in dying with him to the world, they themselves experienced true knowledge of God and true power from God. And the message of the oneness of God intensified their struggle against false gods. To them, the conflict with heathen gods had entered its final stage.

5. Paul S. Minear, *Eyes of Faith* (St. Louis: Bethany Press, 1966), 115.

6. Maurice Friedman, *Martin Buber: The Life of Dialogue*, 242.

7. Ontology is the philosophical concern with the nature of "being" (*ontos*). In the hands of the Christendom church, influenced as it was by Hellenistic/Platonic thinking, theology is more concerned with metaphysics (the branch of philosophy that deals with the first principles of things, including abstract concepts such as being, knowing, substance, cause, identity, time, and space) rather than with physics and is therefore highly speculative by nature. Ontological theology, therefore, focused on God in his eternal Being—his innate nature— rather than on his existential claim on our lives. It is almost impossible to find anything of its kind in the whole of scripture, and yet it became, and still is, the chief concern of theologians in the Western tradition.

Christian belief does not consist in merely saying "There is One God." The devil knows that. Christians respond to God by faith in his deeds, trust in his power, hope in his promise, and passionate abandonment of self to do his will. Only within the context of such a passionate vocation does the knowledge of the one Lord live. And this knowledge necessitates rather than eliminates the struggle with the devil and all his works. Only in unconditional obedience, spurred by infinite passion, infinite resignation, infinite enthusiasm is such "monotheism" wholly manifested in human existence, as for example, in Jesus.[8]

The "jealousy" of God must be understood in this light (Exod. 20:5; 34:14; Deut. 4:24, etc.). It is a refusal in God to share his exclusive claim to rule over the lives of his people. It is not a negative emotional response in God; it is simply the outworking of his claim over against the claim of the idols.[9] God will simply not share us with false gods. But it is because idolatry will damage and fracture us, not because God "feels jealous."

All of Life under God

God is ONE and the task of our lives is to bring *every* aspect of our lives, communal and individual, under this One God, Yahweh. This "practical monotheism" lies at the epicenter of Israel's, and therefore the biblical, concept of faith. From this confession all things flow. Even the concept of *torah* (literally "the instruction") is directed at fulfilling it. When reading the Pentateuch one is immediately struck by the radically nonlinear logic associated with it. It seems to jump from one subject to another, from issues of sublime theology in one verse to seemingly trivial issues in the very next verse.

One verse deals with the Israelite's approach to God in the temple. The very next verse deals with what one does when one's donkey falls into a pit. The next might well deal with the mildew in the kitchen, the next with the female menstrual cycle. It seems to be radically discontinuous and generally lacks the sequential reason that we look for in a text. What is going on here? How can we comprehend the meaning of this?[10]

There is actually a rather profound if somewhat nonlinear "logic" in the Torah, a logic that trains us to relate *all aspects* of life to God. The implications of following the Torah faithfully will be to connect all things in life directly to Yahweh, whether it be the mildew or the temple worship and everything in between. Therefore, everything—one's work, one's domestic life, one's

8. Minear, *Eyes of Faith*, 25–26.
9. My dog Ruby is a jealous dog; when I pat other dogs she pushes her way between myself and them and won't let me get to them. This is an insight into the nature of exclusive claims.
10. Frost and Hirsch, *Shaping of Things to Come*, 126.

health, one's worship—has significance to God. He is concerned with every aspect of the believer's life, not just the so-called spiritual dimensions.

> While in the Western spiritual tradition we have tended to see the "religious" as one category of life among many (we even call nuns and monks the "religious"), the Hebrew mind has no such distinction about a purely "religious" existence but is concerned with all of life. . . . All of life is sacred when it is placed in relationship to the living God.[11]

The Hebraic perspective draws a direct correlation from any and every aspect of life to the eternal purposes of God—this is the intrinsic logic of the Torah. It is a natural extension of the claim of monotheism, namely, that Yahweh is Lord! In fact, the Torah is training in this orientation; Paul even calls it a "schoolteacher" (Gal. 3:19–4:5). That is, *Torah* (simply translated "Law" in most standard English translations) trains us in godliness and in God-orientation, and it leads us to Jesus. This was and is its very function.

To say this more explicitly, there is no such thing as sacred and secular in biblical worldview. It can conceive of no part of the world that does not come under the claim of Yahweh's lordship. All of life belongs to God, and true holiness means bringing all the spheres of our life under God. This is what constitutes biblical worship—this is what it means to love God with all our heart, mind, and strength. We will work out some of the implications later, but we now need to consider how Jesus changes the equation.

Jesus Is Lord

The Incarnation does not alter the nature of God or the fundamental practical monotheism of the scriptures; rather it reinforms and restructures monotheism around the central character in the New Testament—Jesus Christ. Our loyalties are now to be given to the Revealer and Savior. He becomes the focus of our attention and the pivotal point in our relationship to God. We adhere to him—he not only initiates the new covenant, he *is* the New Covenant.

When the early church claims "Jesus is Lord," it does so in precisely the same way, and with exactly the same implications, that Israel claimed God as Lord in the *Shema*. In fact, the fundamental religious situation hadn't shifted all that much (it never really does). Polytheism was still the dominant religious force in their day, as it is in ours. The names of the gods had changed from those of Canaanite ones (Baal, Ashteroth, etc.) to Greco-Roman ones (Venus, Diana, Apollo, etc.) and from there to romantic love, consumerism,

11. Ibid.

and self-help religion in our day, but in essence the confession has the same claim and impact. In fact, this is precisely why they got into trouble with Rome. In Roman theology, Caesar was a physical manifestation of a god that claimed total allegiance. Furthermore, it was the political genius of Rome to gather all the other gods of the subjugated nations and bring them under the lordship of Caesar and so create a religion that gave a deeper religious unity to the diverse political empire. A people group could keep their tribal gods only as long as they were willing to acknowledge that Caesar was lord over them. The fact that they were a conquered people indicated that the Roman god was supreme, and so the people generally submitted (except for Jews and Christians). The effect was to unify the religions of the empire and bind it to the state.[12] Sound familiar?

The early church refused this claim of the overlordship of Caesar; they refused to see Jesus as a mere part of the pantheon of the gods in Rome. In fact, the confession "Jesus is Lord" became in their mouths and in this context a deeply subversive claim that effectively undermined the rule of Caesar. The Christians wanted to bring all of life under the lordship of Jesus, and that meant subverting the lordship of Caesar. The emperors understood this all too clearly; hence, the terrible persecutions that followed. But the point is that our spiritual forebears really understood the inner meaning of monotheism here. They knew that Jesus was Lord and that this lordship effectively excluded all other claims to ultimate loyalty. They knew that this was the heart of the faith, and they could not, would not, surrender it.

This turns out to be exactly the same for the contemporary Chinese underground Christians: they refuse to bow to the claim of the communist state over their lives, a claim which would effectively dethrone the supreme lordship of Christ.[13] It is interesting that this clash of supreme governance is the source of spiritual conflict in both the cases I have chosen to demonstrate the nature of Apostolic Genius. And in both cases, the Christians were willing to die rather than deny their essential affirmation. Herein lies the heart of the Christian confession.

Jesus-Shaped Monotheism

So how has the New Testament revelation conditioned the biblical understanding of monotheism? By affirming that God is indeed triune in nature,

12. In fact, this is exactly what Constantine was attempting to do when he made Christianity the official state religion—to unite church and state under the emperor's rule. In fact, he retained the title *Pontifex Maximus*, that of the high priest in the Roman religious system. It is not coincidental, then, that the pope eventually takes on this title after the demise of the Roman Empire.

13. See Tony Lambert, *China's Christian Missions: The Costly Revival* (London: Monarch, 1999), 193, for a description of lordship theology and the state in China.

the New Testament reveals that each person in the Trinity has a particular role in the human experience of redemption. And while definitely suggesting a complex three-ness of sorts in the divine nature, the overall emphasis in the scriptures falls nonetheless on the oneness of God. The NT Christians did not move one iota from their primary commitment to the *Shema* and monotheism, precisely because, as I have tried to articulate, they understood this monotheism as the central confession of the people of God.[14] Even the kingdom of God is a call to live under the lordship of God (kingdom = rule of God), and so when Jesus says in Matthew 6:33 "But seek first his kingdom and his righteousness, and all these things will be given to you as well," he is entirely consistent with the basic dynamic of the *Shema*. The kingdom is God's claim upon us—it's the "business end" of practical monotheism.

What the New Testament revelation does indicate is that the Second Person of the Trinity takes on a distinct role in relation to redemption, not only by redeeming the world through his death and resurrection, but in an effective lordship at the right hand of the Father (Matt. 26:64; Mark 12:35–36; 14:62; 16:19; Acts 2:32–33; Rom. 8:34, among many other references). To sit at the right hand of a king was immediately understood in those days to be in a favored executive position.

But the teaching about Jesus's executive lordship goes deeper than merely being put in a favored position. Paul suggests that the actual function of lordship, normally associated with the Father, is now passed on to Jesus. "[H]e [God] raised him from the dead and seated him at his right hand in the heavenly realms, far above all rule and authority, power and dominion, and every title that can be given, not only in the present age but also in the one to come. *And God placed all things under his feet and appointed him to be head over everything* for the church, which is his body, the fullness of him who fills everything in every way" (Eph. 1:20–23; emphasis mine). In 1 Corinthians 15:25-28 Paul says, "For he [Jesus] must reign until he has put all his enemies under his feet. . . . When he has done this, then the Son himself will be made subject to him who put everything under him, so that God may be all in all."

This redefinition of biblical monotheism around the role of Jesus I will call christocentric monotheism, because it does realign our loyalties to God around the person and work of Jesus Christ. Jesus thus becomes the pivotal point in our relation to God, and it is to him that we must give our allegiance and loyalty. Jesus is Lord! And this lordship is expressed in exactly the same way that it is in the Old Testament. It is the covenant claim of God over our lives—the unshakable center of the Christian creed and confession. And it is not just about the nature of God himself; it has practical implications for our lives.

14. I have recently come across a thorough exploration of monotheism and Christianity in the writing of the brilliant New Testament scholar N.T. Wright. I refer you to the section "Rethinking God" in his book *Paul: Fresh Perspectives* (London: SPCK, 2005), 83–107, for an extended exploration of NT monotheism.

It is probably best to refer to our Lord himself as it relates to the ongoing validity of the *Shema*:

> One of the teachers of the law came and heard them debating. Noticing that Jesus had given them a good answer, he asked him, "Of all the commandments, which is the most important?" *"The most important one"* answered Jesus, *"is this: 'Hear, O Israel, the Lord our God, the Lord is one. Love the Lord your God with all your heart and with all your soul and with all your mind and with all your strength.' The second is this: 'Love your neighbor as yourself.' There is no commandment greater than these."* (Mark 12:30-31, emphasis mine)

There is an unambiguous expression of the *Shema* throughout the pages of the NT, only now it is christologically redefined—and it is this form of monotheism that infuses all genuinely *biblical* religion.

The Heart of Things

I wish to briefly restate here what seems to be an obvious fact, but one that is often overlooked. For authentic missional Christianity, Jesus the Messiah plays an *absolutely* central role.[15] Our identity as a movement, as well as our destiny as a people, is inextricably linked to Jesus—the Second Person of the Trinity. In fact, our connection to God is only through the Mediator—Jesus is "the Way"; no one comes to the Father except through him (John 14:6). This is what makes us distinctly *Christ*-ian.

At its very heart, Christianity is therefore a messianic movement, one that seeks to consistently embody the life, spirituality, and mission of its Founder. We have made it so many other things, but this is its utter simplicity. Discipleship, becoming like Jesus our Lord and Founder, lies at the epicenter of the church's task. It means that Christology must define all that we do and say. It also means that in order to recover the ethos of authentic Christianity, we need to refocus our attention back to the Root of it all, to recalibrate ourselves and our organizations around the person and work of Jesus the Lord. It will mean taking the Gospels seriously as the primary texts that define us. It will mean acting like Jesus in relation to people outside of the faith; as God's Squad, a significant missional movement to outlaw bikers around the world puts it, "Jesus Christ—friend of the outcasts."

Christianity beyond the Sacred and the Secular

A genuinely messianic monotheism therefore breaks down any notions of a false separation between the "sacred" and the "secular." If the world and all

15. See Frost and Hirsch, *Shaping of Things to Come*, 105–14.

in it belongs to God, and comes under his direct claim over it in and through Jesus, then there can be no sphere of life that is not radically open to the rule of God. There can be no non-God area in our lives and in our culture.

If we take the advice of the current alternative worship movement, of which I am generally deeply appreciative, one of the tasks of the church in a postmodern context is to make "sacred spaces," places filled with rich and fresh symbolism expressed by new forms of media, where people can reconnect with God in new ways. This all sounds right, but when this impulse is divorced, as it often is, from the overarching task of mission (and that of missional contextualization), then it simply becomes another way in which we separate the sacred from the secular. By setting up a place that we call "sacred" because of the lighting, the incense, and the religious feel, what are we thereby saying about the rest of life? Is it not sacred? We cannot escape the conclusion that by setting up so called sacred spaces we, by implication, make all else "not-sacred," thereby assigning a large aspect of life in a non-God, or secular, area. Following the impulses of biblical monotheism rather than setting up some sacred spaces, our task is to make *all* aspects and dimensions of life sacred—family, work, play, conflict, etc.—and not to limit the presence of God to spooky religious zones.[16]

I use this as an example simply to highlight how deeply dualism, including as it does the idea of the sacred/secular divide, penetrates our understanding, and how biblical monotheism helps us to develop an all-of-life perspective. Dualism distorts our experience of God, his people, and his world.

People involved in dualistic spiritual paradigms experience God as a church-based deity, and religion as a largely private affair. Church is largely conceived as a sacred space: the architecture, the music, the liturgies, the language and culture, all collaborate to make this a sacred event not experienced elsewhere in life in quite the same way. In other words, we go to church to experience God, and in truth God is there (he is everywhere and particularly loves to abide with his people), but the *way* this is done can tend to create a perception that is very difficult to break—that God is really encountered only in such places and that it requires an elaborate priestly/ministry paraphernalia to mediate this experience (John 4:20–24).

This dualistic spirituality has been called a number of things, but perhaps the idea of the Sunday-Monday disconnect brings the experience to the fore. We experience a certain type of God on Sunday, but Monday is another matter—"this is 'the real world,' and things work differently here." How many

16. This is not to say that aesthetics does not have a part to play in worship, or in our understanding and experience of church, but simply to point out that divorcing aesthetics from a monotheistic impulse and a missional task is bound to further the sacred-secular divide, and in our case assign spirituality to the realm of the merely private and the religious. This has been basic practice in Christendom, and it has damaged our understanding of the presence of God in all places.

times have we professional ministers heard variations of that phrase? "You don't really understand. It's just not as easy for me as it is for you. You work in the church with Christians," etc. The two "spheres of life," the sacred and the secular, are conceived as being infinitely different and heading in opposite directions. It is left to the believer to live one way in the sacred sphere and to have to live otherwise in the secular. It is the actual way we *do* church that communicates this nonverbal message of dualism. The medium is the message, after all. And it sets people up to see things in an essentially distorted way, where God is limited to the religious sphere. This creates a vacuum that is filled by idols and false, or incomplete, worship.

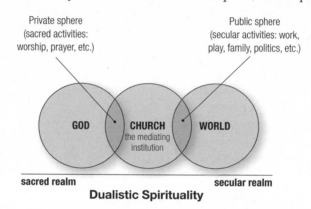

Dualistic Spirituality

Now, using the same elements and realigning them to fit a nondualistic understanding of God, church, and world, we can reconfigure this as follows:

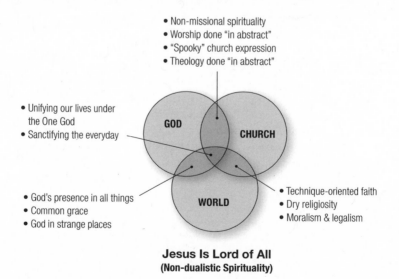

Jesus Is Lord of All
(Non-dualistic Spirituality)

Seeing things this way leads us to embrace an all-of-life perspective to our faith. By refusing the false dualism of sacred or secular, and by committing all of our lives under Jesus, we live out true holiness. There is nothing in our lives that should not and cannot be brought under this rule of God over all. Our task is to integrate the disparate elements that make up our lives and communities and bring them under the One God manifested to us in Jesus Christ.

If we fail to do this, then whilst we might be confessing monotheists, we might end up practicing polytheists. Dualistic expressions of faith always result in practical polytheism. There will be different gods that rule the different spheres of our lives, and the God of the church in this view is largely impotent outside of the privatized religious sphere. Christocentric monotheism demands loyalty precisely where the other gods claim it, and this is true for us as it was for our spiritual forebears. For make no mistake, we are surrounded by the claims of false gods in our own way as the many gods clamor for our loyalties and lives as well—not the least of these the worship of wealth and the associated gods of consumerism. But this is also how apartheid was birthed and developed in South Africa. The white Christians of South Africa would not integrate their national situation under the lordship of Jesus, and so a false god was invoked to rule over white politics. The result was a deeply sinful and ungodly crushing of the people of color in that land. When we fail to bring a sphere under the claim of Jesus, then it becomes autonomous and susceptible to the rule of other gods, and many sins result.

In this way, so many Christians end up being practicing polytheists. Isn't it interesting that most churchgoers report a radical disconnect between the God that rules Sunday and the gods that rule Monday? How many of us live as if there were different gods for every sphere of life? A god for work, another for family, a different one when we are at the movies, or one for our politics. No wonder the average churchgoer can't seem to make sense of it all. All this results from a failure to respond truly to the One God.[17] This failure can be addressed only by a discipleship that responds by offering all the disparate elements of our lives back to God, thus unifying our lives under his lordship.

How Far Is Too Far?

Perhaps we can finish this chapter by exploring how this central force of spiritual mDNA actually guides our missional conduct and activities. As

17. For a thorough theological exposition of the challenge of monotheism in the context of contemporary culture, see H. Richard Niebuhr, *Radical Monotheism and Western Culture* (e-text, available at www.religion-online.org/).

an incarnational missionary, I have often been asked the question "How far can we incarnate? How far is too far?" It's a good question. How can we know when our attempts to incarnate the gospel do not just result in syncretism (a blending of religions)?[18] I believe that the concept of christocentric monotheism as defined above is our guide. When the surrounding culture intrudes on the lordship of Jesus and his exclusive claim over all aspects of our lives, then monotheism functions as the defining criterion by which we can discern between syncretism and incarnational mission.

Syncretism effectively dilutes the claim of the biblical God and creates a religion that merely diminishes the tension of living under the claim of Jesus and ends up merely affirming the religious prejudices of the host culture. Let us further analyze the example of apartheid given above, although we could use any context.[19] What happened in South Africa is that to a large extent, white European Christianity actually sanctioned the racial prejudice and legitimized the oppressive power structures of the white peoples of South Africa in the name of a doctrine called "Christian paternalism." As this little piece of theology played itself out socially and politically, it resulted in what we now know as the policy of apartheid.

Why this was syncretism and not just political expedience is that the vast majority of whites in South Africa lived under a very religious, Calvinist code—they are a deeply religious people (there are traffic jams getting to church on Sunday). It was the theologians who gave apartheid its original legitimacy and sustaining authority. God, under the syncretistic influence of the apartheid theologians, became a racist god who justified the suppression of the "inferior" black peoples. But if we analyze it more simply, we can look at apartheid as simply the refusal to live under the claims of love and justice that are part of what it means to worship the one true God. How can one worship the God of justice by acting unjustly? Clearly, the biblical answer is that one cannot. In this case, acting in love and justice toward the black peoples was perceived as a threat to the ongoing identity and viability of the Afrikaner people, so they put race and politics out of the equation of the lordship of Jesus in the name of racial survival and dominance. Or rather, acting syncretistically, they co-opted God to their racist agenda. Paradoxically, the rest of the culture was deeply Christian, but the god over politics and social life was a different god than the God in the church.

Perhaps another example from Africa will serve to bed this down for us—that of the Rwandan genocide, a murderous frenzy that involved active professing Christians and churches in the slaughter. Lee Camp comments on this as a failure of the lordship of Christ.

18. Syncretism is the blending of religions and worldviews in such a way as to dilute the effect of both and actually create a new subspecies of religion.
19. I do this as someone who grew up in apartheid South Africa (until age twenty-two) and as one who has reflected deeply on the deeply sinful nature of that system.

In fact, the Rwandan genocide highlights a recurrent failure of much historic Christianity. The proclamation of the "gospel" has often failed to emphasize a fundamental element of the teaching of Jesus, and indeed, of orthodox Christian doctrine: *"Jesus is Lord" is a radical claim, one that is ultimately rooted in questions of allegiance, of ultimate authority, of the ultimate norm and standard for human life.* Instead, Christianity has often sought to ally itself comfortably with allegiance to other authorities, be they political, economic, cultural, or ethnic. Could it be that "Jesus is Lord" has become one of the most widespread Christian lies? Have Christians claimed the lordship of Jesus, but systematically set aside the call to obedience to this Lord? At least in Rwanda, with "Christian Hutus" slaughtering "Christian Tutsis" (and vice versa), "Christian" apparently served as a brand name—a "spirituality," or a "religion"—but not a commitment to a common Lord.[20]

What does all this practically mean for those seeking to recover Apostolic Genius in the life of the community of God? For one, it will involve (re)engaging directly the central confession of "Jesus is Lord" and attempting to reorient the church around this life-orienting claim. It will also mean simplifying our core messages, uncluttering our overly complex theologies, and thoroughly evaluating the traditional templates that so shape our behaviors and dominate our consciousness. I have become absolutely convinced that it is Christology, and in particular the primitive, unencumbered Christology of the NT church, that lies at the heart of the renewal of the church at all times and in every age. Sadly history amply demonstrates how we as God's people can so often obscure the centrality of Jesus in our experience of church. There is so much clutter in our "religion," so many competing claims, that this central unifying claim that lies at the heart of the faith is easily lost. It is remarkable how Jesus can be so easily cast out from among his people. Have you ever wondered why in Revelation 3:20 Jesus is seen standing outside of his church knocking at the door and asking to come in? The question we must ask ourselves is "How did he get out from among his people in the first place?!" Honestly asking the question "Is the real Jesus really Lord in my community?" can be a very unnerving exercise indeed.

In order to recover Apostolic Genius we must learn what it means to *recalibrate*, to go back to the basic "formula" of the church—we need to constantly go back to our Founder and reset our faith and communal life on him. It all began with Jesus, it will all end with him, and to Jesus we must constantly return of we are to re-find ourselves again. (At the very least, this is what it means to confess that he is the Alpha and Omega.) Christianity is essentially a "Jesus movement" and not a religion as such. The confession of "Jesus is Lord" is a challenge to take seriously the absolute and ongoing centrality of

20. Lee C. Camp, *Mere Discipleship: Radical Christianity in a Rebellious World* (Grand Rapids, Brazos Press, 2003), 16 (emphasis mine).

Jesus for Christianity as a whole and thus for the local church. As we have seen, the early Christian movement and the Chinese underground church discovered this as their sustaining and guiding center in the midst of a massive adaptive challenge. No less is required of us as we seek to negotiate the challenge of the twenty-first century. The element of Jesus's Lordship never shifted from being the real center of the Christian experience of God; only our focus did. The first step in the recovery of Apostolic Genius is thus the recovery of the Lordship of Jesus in all its utter simplicity.[21] It is also the place to which the church must constantly return in order to renew itself. He is our Touchstone, our Defining Centre, our Founder, and therefore he has preeminence theologically and existentially in the life of his people.

It is a truly difficult thing to truly worship the one true God, but it is central to our life and purpose in this world. And we don't need to analyze large systems like apartheid, or the horrors of the Rwandan genocide, to see this dynamic at work. We need only look into our own lives; when we deliberately sin, or when we refuse to allow his claim to seep into all the dimensions of our lives and respond in obedience, we effectively limit the lordship of Jesus and his claim of absolute rule (e.g., Luke 6:46[22]).

When practicing the missional discipline of incarnation, we need to always have our eye to the Lordship of Jesus and the exclusive claims consistent with his nature. How far is too far? I suggest that it is when we refuse to bring aspects of our cultures and lives under the lordship of Jesus—that simple.

This chapter has sought to identify and articulate the epicenter of spiritual mDNA, and therefore a critical element of Apostolic Genius. The other elements in the structure of spiritual mDNA therefore form themselves around Christocentric monotheism and are guided by it—they assume it. At the heart of the church's call and mission lies a challenge to respond to God with all that we are and all that we have and so complete the meaning of our lives.

---

21. There is a faith community called The Spare Chair in Adelaide, Australia, that decided that the only creed it needs, the only philosophy under which it would legimately operate, is "to live under the Lordship of Jesus in the power of the Spirit."

22. "Why do you call me, 'Lord, Lord,' and do not do what I say?"

4

disciple making

We can only live changes: we cannot think our way to humanity. Every one of us, every group, must become the model of that which we desire to create.

Ivan Illich

The greatest proof of Christianity for others is not how far a man can logically analyze his reasons for believing, but how far in practice he will stake his life on his belief.

T. S. Eliot

As I've indicated on numerous occasions already, all six elements of mDNA must be present for authentic Apostolic Genius to activate and permeate the life of the Christian communities and movements. Each element is a critical component in itself that, when evident, develops missional fitness in the community and draws it closer to the moment of critical mass when all elements amplify, come together, inform each other, and so unleash the potent force of Apostolic Genius. All the elements of mDNA belong together, and they must all be present in significant ways for Apostolic Genius to manifest, but my own experience and observation indicates that perhaps *this* element, namely, that of discipleship and disciple making, is perhaps the most critical element in the mDNA mix. This is so because it is the essential task of discipleship to embody the message of Jesus, the Founder. In other words, this is the *strategic* element and therefore a good place to start. C. S. Lewis rightly understood that the purpose of the church was to draw people to Christ and make them like Christ. He said that the church exists for no other purpose. "If the Church is not doing this, then all the cathedrals, clergy, missions, sermons, even the Bible, are a waste of time."[1]

When dealing with discipleship, and the related capacity to generate authentic followers of Jesus, we are dealing with that single most crucial factor that will in the end determine the quality of the whole—if we fail at this point then we must fail in all the others. In fact if we fail here, it is unlikely that we will even get to doing any of the other elements of mDNA in any significant and lasting way.

But even more significant, this is the very task into which Jesus focused his efforts and invested most of his time and energy, namely in the selection and development of that motley band of followers on whose trembling shoulders he lays the entire redemptive movement that would emerge from his death and resurrection. The founding of the whole Christian movement, the most significant religious movement in history, one that has extended itself through the ages, and into the twenty-first century, was initiated through the simple acts of Jesus investing his life and embedding his teachings in his followers and developing them into authentic disciples.

In the end, Jesus must have trusted his cause to his followers in the belief that they would faithfully stand the test, and that somehow they would adequately embody and transmit his message to the world. And we might well wonder at the sheer risk that God took in handing over the fragile and precarious Jesus movement to this rather unlikely crew. But the fact that it did succeed is directly related to the truth that through their engagement with Jesus, this rather dubious human material had somehow become true disciples. Jesus had, through living with them and showing them God's

---

1. W. Vaus, *Mere Theology: A Guide to the Thought of C. S. Lewis* (Downers Grove, IL: Inter-Varsity, 2004), 167.

way, somehow succeeded in embedding his life and the gospel in them. Talk about rolling the dice! And it almost failed. After all the amazing things they had experienced in their journeys with Jesus, they all, to a man, deserted him at the cross. "The Rock," Simon Peter, denied him three times, no less. If Jesus had failed in this critical task of making disciples out of the people that hung out with him, you would not be reading this book today, and I certainly would not be writing it. I do believe it is *the* critical factor.

It is interesting that when we really look at the dangerous stories of the phenomenal movements, at the most uncomplicated level, they appear to the observer simply as disciple-making systems. But the rather funny thing is that they never appear to get beyond this—they never move beyond mere disciple making. This is because it is at once the starting point, the abiding strategic practice, as well as the key to all lasting missional impact in and through movements. Whether one looks at the Wesleyan, the Franciscan, or the Chinese phenomenon, at core they are essentially composed of, and led by, disciples, and they are absolutely clear on the disciple-making mandate. Take, for instance, the Methodist movement, which was founded in eighteenth-century Britain by John Wesley: Following a life-changing encounter with God, Wesley began to travel throughout Great Britain with a vision for the conversion and discipling of a nation and the renewal of a fallen church. He "sought no less than the recovery of the truth, life and power of earliest Christianity and the expansion of that kind of Christianity."[2] Within a generation, one in thirty people in Britain had become Methodists, and the movement was becoming a worldwide phenomenon. In the opinion of Stephen Addison, a missiologist who has spent much of his professional life studying Christian movements, the key to Methodism's success was the high level of commitment to the Methodist cause that was expected of participants.[3] This cause declined to the degree that the movement had moved away from its original missional ethos or evangelism and disciple making and degenerated into mere religious legalism maintained by institution, rule books, and professional clergy.

For the follower of Jesus, discipleship is not the first step toward a promising career. It is in itself the fulfillment of his or her destiny. We never move from being a disciple *on-the-way*. And yet it seems as if we find little place for radical discipleship in our life together as believers. At best, we tend to think of it as something we do with young converts. The dilemma we face today in regard to this issue is that while we have a historical language of discipleship, our actual practice of discipleship is far from consistent, and as a result this mismatch tends to obscure the centrality of the problem. I think

2. George G. Hunter III, *To Spread the Power: Church Growth in the Wesleyan Spirit* (Nashville: Abingdon, 1987), 40.
3. Addison, "Movement Dynamics," 44.

it is fair to say that in the Western church, we have by and large lost the art of disciple making. We have done so partly because we have reduced it to the intellectual assimilation of ideas, partly because of the abiding impact of cultural Christianity embedded in the Christendom understanding of church, and partly because the phenomenon of consumerism in our own day pushes against a true following of Jesus.

For the above reasons it seems to me that we have lowered the bar for participation in Christian community to the lowest common denominator. However, when we look into this element of mDNA as it appears in the phenomenal movements, we discover how counterintuitive their emphases really are—they seem to flatly contradict so many of our own church growth practices. For instance, far from being "seeker-friendly," by AD 170 the underground Christian movement had developed what they called the *catechisms.* These were not merely the doctrinal confessions they later became; they involved rigorous personal examinations that required the catechumen to demonstrate why he or she was worthy of entry into the confessing community.[4] Not only could proposed converts lose their life, because of the persecution of the time, but they had to prove why they believed they should be allowed to become part of the Christian community in the first place! Many were turned away because they were found unworthy. This is contrary to the "seeker-sensitive" practice so prevalent in our day. And it was this element of vigorous discipleship that characterized the early Christian movement that was blighted by the deluge of worldliness that flooded the post-Constantinian church when the bar was lowered for membership and the culture was "Christianized."

Apart from the very simple strategy to multiply organic, reproducing churches, Neil Cole of Church Multiplication Associates suggests that the key to their remarkable growth to 500 churches in a few short years essentially revolved around their resolute commitment to discipleship. He says of the early period "[W]e started articulating this profound goal for CMA: '*We want to lower the bar of how church is done and raise the bar of what it means to be a disciple.*'" Their rationale was that if the experience of church was simple enough that just about anyone can do it, and is made up of people who have taken up their cross and follow Jesus at any cost, the result will be a movement that empowers the common Christian to do the uncommon works of God. "Churches will become healthy, fertile and reproductive."[5] If this is right, then many of our current practices seem to be the wrong way around . . . we seem to make church complex and discipleship too easy.

4. For an insightful study on conversion processes and catechisms in the early Christian movement, see Alan Kreider, *The Change of Conversion and the Origin of Christendom* (Harrisburg, PA: Trinity, 1999).

5. Cole, "Organic Church," 50.

With the core task of discipleship in mind, they developed the concept of Life Transformation Groups (LTGs), a very simple, duplicable, disciple-making system that was eventually used worldwide, and which, because of its simplicity and reproducibility, has brought many people closer to Jesus and brought growth to their movement. An LTG simply involves a staple of Bible reading, storytelling, personal accountability, and prayer. In the CMA movement it is required that all who call themselves Christians be in an LTG, and this is not just something done in the initial phases of the Christian life. It is an ongoing commitment for all who are involved in the various expressions of CMA, including leadership at every level. In other words, they are basically a disciple-making movement.[6] Neil claims that it is essentially this combination of organic ideas of organization and the primary commitment to discipling the nations that has led to the remarkable growth of CMA. All the other elements of Apostolic Genius are clearly evident in CMA, including missional-incarnational impulse, apostolic environment, and *communitas*, as well as their more stated emphases on organic systems and discipleship. In fact, CMA is an excellent contemporary example of a genuine expression of Apostolic Genius in our day, but we need to heed Cole's emphasis on disciple making as a nonnegotiable essential of any genuine expression of Christianity. It seems that this introverted, unassuming, modern-day apostle has built his ecclesial house on the right foundation (Matt. 7:24–27).

The story of CMA squares with the best thinking in terms of movement dynamics. Steve Addison, a researcher of the nature of movements, discerns five phases in the transmission of ideas through missionary movements.[7] In simple terms, these consist of;

- *White Hot Faith:* By this he means a direct and personal encounter with the living God, followed by social renewal. Whether this be a Paul, a Wesley, a Francis, a Luther, a Wimber, a Mother Teresa, or any other great Christian leader who founded a movement, transformative movements start with a direct and transforming encounter with God.

- *Commitment to the Cause:* The people who are touched in such a way by God give their lives to the cause as articulated by the movement. Commitment levels tend to be significantly high and catalyze a certain kind of synergy that comes through mutual cooperation and commitment.

- *Contagious Relationships:* Ideas travel like a virus. Powerful ideas like the gospel are passed on from one person to another. For movements

6. See N. Cole, *Cultivating a Life for God* (Elgin, IL: Brethren Press, 1999).

7. These headers were taken from a presentation he gave to Forge interns. However, the substance is contained in the as yet unpublished "Movement Dynamics."

to extend themselves beyond a narrow network of people and a single generation, there needs to be a network of relationships that become "contagious."

- *Rapid Mobilization:* There needs to be an apostolic type of leadership and organization that develops to be able to coordinate and maximize the efforts of the adherents of the movement.

- *Dynamic Methods:* It is significant that movements tend to use new, innovative methods and techniques to communicate their message.

I point these out now to underscore why discipleship is so important to missional impact. Dimensions of discipleship can be discerned at every level: *encounter with Jesus, commitment, contagious relationships, mobilization,* excluding, perhaps, *dynamic methods.* In fact, without meaningful discipleship there can be no real movement and therefore no significant impact for the gospel—that is why it is so critical.

"Little Jesus" in Disneyland

Before we can continue with the exploration of the mDNA of discipleship in remarkable Jesus movements, we can recognize the significance of this aspect of Apostolic Genius only once we have understood the cultural situation in which we find ourselves. Discipleship is all about adherence to Christ. And therefore it is always articulated and experienced over against all other competing claims for our loyalty and allegiance. In the time of the apostolic and postapostolic church, their allegiance to Christ was set against the claims of the false religious systems of their day and the demand for complete political loyalty to Caesar. It was the refusal to submit to the claim of "Caesar as Lord" that got them into trouble in the first place. For the Chinese Christians, their loyalty to Jesus is set primarily against the unconditional demands of the totalitarian Communist state, which endures no religious rivals to its power.

Due to my own experience in local ministry, the ones described in the first two chapters of this book, I have come to the conclusion that for we who live in the Western world, the major challenge to the viability of Christianity is not Buddhism, with all its philosophical appeal to the Western mind, nor is it Islam, with all the challenge that it poses to Western culture. It is not the New Age that poses such a threat; in fact, because there is a genuine search going on in new religious movements, it can actually be an asset to we who are willing to share the faith amidst the search. All these are challenges to us, no doubt, but I have come to believe that the major threat to the viability of our faith is that of consumerism. This is a far more heinous and insidious challenge to the gospel, because in so many ways it infects each and every one of us.

I was trained as a marketer and advertiser before I came to Christ, and when I look at the power of consumerism and of the market in our lives, I have little doubt that in consumerism we are now dealing with a very significant religious phenomenon. If the role of religion is to offer a sense of identity, purpose, meaning, and community, then it can be said that consumerism fulfills all these criteria. Because of the competitive situation of the market, advertisers have become so insidious that they are now deliberately co-opting theological ideas and religious symbols in order to sell their products. But this co-option is merely incidental or functional; in so doing it is acting consistently with its own nature, namely that of the official priesthood of a new and all-pervasive religion. The assimilation of religious symbols and rituals merely serves to bolster its appeal to the spiritual dimension of life. An advertising executive recently confessed to me that they are now deliberately stepping into the void that was left by the removal of Christianity from Western culture.

Much of that which goes by the name *advertising* is an explicit offer of a sense of identity, meaning, purpose, and community. Most ads now appeal to one or more of these religious dimensions of life. Take, for instance, a recent car ad in my country in which we are introduced to a fantastic community of very cool people singing along in a car and generally having a great time. Throughout the ad, nothing is mentioned about the qualities of a car, its technical ingenuity, its availability, its price; rather, the advertisement is an explicit appeal to the need for people to be accepted as cool people. The selling point of the ad is an offer of community, status, and acceptance by groovy people: if the consumer would just purchase this vehicle they will achieve this. Analyzed in a religious way, we could see just about all advertising in this light. Buy this and you will be changed (Levi Strauss even used the idea of being born again through the purchase of their products).[8] The astute cultural commentator Douglas Rushkoff in his PBS documentary on consumerism, *The Persuaders,* has noted that advertisers and marketers are now learning from religion in order to sell products. Marketers have now co-opted the language and symbolism of all the major religions in order to sell the product because they know that religion offers the ultimate object of desire and that people will do just about anything to get it. If through advertising marketers can just link their products to this great unfilled void, they *will* sell.

8. Earlier in 2003 a Levi Strauss TV ad for Levi 501 jeans, featuring a woman being baptized in her underwear and coming out of the water wearing jeans, was banned in New Zealand because it was considered inappropriate use of religious imagery.

Much that goes by the name *advertising* has nothing to do with inherent aspects of the products themselves. Rather, advertising has everything to do with managing the value and significance people give to products and the relative status we derive from them. In our day there is little doubt that as a culture we have *totemized* the product.[9] In other words, it has acquired religious significance for us.

There is a real history to this phenomenon, one that is worth unpacking to understand what we are really dealing with.[10] When we talk about secularization in our culture, we are referring to that process whereby the church was taken from the center of culture (as in the Christendom period) and increasingly pushed to the margins. The explicit aim (as in the French Revolution) was to create a secular social field whereby the state is not controlled by the concerns and domination of the church as it was in earlier periods, but one within which a plurality of opinions, ideas, and activities can compete for our attention and allegiances based on rational discourse, individual freedoms, and democracy. This was a significant part of what is called the Enlightenment, or modern, period of Western history. But the end result of this process created a massive spiritual vacuum into which stepped an unprecedented host of cultural forces.

For all its failings, the church, up till the time of the Enlightenment, played the overwhelmingly dominant role in the mediation of identity, meaning, purpose, and community for at least the preceding eleven centuries in the West. Its demise, or rather its forced removal, came about when two or three other major forces were on the rise. These were

- The rise of capitalism and of the free market as the mediator of value
- The rise of the nation-state as the mediator of protection and provision
- The rise of science as the mediator of truth and understanding

These become the public realm, the realm of common truth. Religion, under these conditions, was pushed into the private realm of private opinion, personal values, and individual taste. (We all know that retort, "I'm really glad it works for you, but it's not for me.") We no longer feature in the public sphere. Christianity has become a mere matter of private preference rather than that of public truth.

9. Totemization is the action whereby humans assign religious significance to, or set up a mystical relationship with, an object that in turn serves as the emblem or symbol of the power that people confer on it. It is implied in all religious idolatry. This is partly what Paul is dealing with in 1 Corinthians 8:3–8, 10:18–22. The idol in itself is no god. It is only a representation of the "god." And behind these things that claim our loyalty lies the power of the demonic. Monotheism came to break us from such false allegiances and establishes an abiding loyalty to the One God.

10. I am thankful to Alan Roxburgh for the basis of this analysis of history.

By the time that we got to the mid-twentieth century, these forces had all but completely replaced the church in our culture. One could hardly now doubt the almost total hegemonic power of the economy, the state, and science in our lives. And the upshot is that these are precisely the places where the vast majority of people find their direction and meaning. And as we engage the twenty-first century, the most dominant force of all three—the one that pervades our lives totally—is that of the global economy and the market.[11]

Under this excessive influence of the market, experiences, indeed life itself, tends to become commodified. In such an economy, people are viewed as mere consumptive units. The suburbs all orbit around the central consumerist temple called The Shopping Mall. Teenagers walk aimlessly up and down these soulless corridors as if looking for an answer that somehow evades them in the windows. Their parents saunter through the same malls indulging in a dose of "retail therapy." Disneyland, cruise vacations, extreme sports, drugs, and the like are consumable experiences. It has often been noted that in the postmodern condition we can consume new identities like we do new clothes. We do this either by moving into the groovier inner city, or by dropping out and becoming feral, changing our clothes, changing our friends and looking around for new ones, or buying this or that product that identifies us with new, more desirable networks of people. In this cultural situation everything, even personal identity and religious meaning, becomes a commodity that we can now trade in, depending on the latest fads, and by consuming the latest products. In this light it's easy to see how "church shopping," ecstatic worship experiences, and even Christian spirituality can come to reflect the consumerization of faith.

This is our missional context, and I've come to believe that in dealing with consumerism we are dealing with an exceedingly powerful enemy propagated by a very sophisticated media machine. This is our situation, but it is also our own personal condition—and it must be dealt with if we are going to be effective in the twenty-first century in the West.

Consuming Religion

The problem for the church in this situation is that it is now forced to compete with all the other ideologies and -isms in the marketplace of religions and products for the allegiance of people, and it must do this in a way that mirrors the dynamics of the marketplace—because that is precisely the basis of how people make the countless daily choices in their lives. In the

11. The market has totally triumphed, eclipsing even the state through multinational capital, and by reducing science to technology focused around the profit motive. No wonder historian Francis Fukuyama called it "the end of history."

modern and the postmodern situation, the church is forced into the role of being little more than a *vendor of religious goods and services*. And the end-users of the church's services (namely, us) easily slip into the role of discerning, individualistic consumers, devouring the religious goods and services offered by the latest and best vendor. Worship, rather than being *entertaining* through creatively engaging the hearts and minds of the hearers, now becomes mere *entertainment* that aims at giving the participants transcendent emotional highs, much like the role of the *"feelies"* in Aldous Huxley's *Brave New World*, where people go to the movies merely to get a buzz.

Church growth exponents have explicitly taught us how to market and tailor the product to suit target audiences. They told us to mimic the shopping mall, apply it to the church, and create a one-stop religious shopping experience catering to our every need. In this they were sincere and well intentioned, but they must have been also totally ignorant of the ramifications of their counsel—because in the end the medium has *so* easily overwhelmed the message.[12] Christendom, operating as it does in the attractional mode and run by professionals, was already susceptible to consumerism, but under the influence of contemporary church growth practice, consumerism has actually become the driving ideology of the church's ministry.

The very shape of the church building gives us away (refer to the diagram of the church building in chapter 1). Ninety percent or more of the people who attend our services are passive. In other words, they are consumptive. They are the passive recipients of the religious goods and services being delivered largely by professionals in a slick presentation and service. Just about everything we do in these somewhat standardized services and "box churches," we do in order to attract participants, and to do this we need to make the experience of church more convenient and comfortable. It is the ultimate religious version of one-stop shopping—hassle-free. But alas, all we are achieving by doing this is adding more fuel to the insatiable consumerist flame. I have come to the dreaded conclusion that we simply cannot consume our way into discipleship. Consumerism as it is experienced in the everyday and discipleship as it is intended in the scriptures are simply at odds with each other. And both aim at the mastery over our lives, only in marketing it's called brand loyalty or brand community.

Speaking to the insecurity of the human situation, it was Jesus who said "So do not worry, saying, 'What shall we eat?' or 'What shall we drink?' or 'What shall we wear?' For the pagans *run after* all these things, and your heavenly Father knows that you need them. But seek first his kingdom and his righteousness, and all these things will be given to you as well" (Matt. 6:31–33, emphasis mine). Consumerism is thoroughly pagan. Pagans *run after* these things (Gk. *epizēteō* "seek, desire, want; search for, look for"). Seen in

12. See Frost and Hirsch, *Shaping of Things to Come*, chapter 9, especially 149ff.

this light, *Queer Eye for the Straight Guy, Extreme Makeover, Big Brother,* and other lifestyle shows are of the most pagan, and *paganizing,* shows on TV. Even the perennial favorites about renovating the house paganize us, because they focus us on that which so easily enslaves us. In these the banality of consumerism reaches a climax as we are sold the lie that the thing that will complete us is a new kitchen or a house extension, whereas in fact these only add more stress to our mortgages and our families.[13] These shows are far more successful promoters of unbelief than even outright intellectual atheism, because they hit us at that place where we must render our trust and loyalty. Most people are profoundly susceptible to the idolatrous allure of money and things. We do well to remember what our Lord said about serving two masters and about *running after* things (Matt. 6:24–33).

Mark Sayers, a friend of mine, has noted that one of the most alluring religious appeals of consumerism is that it offers us a new immediacy, a living alternative to what heaven has always stood for in the Judeo-Christian tradition—the fulfillment of all our longings. We have at our fingertips experiences and offerings available only to kings in previous eras. Offered "heaven now," we give up the ultimate quest in pursuit of that which can be immediately consumed, be it a service, product, or pseudo-religious experience. Consumerism has all the distinguishing traits of outright paganism—we need to see it for what it really is.

But this is no mere objective and cold analysis; I have applied this critique to myself and my own ministry and have had to constantly repent. You will remember from chapter 1 my narrating the experience of initiating a significant mission project in the café called Elevation. When the chips were down, we failed to generate stronger commitment from the community members. As a leadership we realized this as our own failure, a failure to develop disciples. By not intentionally focusing on making disciples, we had inadvertently cultivated the already immanent (religious) consumerism. I found out the hard way that if we don't disciple people, the culture sure will. This was a moment of truth for me as leader of the movement, and I vowed that from then on my practice must change and that somehow disciple making must become a central activity of whatever I would do through Christian community in the future.

It seems, then, that we have two basic options before us: (1) We try to redeem the rhythms and structures of consumerism as Pete Ward suggests in his excellent book on missional ecclesiology. He advises that, rather than reject or denounce consumerism, we should see it as an opportunity for the church to rediscover her missional and redemptive nature. He

13. In their groundbreaking book *Affluenza,* economists Hamilton and Denniss detail how having more than ever before has made us unhappier than ever before. *Affluenza: When Too Much Is Never Enough* (Crows Nest, NSW, Aus.: Allen & Unwin, 2005).

maintains that in consumerism there is a massive search going on, and that the church cannot miss out on meaningfully communicating from within this context. He suggests, therefore, that the church must radically reorganize around consumerist principles but maintain its missional edge.[14] (2) Alternatively, we must initiate a thoroughly prophetic challenge to consumerism's overarching control on our lives. These two alternatives become our missional challenge and are each real live options. However, my warning is that if we are going to sup with the devil, we had better have a very long spoon, because we are dealing with a deeply entrenched alternative religious system to which Jesus's disciples need to model an alternative reality.

One of the more effective, countercultural ways in which followers of Jesus are working out disciples is in the new interest and practice of missional and monastic orders. One such group, called the Rutba House, have developed twelve practices, or marks, for a new monasticism to challenge the worldliness of the church.[15] These are:

1. Relocation to abandoned places of the city
2. Sharing economic resources with fellow community members and with the needy
3. Hospitality to the stranger
4. Lament for racial divisions in church and society, combined with an active pursuit of a just reconciliation
5. Humble submission to Christ's Body, the Church
6. Intentional formation in the Way of Christ and the Rule of Community
7. Support for celibate singles alongside monogamous married couples and their children
8. Geographical proximity to community members who share a common rule of life
9. Care for God's earth and supporting local economies
10. Peacemaking in the midst of violence

The reader will no doubt agree that these provide critical points around which we can counter the effects of consumerism on our lives. There are many such orders like these flourishing in Western contexts—InnerChange (United States and Southeast Asia), Urban Neighbors of Hope (Australia and Thailand), YFC-New Zealand, being just a few examples of them.

14. My problem with Pete's work is that I think he underrates the power of consumerism to undermine Christianity, not the other way round. I think we are way too consumerist already, and I think this is inconsistent with the death to self required in following Jesus.

15. Rutba House, *Schools for Conversion: 12 Marks of a New Monasticism* (Eugene, OR: Cascade, 2005).

The Conspiracy of "Little Jesus"

So again, why is discipleship such a critical, perhaps even the central, element of mDNA in Apostolic Genius? It was David Bosch who rightly noted that "discipleship is determined by the relation to Christ himself not by mere conformity to impersonal commands. The context of this is not in the classroom (where "teaching" normally takes place), or even in the church, but in the world.[16] To be true, evangelical *thinking* reverberates with this idea. We emphasize the primacy of our relationship with Jesus and not to mere ideas about him, and we claim that this is an all-of-life phenomenon, but it is our lifestyle practices and not our thinking that constantly let us down in this matter.

Apostolic movements make this a core task, because when we really think about it, this is perhaps the most strategic of all of the church's various activities. When Jesus tasked his people with what has been called the Great Commission, what did he have in mind? Why is our central commission "to make disciples of all nations" (Matt. 28:18–20)?

This question must take us back to the real significance and meaning of discipleship. If the heart of discipleship is to become like Jesus, then it seems to me that a missional reading of this text requires that we see that Jesus's strategy is to get a whole lot of little versions of him infiltrating every nook and cranny of society by reproducing himself in and through his people in every place throughout the world. But this issue goes much deeper than sociological models relating to the transmission of ideas into movements; it goes to one of the central purposes of Christ's mission among us. Jesus not only embodies God in our realm, but also provides the image of the perfect human being. We are told by Paul that it is our eternal destiny to be conformed to this image of Christ (Rom. 8:29; 2 Cor. 3:18). But the relationship between Jesus and his people goes deeper still. Our mystical union with Christ and his indwelling with us lies at the very center of the Christian experience of God—this is seen in all of Paul's teaching about being "in Christ" and he in us, as well as John's theology of "abiding in Christ." All the spiritual disciplines therefore aim us toward one thing—*Christlikeness*. We heed the words ascribed to Mother Teresa: "We must become holy not because we want to feel holy but because Christ must be able to live his life fully in us."

As such, the God-Man Jesus is, and must remain, the abiding epicenter of Christian spirituality and theology. We are constantly reminded that we are to become like Jesus. This notion of the imitation of Christ is one of the undisputed central tenets of both Jesus's teaching and that of the apostles. It is implied in discipleship and imbues it with its meaning. But to be a fol-

16. D. Bosch, *Transforming Mission* (Maryknoll, NY: Orbis, 1991), 67.

lower of Christ does not mean to imitate him literally by mimicking him, but to express him through the medium of one's own life. "A Christian is no unnatural reproduction [clone] of Christ. . . . The task of the Christian consists of transposing Christ into the stuff of his own daily existence."[17] It appears to me that his aim to transmit his message through the uniqueness of the lives of his followers, and this is to be expressed in every conceivable aspect of their lives. In short, his aim is to fill the world with lots of "little Jesuses"—an actively Christlike (redemptive) presence in every neighborhood and every sphere of life. This *is* the Conspiracy of Little Jesus.

As must be the case for a movement to survive beyond the initial impulse, the Founder *literally* must somehow *live on* in his people, and the vitality of the subsequent message would henceforth depend on the willingness and capacity of his people to faithfully embody his message. The dangerous stories and memories of the Founder are alive in them and call them to a holy and integrated life. In a very real and sobering way, we must actually *become the gospel* to the people around us—an expression of the real Jesus through the quality of our lives. We must live our truths. Or as Paul says it, we ourselves are living letters whose message is constantly being read by others (2 Cor. 3:1–3). In the final analysis, the medium *is* the message, and the phenomenal movements of God seemed to be able to express the message authentically through the media of both their personal and common lives together.[18] This is what made it believable and transferable.

Embodiment and Transmission

Closely linked to the idea of the imitation of Christ is the idea of embodiment, which involves patterning and modeling. When we look at the phenomenal movements in history, we find that these people movements found a way to translate the grand themes of the gospel (kingdom of God, redemption, atonement, forgiveness, love, etc.) into concrete life through the embodiment of Jesus in ways that were profoundly relational and attractive. Through this the Jesus phenomenon became a movement of the people and not a closeted religious philosophy mediated by a religious elite, as often happens in the history of religions.

Embodiment literally means to give flesh to the ideas and experiences that animate us. If these ideas and experiences are really believed in and valued, then they must be lived out. Embodiment is an important factor in the healthy leadership of all human organizations but is absolutely crucial

17. Romano Guardini, *The Lord* (London: Longmans, 1956), 452.
18. For a more thorough exploration of the idea of "the medium is the message," see the chapter with that title in my previous book (with Michael Frost), *The Shaping of Things to Come.*

to the viability and witness of the Christian movement and therefore to both discipleship and missional leadership.[19] And this cannot be passed on through mere writing and books: it is always communicated through life itself, by the leader to the community, from teacher to disciple, and from believer to believer.

The idea of the embodiment of our message highlights, as well as substantiates, the truth that we seek to convey. And it is precisely this that Christian discipleship must seek to achieve. Jim Wallis says that "the only way to propagate a message is to live it."[20] When we try to translate this idea of embodiment in terms of missional strategy as to how we impact people with the gospel, it will mean that we ourselves must become a substantial representation of what for many outside of Christ is an otherwise rather nebulous theory. This concept is therefore not just existentially significant for an authentic life, and it is that, it is absolutely crucial both for the transmission of the gospel beyond ourselves, and for the initiating and survival of missional movements. It is critical to the authenticity and vitality of the church's mission. For remarkable examples of this in western church history, we need only look at someone like St. Francis, who lived out his message in a community that embodied his teachings. We can find similar patterns, for instance, in Count Zinzendorf and the Moravians.

With these reflections in mind, listen to Paul. Try to discern the meaning of embodiment, and consider its impact on others in the surrounding social systems.

> *You became imitators of us and of the Lord;* in spite of severe suffering, you welcomed the message with the joy given by the Holy Spirit. *And so you became a model* to *all the believers* in Macedonia and Achaia. *The Lord's message rang out from you* not only in Macedonia and Achaia—*your faith in God has become known everywhere. Therefore we do not need to say anything about it,* for they themselves report what kind of reception you gave us. They tell how you turned to God from idols to serve the living and true God.
>
> 1 Thess. 1:6–9 (emphases mine)

> Join with others in following my example, brothers, and take note of those who live according to the pattern we gave you.
>
> Phil. 3:17

19. In some significant way for believers, the idea of embodying our beliefs and messages must take us back to the literal embodiment of God in the Incarnation. In Jesus the medium is the message. He *is* love. His life communicates his message fully and completely. Not only did he proclaim the gospel, he actually is the gospel. This is why he impacted his world so profoundly, and does still to ours, and throughout history.

20. Jim Wallis, *Call to Conversion*. Quoted by Len Hjalmarson, "Toward a Theology of Public Presence," at www.allelon.org/articles/article.cfm?id=143&page=1.

We did this, not because we do not have the right to such help, but in order
to make ourselves a model for you to follow.

2 Thess. 3:9

In everything set them an example by doing what is good. In your teaching
show integrity, seriousness and soundness of speech that cannot be condemned,
so that those who oppose you may be ashamed because they have nothing
bad to say about us.

Titus 2:7–8

Follow my example, as I follow the example of Christ.

1 Cor. 11:1

Because the apostles were essentially the custodians of the DNA of God's
people, the embodiment of the gospel had to be observed as *living integrity*
in their lives for the message to have any lasting effect. It is this consistency
between message and messenger that authenticated the apostolic message
and cultivated receptivity in the hearers. The Pauline churches in turn could
be faithful because they had observed in Paul a living model of faithfulness.
Consequently, Paul's converts modeled and embodied it so others could
see, and this led to lasting impact. The teachings must embed themselves
in the lives of the followers, and this can be achieved only through the
discipling relationship.

To be effective, movements, and the central ideas associated with them,
must take root in the lives of their followers. If they do not, the movement
simply will not ignite. And again, it's not just an issue of personal integrity;
it's also about patterning. The pattern of a movement is usually set in a definitive sense by its founder. Therefore, in terms of the movement dynamics
and mission of the Christian church, this notion of modeling the message is
absolutely crucial to the transmission of the original message beyond our
Founder to subsequent generations.

Inspirational Leadership

The Academy Award-winning movie depicting the life of Mohandas
Gandhi opens with the state funeral of the remarkable man who had so
transformed India. An American radio commentator narrates the meaning
of his life to the rest of the world. In his narration, he observes that before
them was a man who was never an "official" leader, a man who never
held political office or headed up any government, who never held any
official title at all and regarded himself as a humble weaver of cloth, and
yet one who in so many ways had transformed the history of his people

and determined the destiny of nations in the modern world. He altered his world, not through political maneuvering or institutional power, but rather through the sheer inspirational power of an integrated life based on religious, moral, and social virtues. And because he was such a remarkable model of leadership, he still influences the world today. It is well known that he was Martin Luther King Jr.'s model and inspiration for his stand in the American civil rights movement.

Gandhi was indeed a remarkable person and one well worth studying in relation to leadership and social movements. But what is particularly remarkable is that he achieved his vision of an independent India by renouncing violence and shunning all forms of institutional power and authority. He based his message solely on what has been called "moral authority." In our case we can also call it spiritual authority or inspirational leadership. Inspirational leadership can be described as a unique kind of social power that comes from the personal integration and embodiment of great ideas, as opposed to the power that comes from some form of authorization of external and structural authority like that of government, corporation, or religious institution. For example, a president's power comes primarily from the office that he or she holds, so too a general, a CEO, or a denominational leader, and so forth. In institutional power, it is the human institution that confers the power to an individual to perform a certain task. It is therefore primarily an external source of power that drives the role. Not so with inspirational leadership. Inspirational leadership involves a relationship between leaders and followers in which each influences the other to pursue common objectives, with the aim of transforming followers into leaders in their own right. It does this by appealing to values and calling without offering material incentives. It is based largely on moral power and is therefore primarily internal.

The interesting thing about Gandhi is that when probed about the ideological roots of his philosophy, he claimed absolutely no originality for his ideas: he said that he learned all this from Jesus indirectly, via Tolstoy. And so it is that we find our attention directed back to our Founder again. So let's look at him. When we examine the life and ministry of Jesus, we find that he too had no official titles or office. He had no accredited learning, he led no armies, opposed the use of violence, and taught us rather about the transforming spiritual power of love and forgiveness, and yet he changed the world forever. And in the greatest act of spiritual influence in the history of the world, sacrificially gave himself for the redemption of the world. The kind of power inherent in that supreme act of sacrifice, like that of all sacrificial acts, is a noncoercive power that influences people though sheer spiritual power—it draws people into its influence and changes them by calling out a moral and spiritual response in those who come into its orbit. Jesus is fully aware of this power when he says in John 12:32, "I, when I am lifted up from the earth, will *draw* all people to myself." It is the power of his teachings and the sheer quality of his life that change the world. He changed the world forever without being an official leader, politician, or general. This is authentic spiritual leadership, and Christian leadership is authentic only to the degree that it reflects this type of spiritual authority and power.

If we need any other biblical examples, we need look no further than Paul. Whenever he defends his own apostolic role against that of the "false apostles" (e.g., 2 Corinthians), he does not refer to some act of "ordination" by an institution that did not yet exist; rather he refers his readers to his suffering for the cause, his integrity in dealing with this, his calling to be an apostle by Jesus himself, his spiritual experiences, and his humility and "powerlessness" in human terms (cf. 2 Cor. 1:1 and Gal. 1:1). Hardly a description of a top-down, charismatic, fully empowered CEO; but here again we encounter the source of true spiritual power behind great leadership. It is not found in externalities, but rather in the mixture of calling, gifting, and personal integrity.

Influence is a hard thing to quantify. But you know it when you encounter it. It is interesting as well as profound that the NT word for authority is *exousia*, which quite literally means "out of oneself" (out of one's own substance). When one probes the nature of spiritual authority in scripture, it is clear that authority does come primarily out of oneself, and only secondarily from external sources. Or, to be more accurate, moral authority arises out of the mix of personal integrity, one's relationship to God, and the wealth of our relationships to others around us. And it is these qualities that should characterize a leadership that gets its inspiration from Jesus Christ.[21] So many of the problems in the world relate to the wrong use of power and authority—and in the history of Christendom it is to our great shame that the church has too often led the way. One has only to look at the Crusades, the Inquisition, the persecution of nonconformist Christians, and the treatment of Jews to see how we have so missed the mark in relation to authentic moral leadership.

I have recently been reminded that the best critique of the bad is the practice of the better. So what, then, is the practice of the better in this case? To find this "better" we must seek it where leadership *really* does work—in the remarkable Jesus movements of history. It is remarkable that most leaders in these mission movements would lack the qualifications necessary to lead in our Western churches, and yet by and large the impact of their influence across decentralized networks is exponentially greater than that of their western counterparts in centralized institutions. How can we account for this?!

---

21. Or, as Steve McKinnon, one of my Forge colleagues, once noted, "George Bush has power; Mother Teresa had *authority*!"

As mentioned previously, I was recently exposed to a remarkable apostolic leader from the underground church in China, "Uncle L," who was leading an underground house church movement of three million Christians. This man exemplified spiritual authority. He had no official learning, had no "office" and associated titles, and no real central institution to help in the administration and control of the tens of thousands of house churches, and yet his influence and teaching were felt throughout his movement. How did he do this? The only way that this is achieved is through the exercise of a genuinely spiritual authorizing for leadership.

Leadership as an Extension of Discipleship

If this is not already obvious by now, let me say it more explicitly: the quality of the church's leadership is directly proportional to the quality of discipleship. If we fail in the area of making disciples, we should not be surprised if we fail in the area of leadership development. I think many of the problems that the church faces in trying to cultivate missional leadership for the challenges of the twenty-first century would be resolved if we were to focus the solution to the problem on something prior to leadership development per se, namely, that of discipleship first. Discipleship is primary; leadership is always secondary. And leadership, to be genuinely Christian, must always reflect Christlikeness and therefore . . . discipleship.

If we stated this in terms of movement dynamics, it can be said that the reach of any movement is directly proportional to the breadth of its leadership base. And leadership in turn is directly related to the quality of discipleship. Only to the extent that we can develop self-initiating, reproducing, fully devoted disciples can we hope to get the task of Jesus's mission done.[22] There is no other way of developing genuine transformational movements than through the critical task of disciple making. Or as Neil Cole wryly notes, "If you can't reproduce disciples, you can't reproduce leaders. If you can't reproduce leaders, you can't reproduce churches. If you can't reproduce churches, you can't reproduce movements."[23]

If we wish to develop and engender a genuinely missional leadership, then we have to first plant the seed of obligation to the mission of God in the world in the earlier and more elementary phases of discipleship. This seed should be cultivated into full-blown missional leadership later on. This is not being coercive and manipulative, but simply recognizing that as disciples we are active participants in the missio Dei. We can't merely create missional leadership when the DNA of missional leadership was not first laid down in

22. See http://onmovements.com/?p=101
23. Given in a presentation in Melbourne, May 2006.

the seeds of discipleship. And this is exactly how Jesus does discipleship: he organizes it around mission. As soon as they are called he takes the disciples on an adventurous journey of mission, ministry, and learning. Straightaway they are involved in proclaiming the kingdom of God, serving the poor, healing, and casting out demons. It is active and direct disciple making in the context of mission. And all great people movements are the same. Even the newest convert is engaged in the mission from the start; even he or she can become a spiritual hero. If we accept that Jesus forms the primary pattern of disciple making for the church, then we must say that discipleship is our core task. But if disciple making lies at the heart of our commission, then we must organize it around mission, because mission is the catalyzing principle of discipleship. In Jesus they are inexorably linked.

This takes us to the final section of this chapter, which lays out something of the way in which we could follow more consistently the biblical pattern of disciple making.

Hitting the Road with Jesus

We are all familiar with the gospel stories where Jesus selects a band of disciples, lives his life with them, ministers with them, and mentors them. This approach to the formation of followers was common in the Israel of Jesus's day. Most rabbis would initiate and develop their schools of thought through similar means. It was this life-on-life phenomenon that facilitated the transfer of information and ideas into concrete historical situations. This has already been described above and so will not be pursued here. I simply note that this is the way that Jesus formed his disciples and that we should not think that we could generate authentic disciples in any other way.

Few would deny that in our day we have a crisis in leadership in the church in the West. We find ourselves facing an adaptive challenge that will necessitate a certain type of leadership to be able to guide us through the complexities of the twenty-first century. In this book and others, this type of leadership has been tagged "missional." And it is missional leadership that we need. The problem is that most of our training institutions are geared toward training a more *maintenance type* of leader. One has only to survey the types of subjects and the people teaching them for the point to be proved. If we are going to learn from the dangerous stories of the Jesus movements and attempt to gear ourselves around Apostolic Genius, then we simply have to find "the better way" of forming leaders.

I have long believed that leadership, or the lack of it, is a significant key to either the renewal or the decline of the church. If this is true, that leadership is critical to our success or failure, then we *must* ask why we are in our current state of demise, and then seek to remedy the situation. This is of strategic importance. And if we pursue this a little further, we must in the end center our attention on the agencies and people that have been responsible for the training and endorsing of a leadership that has overseen the massive decline of Christianity in the last two centuries. Some hard questions must be asked about the way we train and develop leadership.

Perhaps the single most significant source of the malaise of leadership in our day comes from the way, and the context, in which we form leaders. For the most part, the would-be leader is withdrawn from the context of ordinary life and ministry in order to study in a somewhat cloistered environment, for up to seven years in some cases. During that period they are subjected to an immense amount of complex information relating to the biblical disciplines, theology, ethics, church history, pastoral theology, etc. And while the vast majority of this information is useful and correct, what is dangerous to discipleship in that setting is the actual *socialization* processes that the student undergoes along the way. In effect, he or she is socialized out of ordinary life and develops a kind of language and thinking that is seldom understood and expressed outside of the seminary. It's as if in order to learn about ministry and theology, we leave our places of habitation and take a flight into the wonderfully abstracted world of abstraction, we fly around there for a long period of time, and then wonder why we have trouble landing again.

(noncontextual) academy-based training

missional / leadership / ministry context

Please don't get me wrong, we need serious intellectual engagement with the key ideas of our time. What is truly of concern is that such engagement takes place largely in the passive environments of the classroom. To love God fully with our whole being, leadership development must inculcate in the disciple the lifelong love of learning, but this can be done in a way far more consistent with the ethos of discipleship than that of the academy.

This is simply not the way that Jesus taught us how to develop disciples. And it is not that Jesus lacked an appropriate model of the Academy—the Greeks had developed it hundreds of years before Christ, and it was well entrenched in the Greco-Roman world. The Hebrew worldview was a life-oriented one and was not primarily concerned with concepts and ideas *in themselves*. On the other hand, it appears to me that the Academy is almost solely organized around the transfer of concepts and ideas. And so the seminaries, or institutions built on a similar academic model, are largely unable to produce disciples and missional leaders. It's not that they don't want to. The problem inherent in the seminary is that the in-tray of information is piled high while the out-tray of action and obedience is just about empty. The academy demands passivity in the student, whereas discipleship requires activity. If discipleship has to do primarily with becoming like Jesus, then it cannot be achieved by the mere transfer of information outside of the context of ordinary lived life. As I will attempt to show below, I simply do not believe that we can continue to try and *think* our way into a new way of acting, but rather, we need to *act* our way into new way of thinking.[24]

How have we moved so far from the ethos of discipleship passed on to us by our Lord? And how do we recover it again?

The answer to the first question is that Western Christendom was so deeply influenced by Greek or Hellenistic ideas of knowledge. By the fourth century AD the Platonic worldview had almost completely triumphed over the Hebraic one in the church. Later on it was Aristotle who became the predominant philosopher for the church. He too operated under a Hellenistic framework. Essentially, a Hellenistic view of knowledge is concerned with concepts, ideas, the nature of being, types, and forms. The Hebraic view, on the other hand, is primarily concerned with issues of concrete existence, obedience, life-oriented wisdom, and the interrelationship of all things under God. It is quite clear that, as Jews, Jesus and the early church operated primarily out of a Hebraic understanding, rather than a Hellenistic one.

The diagram below tries to illustrate this distinction. If our starting point is *old thinking* and *old behavior* in a person or church, and we see it as our task to change that situation, taking the Hellenistic approach will mean that we provide information through books and classrooms, to try and get the person/church to a new way of thinking, and hopefully from there to a new way of acting. The problem is that by merely addressing intellectual aspects of the person, we fail to be able to change behavior.

The assumption in Hellenistic thinking is that if people get the right ideas, they will simply change their behavior. The Hellenistic approach therefore can be characterized as an attempt to try to *think our way into a new way of acting*. Both experience and history show the fallacy of such thinking. And it certainly does not make disciples. All we do is change the way a person *thinks*; the problem is that his or her behaviors remain largely unaffected. This can be a very frustrating exercise, because once a person is in any new

24. I have borrowed this very useful phrase from the authors of *Surfing the Edge of Chaos*, 14.

paradigm of thinking, it is very hard for that person to deal with the situation from which he or she came.

Many church leaders experience this on a regular basis: it starts with recognition of some sort of problem in the local church together with a desire to address it. So laboring as they are under a system influenced by Hellenistic views of knowledge, they either go to a conference or go to a seminary to access a whole lot of new ideas about church renewal, leadership, and mission. The problem is that this is all they get—*new thinking*. They still have to deal with an unchanged congregation. And on a deeper look they soon realize that their own behaviors remain unchanged. It is genuinely hard to change one's behaviors by merely getting new ideas, as behaviors are deeply entrenched in us via our ingrained habits, upbringing, cultural norms, erroneous thinking, etc. Even though gaining knowledge is essential to transformation, we soon discover that it's going to take a whole lot more than new thinking to transform us. Anyone who has struggled with an addiction knows this.

I have belabored this point because this type of approach is so deeply entrenched in the Western church that we need to see it for what it is before we can find a better way. So what is that better way? You will not be surprised to find out that it is found in the ancient art of disciple making. Disciple making operates best with the Hebrew understanding of knowledge in mind. In other words, we need to take a whole person into account in seeking to transform that person. We also need to understand that we have to educate these whole people in the context *of* life and *for* life. The way we do this, indeed the way Jesus did it, is *to act our way into a new way of thinking*. This is clearly how Jesus formed his disciples. They not only lived with him and observed him in every possible circumstance, but also ministered with him and made mistakes and were corrected by him, all in the context of everyday life. And once again, these practices are found in all phenomenal movements of God.

So whether we find ourselves with old thinking and old behavior, or new thinking and old behavior, the way forward is to put actions into the equation. This is not as strange as it sounds at first. Human beings are sentient, thinking creatures with a deep desire to understand our lives and our world. This being so, we tend to process things *as we go*. Ideas and information are important, but they are generally needed to guide action and are best assimilated and understood in the context of life application. The assumption is that we bring all these dynamic thinking processes with us into our actions. It is all about context (not just content). We do not, as is supposed by the Hellenistic model, leave our thinking behind when we are doing our actions. We think while we are acting and act while we are thinking. In fact, this is precisely the way that all of us learned to walk, talk, socialize, and rationalize in the first place. Why would we assume that our mode of learning should change as we grow older?[25] So what I am proposing looks something like this:

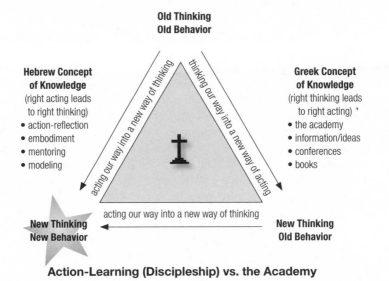

Action-Learning (Discipleship) vs. the Academy

Before we leave this chapter, I would like to provide the reader with a living example of how some training systems are beginning to reorient themselves to a disciple-making ethos in the attempt to form missional leaders. At Forge Mission Training Network we have built the entire system around this concept of action-learning discipleship. Our twin aims are to develop missionaries to the west and to develop a distinctly pioneering/missional mode of leadership. To do this we host an internship, where the intern is placed in an environment where he or she is somewhat out of his or her depth. We do this because when people are placed in a situation requiring something beyond their current repertoire of skills and gifts, they will be much more open to real learning. It's called jumping in at the deep end. The vast majority of the interns' learning is by "having a go" and actually doing things. They meet regularly (at least weekly) with the coach, who will debrief them, identify problems, suggest actions, and refer them to resources, including books and conferences. We *do* hold inspiring learning intensives where we pass on a lot of information, but this information is communicated only by those who have demonstrated their own capacity to do exactly what they are teaching—we allow only active missional practitioners to teach. Engaging in training in this way, the intern increases his

25. The following diagram is inspired by the work of Dave Ridgway and James Jesudason in their notes on the learning process.

or her ability to grasp the issues, to resolve and integrate them. Mission is, and always was, the mother of good theology.

We can't but be genuinely inspired by those amazing Jesus movements that seem to just instinctively get it right without a whole lot of theory. This has to be one of the secret works of the Holy Spirit, but I also believe that it is an inextricable part of the mDNA that constitutes Apostolic Genius. As such, it is latent in the church and birthed in situations where adaptation is demanded, just like some forgotten memory that has somehow been remembered again when a situation requires it. And here is the secret of how the faith is passed on from person to person down the generations—the ongoing and dynamic megaconspiracy of "Little Jesus."

5

missional-incarnational impulse

The Bible tells us that the Christian is in the world, and that there he or she must remain. Christians have not been created in order to separate themselves from, or to live aloof from, the world. When this separation is effected, it will be God's own doing, not man's. . . . The Christian community must never be a closed body.

Jacques Ellul, *The Presence of the Kingdom*

It should not bother us that [during different epochs] the Christian faith was perceived and experienced in new and different ways. The Christian faith is intrinsically incarnational; therefore unless the church chooses to remain a foreign entity, it will always enter into the context in which it happens to find itself.

David Bosch, *Transforming Mission*

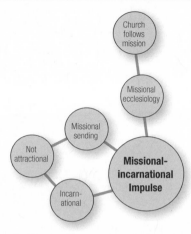

"Starting a single church was not an option for us; we would settle for nothing less than a church multiplication movement and we would abandon all things, even successful ones that would hold us back from that goal. I have found that there are many effective ministry methods that will also hold back multiplication. We were willing to abandon anything that would not multiply indigenous disciples, leaders, churches and movements."[1] With these fighting words Church Multiplication Associates (CMA) was born in the urban center of Long Beach, California. And in these words we can discern the echoes of ancient impulses inherent in the gospel of Jesus Christ itself.

In this chapter we will look at the impetus and patterning of Jesus movements over space and time, something I have chosen to call the missional-incarnational impulse. The purpose in combining these words is to link two practices that in essence form one and the same action. It is the thesis of this chapter that unless we embrace this mode, we will in effect lock up the genius of the apostolic church, namely, to seed and embed the gospel in different groups' cultures and societies and to thus sow the seeds of rapid multiplication.

This is important not only for practical reasons related to movements, but because so much of the theology of mission and incarnation is focused and concentrated in this impulse. The missional-incarnational impulse is, in effect, the practical outworking of the mission of God (the *missio Dei*) *and* of the Incarnation. It is thus rooted in the very way that God has redeemed the world, and in how God revealed himself to us.

And yet as decisive as this element of mDNA is, it one of the most easily overlooked because it is obscured by very sincere thinking that is shaped in another mode and captured by another imagination—the *evangelistic-attractional*. It's hard to critique the genuine sincerity of outreach and evangelism that aims at growing the church. In so many ways, it is right, and it feels right,

1. Cole, *Organic Church*, 27.

and at times it has been very effective. But I have come to believe it was not the way the early church operated, and neither is it present in other genuine expressions of Apostolic Genius. So critique it we must, because it is the evangelistic-attractional mode that is keeping us from experiencing that authentic impulse that reverberates through authentic apostolic movements.

Theological Roots

Because it goes against the grain of our inherited and ingrained practices, it is important to grasp the theological dynamics of the missional-incarnational impulse and the ways in which these two intertwined foundations of essential Christian theology inform our practices and behaviors.

The Mission of God

Over the last forty or so years, there has been a massive shift in the way we view missions. Some have articulated this shift as being from a church-centered one to a God-centered one, as Darrell Guder does, below:

> We have come to see that mission is not merely an activity of the church. Rather mission is the result of God's initiative, rooted in God's purposes to restore and heal creation. Mission means 'sending,' and it is the central biblical theme describing the purpose of God's action in human history. God's mission began with the call of Israel to receive God's blessings in order to be a blessing to the nations. God's mission unfolded in the history of God's people across the centuries recorded in Scripture, and it reached its revelatory climax in the incarnation of God's work of salvation in Jesus ministering, crucified, and resurrected. . . . It continues today in the worldwide witness of churches in every culture to the gospel of Jesus Christ.[2]

Guder concludes, "We have learned to speak of God as a "missionary God." Thus we have learned to understand the church as a "sent people." "As the Father sent me, I am sending you" (John 20:21; cf. 5:36–37, 6:44, 8:16–18, 17:18).[3] As God sent the Son into the world, so we are at core a sent or simply a *missionary* people.

This "sending" is embodied and lived out in the *missional impulse*. This is in essence an outwardly bound movement from one community or individual to another. It is the outward thrust rooted in God's mission that compels the church to reach a lost world. Therefore, a genuine missional impulse is a *sending* rather than an *attractional* one. The NT pattern of mission is centrifugal

---

2. See Guder, *Missional Church*, 4.
3. Ibid., 4.

rather than centripetal. And this cannot be emphasized more highly. When Jesus likens the kingdom of God to seeds being sown, he is not kidding. But applied in our missional practices it will look something like this:

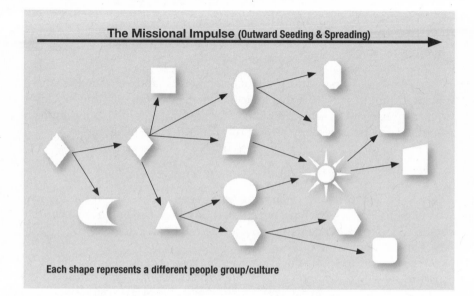

The Missional Impulse (Outward Seeding & Spreading)

Each shape represents a different people group/culture

All genuine mission is inspired by this, so it should not be *too* strange to us (turn it another way, and it looks like a spiritual family tree). What is more unfamiliar, perhaps, is the application of this approach to our own settings. We have tended to see mission as something we do in "heathen nations" and not on home base. We evangelize here and do mission there. This has rightly been called the "geographic myth." Thankfully, this is now changing.

We can see the "sneezelike" nature of the missional impulse in the diagram. But the diagram also enables us to see exactly how it is that we have inhibited this outward-flowing movement. The Christendom template tends to bolt down this missional impulse by substituting it with an attractional one. So while the local church genuinely does forms of evangelism and outreach, because it measures effectiveness through numerical growth, better programming, and increase of plant and resources, it requires the attractional impulse to support it. The exchange is subtle but profound, and the net effect is to unwittingly block the outward-bound movement that is built into the gospel. Instead of being sown in the wind, the seeds are put into ecclesial storehouses, thus effectively extinguishing the purpose they were made for.[4] Or, to go back to the sneeze metaphor, we suppress the "sneeze" by holding back the impulse to sneeze in the first place. And because of this, the attractional model quite simply can never hope to impact the broader culture as Jesus movements are able to.

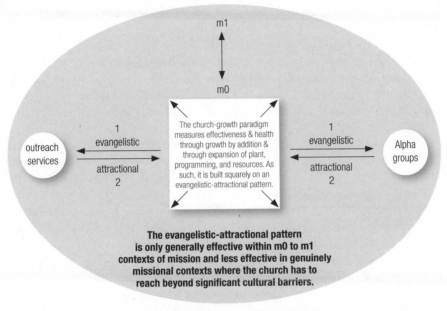

The church-growth paradigm measures effectiveness & health through growth by addition & through expansion of plant, programming, and resources. As such, it is built squarely on an evangelistic-attractional pattern.

The evangelistic-attractional pattern is only generally effective within m0 to m1 contexts of mission and less effective in genuinely missional contexts where the church has to reach beyond significant cultural barriers.

The Evangelistic-Attractional Impulse

The Incarnation

John 1:1–18 forms the central defining scriptural text narrating to us the marvelous coming of God into human history. But this text is far from the only one to probe this mystery. All Christians acknowledge that in Jesus Christ God was fully present and that he moved into our neighborhood in an act of humble love the likes of which the world has never known.

> When we talk of the Incarnation with a capital "I" we refer to that act of sublime love and humility whereby God takes it upon himself to enter into the depths of our world, our life, our reality in order that the redemption and consequent union between God and humanity may be brought about. This "enfleshing" of God is so radical and total that it qualifies all subsequent acts of God in his world.[5]

4. This is easily corrected—just embed mDNA, let go, and stop insisting on attractional church. We will have to learn to trust the kingdom of God to do the job of scattering, watering, and growing the seeds (1 Cor. 3:6–7). But as simple as it sounds, it's a hard lesson for control freaks to learn.

5. Frost and Hirsch, *Shaping of Things to Come*, 35. See 35–40 for further exploration on the implications of incarnational reality.

When God came into our world in and through Jesus, the Eternal moved into the neighborhood and took up residence among us (John 1:14). And the central thrust of the Incarnation, as far as we can penetrate its mystery, was that by becoming one of us, God was able to achieve redemption for the human race. But the Incarnation, and Christ's work flowing out of it, achieved more than our salvation; it was an act of profound affinity, a radical *identification* with all that it means to be human—an act that unleashes all kinds of potential in the one being identified with. But beyond identification, it is *revelation*: by taking upon himself all aspects of humanity, Jesus is for us, quite literally the human Image of God. If we wish to know what God is like, we need look no further than Jesus. We can understand him because he is one of us. He knows us and can show us the way.

Following from this, we can identify at least four dimensions that frame our understanding of the Incarnation of God in Jesus the Messiah.[6] They are

- *Presence:* In Jesus the eternal God is fully present to us. Jesus was no mere representative or prophet sent from God; he was God in the flesh (John 1:1–15; Col. 2:9).
- *Proximity:* God in Christ has approached us not only in a way we can understand, but in a way that we can access. He not only called people to repentance and proclaimed the direct presence of God (Mark 1:15), but befriended outcast people and lived life in proximity with the broken and "the lost" (Luke 19:10).
- *Powerlessness:* In becoming "one of us," God takes the form of a servant and not that of someone who rules over us (Phil. 2:6ff.; Luke 22:25–27). He does not stun us with sound and laser shows, but instead he lives as a humble carpenter in backwater Galilee for thirty years before activating his messianic destiny. In acting thus he shuns all normal notions of coercive power and demonstrates for us how love and humility (powerlessness) reflect the true nature of God and are the key means to transform human society.
- *Proclamation:* Not only did the Presence of God directly dignify all that is human, but he heralded the reign of God and called people to respond in repentance and faith. In this he initiates the gospel invitation, which is active to this very day.

Perhaps we can illustrate these dimensions in the following way:

6. I have adapted this 4 P's grid from the teaching material of Forge colleague Michael Frost.

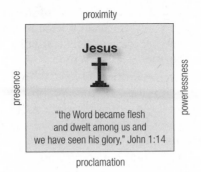

proximity

Jesus

presence

powerlessness

"the Word became flesh
and dwelt among us and
we have seen his glory," John 1:14

proclamation

The Incarnation

Incarnational Lifestyle

The Incarnation not only qualifies God's acts in the world, but must also qualify ours. If God's central way of reaching his world was to incarnate himself in Jesus, then our way of reaching the world should likewise be *incarnational*. To act incarnationally therefore will mean in part that in our mission to those outside of the faith we will need to exercise a genuine identification and affinity with those we are attempting to reach. At the very least, it will probably mean moving into common geography/space and so set up a real and abiding presence among the group. But the basic motive of incarnational ministry is also *revelatory*—that they may come to know God through Jesus.

To say the Incarnation should inform all the dimensions of individual and communal life is surely an understatement. In becoming one of us God has given us the archetypal model of what true humanity, and by implication true community, should look and behave like. This has major implications for our lives as well as our mission. So using the same grid, let us apply this to the mission of God's people.

- *Presence:* The fact that God was in the Nazarene neighborhood for thirty years and no one noticed should be profoundly disturbing to our normal ways of engaging mission. Not only does it have implications for our affirmation of normal human living, it says something about the timing as well as the relative anonymity of incarnational ways of engaging in mission. There is a time for "in-your-face" approaches to mission, but there is also a time to simply become part of the very fabric of a community and to engage in the humanity of it all. Furthermore, the idea of presence highlights the role of relationships in mission. If relationship is the key means in the transfer of the gospel, then it simply means we are going to have to be directly present to the people in our circle. Our very lives are our messages, and we cannot take ourselves out of the equation of mission. But one of the profound implications of our presence as representatives of Jesus is that Jesus actually likes to hang out with the people we hang out with. They get the implied message that God actually likes them. Do They?

- *Proximity:* Jesus mixed with people from every level of society. He ate with Pharisees as well as tax collectors and prostitutes. If we are to follow in his footsteps, his people will need to be directly and actively involved in the lives of the people we are seeking to reach. This assumes not only presence but also genuine availability, which will involve spontaneity as well as regularity in the friendships and communities we inhabit.

- *Powerlessness:* In seeking to act in a Christlike way, we cannot rely on normal forms of power to communicate the gospel but have to take Jesus's model with absolute seriousness (Matt. 23:25–28; Phil. 2:5ff.).[7] This commits us to servanthood and humility in our relationships with each other and the world. Sadly, much of church history shows how little we have assimilated this aspect of incarnational Christlikeness into our understanding of church, leadership, and mission.

- *Proclamation:* The gospel invitation initiated in the ministry of Jesus remains alive and active to this very day. A genuine incarnational approach will require that we be always willing to share the gospel story with those within our world. We simply cannot take this aspect out of the equation of mission and remain faithful to our calling in the world. We are essentially a "message tribe," and that means we must ensure the faithful transmission of the message we carry through proclamation.

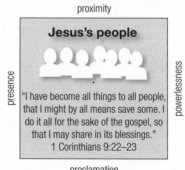

Incarnational Mission

7. Jesus is quite explicit about this: "Jesus called them together and said, 'You know that the rulers of the Gentiles lord it over them, and their high officials exercise authority over them. Not so with you. Instead, whoever wants to become great among you must be your servant, and whoever wants to be first must be your slave just as the Son of Man did not come to be served, but to serve, and to give his life as a ransom for many'" (Matt. 23:25–28).

By living incarnationally we not only model the pattern of humanity set up in the Incarnation but also create space for mission to take place in organic ways. In this way mission becomes something that "fits" seamlessly into the ordinary rhythms of life, friendships, and community and is thus thoroughly *contextualized*. Thus these "practices" form a working basis for genuine incarnational mission, but they also provide us with an entry point into an authentic experience of Jesus and his mission. Lindy Croucher, a missionary to the poor in an order called UNOH, likens living incarnationally to the scene in Mary Poppins where Mary takes hold of the children's hands and steps into the painting. She says that for her, incarnational mission has been like "stepping into the Gospels." She feels that she is "living inside the Gospels" for the first time.[8]

The incarnation must therefore inform the way we engage the complex multicultural world around us. The members of InnerChange (a missional order among the poor) in San Francisco, Los Angeles, Vietnam, and Cambodia take this very seriously. Not only because they work with the poor and that identification with people in their poverty is essential to a meaningful dialogue with them, but also because it is so thoroughly biblical. It fully reverberates with God's own means of reaching us. In order to identify with the poor, all InnerChange workers live voluntarily under the poverty line, spend 80 percent of their time in the neighborhood, and work to support themselves so that people cannot say "You are paid to be among us." They also plant indigenous faith communities that become a genuine part of the various people groups they are trying to reach.

This practice of incarnating the gospel informs some of the most remarkable people movements around today. God's Squad, a missionary order doing mission among outlaw biker gangs, takes the same approach. Over the years, they have become an actual part of the fabric of the subculture and are there when people get to talk about God, Jesus, and meaning, as all people do in their own way. They have brought Jesus into the imagination of the underground biker culture of which they are such a vital part. But this practice need not be limited to subcultures, the poor, and ethnic groups. It must become part of our practice in dealing with the many people that exist around us in everyday life. There are now over sixty pub churches in Australia and no doubt many more in the United Kingdom and the United States. In the desire to incarnate the gospel into a pub we can see the same impulse at work.

Incarnational ministry essentially means taking the church to the people, rather than bringing people to the church. In San Francisco, a remarkable urban missionary named Mark Scandrette embodies the "4 P's" of incarnational practice in his neighborhood. By actively being part of numerous local groups of artists, community activists, and businesses, he brings the presence

8. From a personal communication to the author.

of Jesus into the lives of people significantly alienated from the church as they know it. His ministry is hard to measure in purely numerical terms, *How?* but what is unmistakable is that this invaluable ministry has brought the kingdom of God much closer to many unchurched people than before.

In the Seattle/Tacoma region, two churches (Soma and Zoë) have chosen to collaborate in reaching students and musicians by actively moving into the social rhythms of these groups and "de-churchifying" their previous expressions of ministry. In order to do this they have rented and purchased buildings and developed them as nightclubs and coffee shops, and have established recording studios with direct links to the various musicians in the area. Zoë in particular has taken drastic measures to limit the attractional appeal of the ministry in order to wean members off the consumptive attendance at a "service" and to get them all involved in local expressions of mission. While passive *attendance* at services is down, the community is now highly engaged in various expressions of local community, and the missional reach has been significantly increased through incarnational practices. They all feel that they are now much closer to what it means to be disciples in community.

The Navigators in the United States are undergoing a major rethinking around missional approaches. One of the newest arms of the movement is called BetterTogether or just B2G. Led by visionary Gary Bradley, groups of friends are partnering to bring the gospel of Jesus and his kingdom into their daily environments, as channels of grace and blessing. Alert to where God is working, their aim is to join him in the realities of discipleship *in the missional context*. Their credo? "Right where you are, God is moving to draw and connect people in the depth, risk and reality of knowing Christ." They also aim at the development of transforming communities incarnating in every sphere of life. Gary's aim is "to see the story of Jesus planted in new ways among the next generation."[9]

In Melbourne a major Pentecostal church has rented its substantial property and buildings to rent in a local shopping mall and to become a direct and active presence in this heart of suburban social life. In the mall they will be fully responsible for creating the social fabric and injecting spirituality into these all-too-soulless aspects of modern life. Not only are they financial stakeholders in a profitable project, they are in a real sense bringing the kingdom into the places where people inhabit on a daily basis. Christian worship and presence has come into the public space.[10]

These are just some of the many ways in which individuals, churches, and missional agencies are moving away from the safety of attractional church and engaging in ways that are missional and incarnational. The net effect of these various expressions of incarnational mission is to seed the gospel

9. http://home.navigators.org/us/b2g/index.cfm.
10. http://www.urbanlife.org.au/.

into local areas or people groups and thus make it part of the intrinsic fabric of the culture. Furthermore, genuine incarnational presence gives a deeply personal feel to mission as well as creating credibility for proclamation and response. We must never underestimate the power of incarnational practices to bring the gospel near to any people group.

By way of contrast we have distorted the meaning of incarnational mission when as Western missionaries we have imposed fledged denominational templates on Third World nations. Not only does this diminish the validity of local culture, but it alienates the local Christians from their cultural surroundings by transposing a Western cultural expression in the place of local ones. The net result is a poor black man in the middle of the bush in Africa, dressed in robes and standing outside of a gothic style church building, calling people to worship in ways that barely make sense even to the cultures that started them. In these cases no attempt is made to contextualize (localize) either gospel or church, and yet we wonder why these have little lasting effect on the surrounding populations. While the error is easier to spot in the middle of Africa, we do the same thing all across the now highly tribalized West.

Incarnational Impulses

So much for the local dynamics of incarnational mission. When we look to the patterns that incarnational practice creates over time we see something really important, something that takes us right back to Apostolic Genius. As far as the *missional impulses* of remarkable Jesus movements are concerned, we discover that the incarnational practices are all about embedding and deepening the gospel in every people group so that they too might become God's people. So, diagrammatically the incarnational impulse will look something like this:

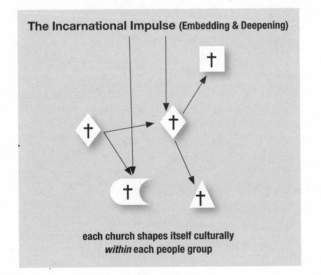

The Incarnational Impulse (Embedding & Deepening)

each church shapes itself culturally
***within* each people group**

By acting incarnationally, missionaries ensure that the people of any given tribe embrace the gospel and live it out in ways that are *meaningful* to their tribe. The culture as a whole thus finds its completion and redemption in Jesus. The gospel thus transforms the tribe *from the inside,* so to speak. We are reminded in Revelation 21–22 that in the great redemption there will be a genuine expression of redeemed culture as people from every tribe and language group and nation will give praise to God for what he has done for them. It is from within their own cultural expressions that the nations will worship.

Missional-Incarnational

The *incarnational* impulse draws its inspiration from the Incarnation, and the missional impulse is energized by the *mission of God*. In the dangerous stories of the phenomenal Jesus movements, these impulses effectively join together to form one single approach, namely, the missional-incarnational impulse. This two-in-one action operates much like the two blades of a scissors that make it an effective cutting tool. This is so vital to missional movements that I have come to believe that this is one of the more clearly identifiable elements of Apostolic Genius and therefore intrinsic to the church in its apostolic form. So this fusing of the missional and the incarnational impulses will look something like this:

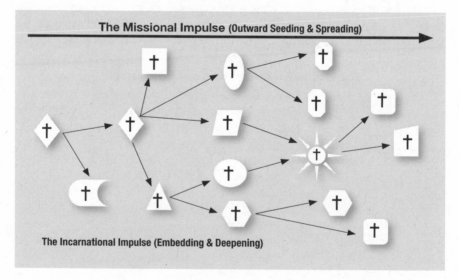

As the mission extends itself, so too the gospel seeds itself into the host culture. What we get are communities of faith that form an actual part of the culture they inhabit as well as are themselves missional. In turn they extend the mission that they received by initiating new missionary works to different tribes and people groups. If this sounds a little theoretical, concretely it looks like Church Multiplication Associates, Urban Neighbours of Hope, God's Squad, InnerChange, BetterTogether, Stadia, and the many other movements that take this approach seriously. This diagram clearly illustrates the actions of these and other movements that follow this impulse even if they don't use the language used in this book. And it's certainly an aspect of the phenomenal movements of early Christianity and China.

Let's try and work out some of the implications of this.

Making Babies Is Fun

Firstly, it is not hard to see that the reproductive capacities of the church are directly linked to this impulse. It is not coincidental that this looks awfully similar to the way in which all organic systems reproduce and procreate themselves. (It looks like a genealogy doesn't it?) We will explore this further when we look at the element of mDNA called organic systems, but it is important to note here that herein lies the impulse for the seeding and reproduction of God's people into every culture and group of people. In this view each unit of church can be conceived as a pod filled with seeds: each church "pregnant" with other churches. And it is in following this impulse that the apostolic church extends itself. To frustrate this impulse is to block the church's innate reproductive capacity.

If you think about it, this is actually how all powerful movements start. It begins with a group of people impassioned with a cause that reproduces itself through multiplication systems. It is fully consistent with the theory of how new movements begin, but sadly, not how they end. Something happens when we try to control things too much that serves to lock up the power of multiplication, and the movement moves on to addition and then on to subtraction. This is exactly what happened in Wesley's revolutionary movement, for instance. Wesleyanism was at its most influential when it was a people movement that was reproducing like mad. It eventually centralized, and as people sought to control what was happening, it lost much of its power to really change the world.

Neil Cole reports that only 4 percent of Southern Baptist churches in America will plant a daughter church. Extrapolated across the denominations, that means that 96 percent of the conventional churches in America will never give birth.[11] Cole goes on to say,

11. http://www.onmission.com/site/c.cnKHIPNuEoG/b.830269/k.AE98/Assisting_in_Church_planting.htm

Many think this is fine. I have heard people say, "We have plenty of churches. There are churches all over the place that sit empty, why start new ones? We don't need more churches but better ones." Can you imagine making such a statement about people? "We have plenty of people. We don't need more people, just better ones. Why have more babies?" This is short-range thinking. No matter how inflated you think the world population is, we are only one generation away from extinction if we do not have babies. . . . Imagine the headlines if suddenly it was discovered that 96% of the women in America were no longer fertile and could not have babies. We would instantly know two things: this is not natural so there is something wrong with their health. We would also know that our future is in serious jeopardy."[12]

The missional-incarnational impulse is a fundamental indicator of ecclesial health.

Getting into the Rhythm of Things

Second, the missional-incarnational impulse requires that as missionaries-to-the-West we seek to embed the gospel and, by extension, the church in such a way that these become an actual organic element of the fabric of the host community. Whereas the missional impulse means that we will always take people groups seriously as distinct cultural systems, the incarnational impulse will require that we always take seriously the specific culture of a group of people—seriously enough to develop a community of faith that is both true to the gospel and relevant to the culture it is seeking to evangelize. This is what is meant by contextualizing the gospel and the church. When we frontload mission with a certain culturally bound model of the church, we cannot avoid simply imposing a prefabricated notion of church on a given community. Subsequently, the church always remains somewhat alien within the broader community. Far more powerful is the approach that indicates we must seek to develop genuine Jesus communities in the midst of a people, communities that seek to become an actual functioning part of the existing culture and life of that people group. A genuinely missional form of church will seek to understand from the inside the issues that a people group faces: what excites them, what turns them off, what God means for them, and where they seek redemption. It will seek to observe and understand the social rhythms as well as relational networks of the people group it is trying to reach. It seeks to appreciate where and how they meet, what such gatherings look and feel like, and then it will try and articulate the gospel and the faith community into these groups in such a way as to become a genuine part of the culture, not something artificial and alien to it. The missional-incarnational approach requires identification

12. Cole, *Organic Church*, 119.

with a local people group, cultural sensitivity, and courageous innovation to authentically fulfill its mission.

Because it respects the culture and the integrity of a people group, missional-incarnational practice enhances the relational fabric of a given host culture. This is important, because the gospel, and therefore the conversion process, always travels along the relational fabric of a given culture. Addison notes that preexisting relationships are a critical factor for the exponential growth of a movement. "New religious movements fail when they become closed or semi-closed networks. For continued exponential growth, a movement must maintain open relationships with outsiders. They must reach out into new, adjacent social networks."[13] Stark argues that as movements grow, their "social surface" expands exponentially. Each new member opens up new networks of relationships between the movement and potential members—provided the movement continues to remain an open system. The forms of social networks will differ from culture to culture, but "however people constitute structures of direct interpersonal attachments, those structures will define the lines through which conversion will most readily proceed."[14]

There are many wonderful experiments in this approach that are going on throughout the West. For instance, a new flowering of this approach is being expressed in the suburban family environment of Perth by a wonderful group of grassroots Christians who go by the name of Upstream Communities (formerly called Backyard Missionaries). Through Christlike engagement and serving their community, a relatively small group of people has had *how?* significant impact on their neighborhood. Many established churches are also adapting to the new conditions by totally reworking their buildings and resources to allow for more genuine participation by the broader community around it, for example, sports venues, learning centers, cafés, and *why?* medical centers. I have been privileged to journey with well-established churches that have sold their church property and bought into shopping centers and main streets. One of them purchased a nightclub and is turning it into a community center. Still others have taken a more movement-style approach. For instance, through Missio, a church-planting movement and training center based in Denver, this missional-incarnational approach is being infused into church planters from the start. The leader of Missio, Hugh Halter, says it this way:[15]

- We move from an *"attraction model"* to an *"incarnational community"* approach.

13. Addison, "Movement Dynamics," 52.

14. Stark, *Rise of Chrstianity*, 22.

15. Material from *Missio's* Zer0rientation training advertising. Used with permission of Hugh Halter. See also http://www.missio.us/train.html.

- We limit transfer growth and build momentum from a spiritually curious culture.
- We learn how to "enflesh" the gospel in ways that make sense to saints and sojourners.
- We bring big values to a valueless culture: no need for "seeker services."
- We structure our lives as leaders, our money, and people in ways that propel missional activity.

But this ethos seems to be a significant missing factor in the way most local churches generally engage with their contexts. And so their potential influence and impact is minimized. Not only does attractional church lock up the outward-bound impulse of the Jesus movement, it tends to invalidate the incarnational impulse as well. Attractional church demands that in order to hear the gospel, people come to us, on our turf, and in our cultural zone. In effect, they must become one of us if they want to follow Christ. I can't emphasize how deeply alienating this is for most non-Christian people who are generally happy to explore Jesus but don't particularly want to be "churched" in the process. The biblical mode, on the other hand, is not so much to bring people to church but to take Jesus (and the church) to the people.

Missional Ecclesiology or . . . *Putting First Things First*

Another fundamental part of this aspect of mDNA relates to the theological and methodological flow of missional church. At Forge Mission Training Network, a missional leadership training system of which I am a part, we work hard to embed the following "formula" for engaging in mission in a post-Christian culture: *Christology determines missiology, and missiology determines ecclesiology*. This is just a smart-aleck's way of saying that in order to align ourselves correctly as a missional movement, we first need to return to the Founder of Christianity and, having done that, recalibrate our approach from that point on. Christian mission always starts with Jesus and is defined by him. Jesus is our constant reference point—we always begin and always end with him. It is Jesus who determines the church's mission in the world, and therefore our sense of purpose and mission comes from being sent by him into the world.[16]

When we go back to Jesus and learn about missional engagement from him, we discover a whole new way of going about it. We rediscover that

16. The christological dimensions of this statement are worked out more thoroughly in *The Shaping of Things to Come,* 112ff.

strange kind of holiness that was so profoundly attractive to nonreligious people and offensive to the religious ones. I live in the red-light and drug district of Melbourne, and from my experience these people do not generally like Christians; and yet in Jesus's day they loved being around Jesus, and he with them. This must mean something to us. I suggest that in a missional context, we must relearn the "how to's" of mission from him. From Jesus we learn how to engage with people in an entirely fresh "non-churchy" way. He hung out with "sinners," and he frequented the bars/pubs of his day (Matt. 11:19). He openly feasted, fasted, celebrated, prophesied, and mourned in such a way as to make the kingdom of God accessible and alluring to the average person. It's back to Jesus for us.

Not only our purpose is defined by the person and work of Jesus, but our methodology as well. These set the agenda of our missiology. Our missiology (our sense of purpose in the world) must then go on to inform the nature and functions, as well as the forms, of the church. In my opinion, it is absolutely vital that we get the order right. It is Christ who determines our purpose and mission in the world, and then it is our mission that must drive our search for modes of being-in-the-world. It can be represented like this:

Church Follows Mission

By my reading of the scriptures, ecclesiology is the most fluid of the doctrines. The church is a dynamic cultural expression of the people of God in any given place. Worship style, social dynamics, liturgical expressions must result from the process of contextualizing the gospel in any given culture. *Church must follow mission.*[17] The leaders guiding the Church of England in its quest to recover a missional edge encourage church planters to ensure that mission questions drive the church's answers, not vice versa. "Those who start with the questions about the relationship to the existing Church have already made the most common and most dangerous mistake. Start with the Church and the mission will probably get lost. Start with mission and it is likely that the Church will be found."[18] We engage first in incarna-

17. I have borrowed this phrase from Milton Oliver, a Forge colleague and friend.

18. Graham Cray, ed., *The Mission Shaped Church: Church Planting and Fresh Expressions of Church in a Changing Context* (Brookvale, NSW, Aus.: Willow Publishing, 2005), 116. "The early Christians were not focused on the church but rather on following Jesus and doing His mission, and the church emerged from that." Martin Robinson and Dwight Smith, *Invading Secular Space: Strategies for Tomorrow's Church* (London: Monarch, 2003), 40.

tional mission, and the church, so to speak, comes out the back of it. But if it is consistent with incarnational practices, that church will take the shape of the cultural group it is trying to reach. Mission in the incarnational mode is highly sensitive to the cultural forms and rhythms of a people group, because these are the means of meaningful relationship and influence. Incarnational mission thus engages people from *within* their cultural expression. Once this essential missional listening, observation, connecting, and networking has been done, then the forming of Jesus communities can take place. This is the only way to ensure that the Christian community truly incarnates itself and is fully contextualized. This can be diagrammatically represented as follows:

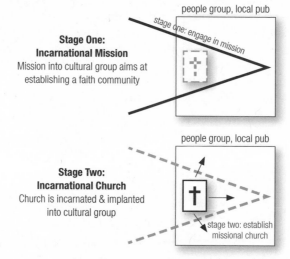

Stage One:
Incarnational Mission
Mission into cultural group aims at establishing a faith community

people group, local pub
stage one: engage in mission

Stage Two:
Incarnational Church
Church is incarnated & implanted into cultural group

people group, local pub
stage two: establish missional church

Church Follows Mission

Only in this way can the church actually become part of the cultural fabric and social rhythms of the host community. Once it has achieved this, it can therefore influence it from within. And it doesn't matter what group that might be. In our neighborhoods there are literally hundreds of different "tribes" that can be meaningfully reached by such means. Through the missional-incarnational approach, Jesus is introduced into their imaginations and conversations in a really evocative way.

Third Place Communities (TPC): A Test Case in Missional-Incarnational Impulse

To close this exploration into missional-incarnational impulse, it is worth looking at an excellent example of a group of spunky people doing it in about every possible social context they find themselves. The story is that of Third Place Communities (TPC), a mission agency that was set up to incarnate Jesus communities in *third places*. For those who are unaware of the term, our first place is the home, our second place is work/school, and our third place is where we spend our time when we have time off. Anywhere people gather for social reasons could be a good place for missional engagement. Third places are pubs, cafés, hobby clubs, sports centers, etc. For these communities "church" takes place wherever they are. Through this approach TPC has made a significant impact on Hobart (Australia) by just hanging out and being the people of God in public spaces. The vast majority of the people who hang out with them are very inquisitive non-Christians.

TPC is now in its fourth year of mission. These are still early days, and they feel that they have just started to find their groove and move more closely into their sense of calling, but they recognize that they are in it for the long haul. Being involved incarnationally has meant the members of the community have been transformed into genuine missionaries to their city.

In just over three years they have found themselves profoundly connected with a large range of people in the broader (non-Christian) community. Many of these relationships have become deep and intimate as over this period they experienced life together through the celebration of engagements, weddings, birthdays, births, and life in general. Their missional rhythms include weekly hospitality around tables, serving the community together, raising money for those in need, enjoying and sponsoring local art and music, burying loved ones, sharing ideas about life, praying together, and exploring the stories about Jesus in the context of life. They have seen some come to active faith in Jesus, and many others are close to it. Some are of course still exploring, and still others just love being part of the community and are involved at deep levels but are content not to explore further at this stage. But for all of these people, whether they realize it or not, Jesus now inhabits their worlds in ways they are meaningful and tangible. Now when they think about themselves, the world around them, or their work and play, Jesus is part of the equation, where he was not before.

But it's not just all parties and rabid socializing. TPC organizes on a number of levels: some of these include . . .

(RE)VERB MISSION COMMUNITY

This is their explicit Jesus community (church). Adopting a distinctly missional-incarnational approach has led them to encourage church to emerge from mission, rather than mission emerging from a particular expression of church. The mission context therefore influences the way the faith community gathers. The goal is to establish many different Christ-centered groups of people who express their Christian spirituality within their local cultural context. So, rather than bringing people to church, they attempt to build church around people where they are. The members of (re)verb therefore spend most of their time building relationships with people through social gatherings and time spent in local third places. But they also gather in smaller groups for prayer, worship, discipleship, and Christian companionship.

MARKETPLACE

Because TPC is so involved in the lives of non-Christian people (they make up about 60 percent of the community), it didn't take them long to discover that most people were up for healthy dialogue on existential matters when sitting as friends together in the pub over a beer. After some time they sensed God inviting them to support these conversations by providing an environment in which existential themes could be explored. Marketplace was the result: a neutral, no-proselytizing forum where people explore ideas and philosophies about life, meaning, culture, identity, and spirituality. It might be surprising that a group defining themselves primarily as missional created a neutral, no-proselytizing zone. In this, they were quite intentional. With the legacy of suspicion and mistrust toward Christianity in Australia, they wanted people to feel this was a safe environment to explore ideas related to life and meaning. With music playing in the background, people arrive at around 8:00 p.m., grab a drink from the bar, and chat with others. Half an hour later they formally welcome everyone, remind them of "marketplace manners" (respect for each other's beliefs and opinions), and then introduce the presenter for the night. The invited speaker (not necessarily a Christian) presents ideas and thoughts on the chosen theme, receiving questions and comments. Most people hang around and engage in a time of informal dialogue over a few drinks. Some amazing conversations have resulted from these nights, and it has actually become a bit of a cultural event in Hobart.

WEDDINGS, PARTIES, ANYTHING . . . (RITE OF PASSAGE CELEBRATIONS)

Over time and through meaningful relationships, TPC has had the privilege of being invited to conduct a number of these events for people they met at the pub, work, home, or university. It's a huge invitation into the world of the people TPC aims to serve. They have found the rites of passage celebrations to be an excellent way to build meaningful relationships that open people to issues of spirituality, and they have found that sharing these deeply significant rites of passage ceremonies with people has been a profoundly missional experience. This has become a major aspect of the TPC mission—and they do it well.

IMAGINE TASMANIA

In addition to these activities, Darryn (the leader of TPC) and a few businesspeople have started a project called Imagine Tasmania.[19] The aim of this grouping is to dream up, and work toward, making Tasmania a better place for everyone to live. The group is largely non-Christian. But as one of the pioneers of this project, Darryn has been able to open up significant relationships with the many people who would like to make their world a better place. These conversations would not have come about if not for Darryn's desire to create an incarnational presence in them. Imagine Tasmania is the kind of engagement that Mike Frost and I refer to as "shared projects" in *The Shaping of Things to Come*[20]—powerful means of missional engagement within the cultures in which we minister.

In concluding this chapter, it is important to reiterate that the missional-incarnational impulse is perhaps one of the most important aspects of Apostolic Genius because by adopting this approach we will be led into the natural discovery of many of the other aspects of mDNA. It is critical because without it we will not be going anywhere, but we will remain trapped in the Christendom mode of the church. To adapt ourselves to the challenges of the twenty-first century, we need to undergo a fundamental change at the level of our primary impulses. We need to move from evangelistic-attractional to missional-incarnational. This transition can best be recovered by seeing mission as an activity of God and not primarily an activity of the church. We participate in God's mission and not the other way around. If this is conceded, then it follows that we must engage in ways that mirror God's engagement with the world . . . and that takes us directly to the missional-incarnational impulse that clearly marks the phenomenal Jesus movements in history.

In its very simplest form, this will mean allowing Jesus to lead us into the marketplaces, the *third places,* and the homes of the various people in our lives, and there teach us about how we ought to engage in ways that are truly Christlike. He will teach us how to become redemptive, incarnated expressions of the gospel in every nook and cranny of our culture. WWJD? He has already given us the answer.

---

19. Tasmania is the state they live in. This type of approach was started in Chicago. It is called Imagine Chicago, and it has proven to be a really effective way to involve a diverse group of people in urban and cultural renewal of Chicago.

20. Frost and Hirsch, *Shaping of Things to Come,* 24.

6

apostolic environment

Purpose and principle, clearly understood and articulated, and commonly shared, are the genetic code of any healthy organization. To the degree that you hold purpose and principles in common among you, you can dispense with command and control. People will know how to behave in accordance with them, and they'll do it in thousands of unimaginable, creative ways. The organization will become a vital, living set of beliefs.

Dee Hock, *The Birth of the Chaordic Age*

The first responsibility of a leader is to define reality.

Max DePree, in *Credibility*

Recently I was privileged to hear a remarkable leader, affectionately called "Uncle L,"[1] from the underground church in China. He was a small, bent, soft-spoken old man, who at that point was leading an underground house-church movement of three million Christians! He has no degrees but exhibits an amazing intellect imbued with a savvy, life-oriented wisdom. He has no "office" or associated titles and yet exercises a remarkable gift of leadership and calling. He has no central institution to help in the administration and control of the tens of thousands of house churches, and yet his influence and teaching are felt throughout his movement. I assume that he employed only a very few people, and yet he leads millions. He has been imprisoned and had suffered much for his faith and yet has continued in his old age to defy the state through his involvement in the underground movement. I had no doubt that in this inspiring old man I had encountered an authentic apostle. Philip Yancey reports a similar experience on a recent trip to China, where he met a bright and passionate forty-four-year-old leader called Brother Shi. As a teenager Shi headed up his province's Communist Youth League and later served as a Red Guard. When he became a Christian, he was kicked out of his home and was hunted down by the authorities. Yancey writes, "Shi must travel constantly, eluding police through narrow escapes. The house churches, recognizing his leadership skills, have promoted him so that he now supervises 260,000 Christians in his province!"[2] Yancey rightly says that in wonderment, given his own context in America, where megachurches are made up of 1,000 to 20,000 members but require sophisticated organizations to operate them. Peter Wenz, an apostolic leader from Stuttgart, Germany, leads a network of house churches that grew rapidly to around 250. Around 6,000 people have a weekly celebration in the city. He coaches about forty other networks as well.

The introduction of these remarkable apostolic leaders forms a good starting point for this chapter, because it takes us back to the same kind of questions that initially drove me to search for that "magical" something that seems to animate the phenomenal Jesus movements of history. The question that bugged me then, and continues to do so now, is "How did they do it?" One of the clear answers is that they didn't do it without significant leadership. But that just merely raised another question: "What *kind* of leadership?" We have all sorts of leadership and training resources today, yet we are in serious decline. So, what was/is the difference? It's a good question, and it deserves an equally good answer in response.

In every manifestation of Apostolic Genius there is a powerful form of catalytic influence that weaves its way through the seemingly chaotic network of churches and believers. There is no substantial word for this catalytic

1. His name is being withheld because of the situation in China.
2. Philip Yancey, "Discreet and Dynamic," *Christianity Today*, July 2004, vol. 48, no. 7, 72.

social power other than, to reinvoke biblical language, *apostolic*.[3] And this is not just the power of the gospel/apostolic doctrine (as powerful as that is in sustaining the faith) but also that of a certain category of leadership, namely, that of the apostolic person. I can find no situation where the church has significantly extended the mission of God, let alone where the church has achieved rapid metabolic growth, where apostolic leadership cannot be found in some form or another. In fact, the more significant the mission impact, the easier it is to discern this mode of leadership.

Apostolic leadership, as in all types of influence, is both identified and measured by the *effect* it has on the social environment in which it operates. And in these terms it is *always* present in periods of significant missional extension. Such people might not always call themselves "Apostles," but the apostolic nature and effect of their ministry and influence are undeniable.

If You Want Missional Church, Then . . .

It is worth noting again at this point that the church in the West is facing a massive adaptive challenge—positively in the form of compelling opportunity and negatively in the form of rapid, discontinuous change.[4] These twin challenges constitute a considerable threat to Christianity, locked as it is into the prevailing Constantinian (Christendom) form of church, with all its associated institutional rigidity. Our situation is what Canadian missiologist Alan Roxburgh calls *liminality*. Liminality, in his view, is the transition from one fundamental form of the church to another, *necessitating the apostolic role*.[5] Environments of discontinuous change require adaptive organizations and leadership.[6] As the apostolic role is responsible and gifted for the extension of Christianity, so too the missionary situation requires a pioneering and innovative mode of leadership to help the church negotiate the new territory in which it finds itself. This is clear enough when we consider the emerging missional church, which relies heavily on an innovative pioneering spirit and is therefore fundamentally apostolic in nature. But it is equally true for established churches.

3. Opting for more technical (and descriptive) terminology rather than biblical, Garrison calls these "Strategy Coodinators." D. Garrison, *Church Planting Movements* (Midlothian, VA: WIGTake Resources, 2004), 17.

4. See appendix for development of the idea of adaptive challenge.

5. A. J. Roxburgh, *The Missionary Congregation, Leadership & Liminality* (Harrisburg, PA: Trinity, 1997), 61.

6. This is no small task, and it requires a particular mode of leadership. An adaptive challenge requires an adaptive organization. In living systems, adaptivity is the capacity of an organism to change behavior in various environments. Applied to churches and organizations, it requires those who understand the essential mDNA of the church and gospel dynamic coupled with the know-how of how to reapply it in different contexts.

The apostolic person's calling is essentially the extension of Christianity. As such, he or she calls the church to its essential calling and helps guide it into its destiny as a missionary people with a transformative message for the world. All other functions of the church must be qualified by its mission to extend the redemptive mission of God through its life and witness. The apostolic leader thus embodies, symbolizes, and *re*-presents the apostolic mission to the missional community. Furthermore, he or she calls forth and develops the gifts and callings of all of God's people. Without apostolic ministry the church either forgets its high calling or fails to implement it successfully. Sadly, in declining denominational systems, such people are commonly "frozen out" or exiled because they disturb the equilibrium of a system in stasis. This "loss" of the apostolic influencer accounts for one of the major reasons for mainstream denominational decline. If we really want missional church, then we must have a missional leadership system to drive it—it's that simple.

really?

I am well aware of the various reactions that this subject can evoke. This is so partly because of the confusion between the unique role and calling of the original apostles and that of present-day apostol-*ic* ministry, that is, a ministry gifting that further extends and substantiates the original apostolic work but does not in any way alter it. But another reason for negative reaction has been that many who have claimed "apostleship" do it no justice and in the end discredit this vital role. Sadly, church history is littered with false apostles.[7]

The only conclusion from the research and study undergirding this book is that apostolic ministry is a distinct element of Apostolic Genius, and because of this we need to find a way to understand and re-embrace it if we want to become a genuinely missional church. Quite simply, a missional church needs missional leadership, and it is going to take more than the traditional pastor-teacher mode of leadership to pull this off.[8] Leadership always pro-

---

7. If it helps us understand the issue more clearly, the New Testament apostles struggled with precisely the same problem. Much of their struggle in founding the initial Jesus movement was against the so-called false apostles of their day. But because of this, the original apostles found no reason to dismiss the apostolic function *holus bolus*. We don't see Paul renouncing his apostleship because there were false ones around. Quite the contrary, he seems to argue all the more for the validity and authority of his own apostleship over against the claims of the false ones. And by the providence of God, these Pauline texts have come to form the authoritative basis of testing the authenticity of all subsequent claims to apostolic ministries.

8. Roxburgh goes further in saying that in actual practice, a predominantly pastoral conception of the church and ministry now actually constitutes a major hindrance to the church reconceiving itself as a missional agency. He also says, in relation to the institutionalization and dominance of the pastoral function embodied in ordination, that "the guild of the ordained will have to be removed; this is one social function that will not move us through liminality." In A. J. Roxburgh, *The Missionary Congregation, Leadership, & Liminality* (Harrisburg, PA: Trinity, 1997), 64–65.

vides a strategic point of leverage for missional change and renewal. If this is conceded, then the question of *what type of leadership* naturally follows. The natural answer is *missional* and therefore must include the idea of the *apostolic*. We simply have to get over our historical cringe in this matter if we are going to grow and mature as a missional movement (Eph. 4:11ff.). It is no mere coincidence that all the historical denominations that by and large have rejected apostolic leadership find themselves in long-term, systematic decline in every context in the West. This chapter will therefore focus on *why* apostolic ministry is needed and *why* it is an irreplaceable aspect of mDNA.

An Apostolic Job Description

Apostolic ministry is basically a function and not an office. *Office* as we normally conceive it, relates to a position in an established, centralized institution, and it gets its authority from being an "official" in an institutional structure. One simply cannot find this level of "institution" in the really? New Testament and in the postbiblical period. On the other hand, the New Testament church has all the hallmarks of an emergent people movement with little or no centralized structures, no "ordained" or professional ministry class, and no official "church" buildings. Besides, in the context of persecution, any latent institutional inclinations the church might have had were effectively removed by sheer external pressure beyond its control. Apostolic ministry, which was very much alive in the early church, was perceived as a gifting and a calling by God, was authenticated by a life lived consistent with the message, and was recognized by its effects on the movement and its context, namely, the extension of the mission of God and in the sustainability and health of the churches. And it was quite clearly crucial to the survival and growth of the movement. It is hard to see Christianity surviving at all without this form of influence and leadership.

Why this particular ministry is so vitally important and seemingly irreplaceable is best answered by describing the apostle as *the custodian of Apostolic Genius* and of the gospel itself. All subsequent apostolic ministry models itself on this archetypal ministry of the original, and authoritative, apostles. This is to say that he/she is the person who imparts and embeds mDNA.[9] And once the mDNA is embedded in local communities, apostolic

9. First Corinthians 3:9–11 gives a clue to this aspect of apostolic ministry: "For we are God's fellow workers; you are God's field, God's building. By the grace God has given me, I laid a foundation as an expert builder, and someone else is building on it. But each one should be careful how he builds. For no one can lay any foundation other than the one already laid, which is Jesus Christ." Apostolic ministry is about laying foundations, or, in the terminology

ministry works to ensure that the resultant churches remain true to it and that they do not mutate into something other than God intended them to be. As well as pioneering new churches, the apostolic ministry lays foundations in those that have none. The circuit riders of the American West were classic examples of this. They rode out to small towns and small population zones, preached the gospel, brought people to Christ, established churches, and then went on to the next town, only to return the following year on their circuit. The apostles of the Chinese church operated in precisely the same way.[10]

But the importance of apostolic ministry is not limited to new missionary movements. It has ongoing relevance for established denominations as well. In fact, it is crucial to the revitalization process. Steve Addison, consultant on mission and church growth notes that

> The apostolic role within established churches and denominations requires the reinterpreting of the denomination's foundational values in the light of the demands of its mission today. The ultimate goal of these apostolic leaders is to call the denomination away from maintenance, back to mission. The apostolic denominational leader needs to be a visionary, who can outlast significant opposition from within the denominational structures and can build alliances with those who desire change. Furthermore, the strategy of the apostolic leader could involve casting vision and winning approval for a shift from maintenance to mission. In addition the leader has to encourage signs of life within the existing structures and raise up a new generation of leaders and churches from the old. The apostolic denominational leader needs to ensure the new generation is not "frozen out" by those who resist change. Finally, such a leader must restructure the denomination's institutions so that they serve mission purposes."[11]

At core, the apostolic task is about the expansion of Christianity both *physically* in the form of pioneering missionary effort and church planting, as well as *theologically* through integration of apostolic doctrine into the life of the individual Christians and the communities they are part of. But more than that, as custodian of Apostolic Genius, he or she is the person who provides the personal reference point as well as the spiritual context for the other ministries of God's people.

So I want to suggest that there are three primary functions of apostolic ministry, illustrated as follows:

---

of this book, embedding the mDNA of the church and the gospel. The reader should also note the indissoluble link between Christology and the church.

10. Research notes by Curtis Sergeant, acknowledged as a leading expert on the Chinese phenomenon.

11. Stephen Addison, "A Basis for the Continuing Ministry of the Apostle in the Church's Mission," D.Min. diss., Fuller Theological Seminary, 1995, 190.

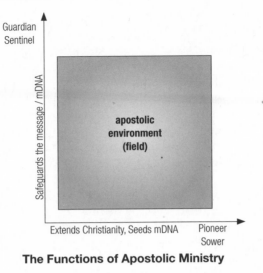

The Functions of Apostolic Ministry

1. To embed mDNA through pioneering new ground for the gospel and church

As custodian (steward) of the DNA of Jesus's people, the apostle is both the messenger and the carrier of the mDNA of Christianity. As "the one who is sent,"[12] he or she advances the gospel into new missional contexts and embeds the DNA of God's people into the new churches that emerge in those places. At heart, the apostle is a pioneer, and it is this pioneering, innovative spirit that marks it as unique in relation to the other ministries. "It is of special significance that those entrusted with translocal, apostolic, leadership are pioneers. The church is called to be a dynamic movement rather than a static institution. For that reason, its leadership is to be drawn from those on the front line of the expansion of the church."[13]

2. To guard mDNA through the application and integration of apostolic theology

But for the custodian of the DNA of Christ's people, the responsibility of apostolic ministry does not end with pioneering missionary work. He or she is also mandated with the task of ensuring that the churches remain true to the gospel and its ethos. This aspect of apostolic ministry can be described as creating and maintaining the *web of meaning* that holds the movement

12. The name *apostle* means "one who is sent."
13. Addison, "Basis for the Continuing," 80.

together. Apostolic ministry does this by reawakening the people to the gospel and embedding it in the organizational framework in ways that are meaningful. It is out of this apostolic web of meaning that the movement maintains itself over the long haul. And it's critical to translocal mission. Watch what the biblical apostles do; they engage in missionary work, establish new churches, and once established they move off to new frontiers. But they also see as essential networking the churches and exhorting the disciples by traversing between them, cultivating leadership, and issuing guidance to ensure a correct apprehension and integration of the gospel message in the common and individual lives of the hearers. They are quick to weed out heresy and error—removing potential mutations in the mDNA.

All authentic apostolic ministry does this. Apostles are not just hot-headed entrepreneurs; they are also working theologians—or at least ought to be if genuinely apostolic. This impulse to ensure doctrinal integrity is therefore another key characteristic of apostolic ministry, and without it we would not be here today, as it forms the basis of the Christian faith. While acknowledging that the unique teaching authority of "the twelve" was foundational and authoritative and constitutes the base theology of the church, apostolic ministry throughout the ages has both these elements in it. Witness the ministry of Patrick, John Wesley, Ignatius of Loyola, John Wimber, William Booth, William Carey, and the countless unnamed apostles of the Chinese underground church, for example, and you will see this dual element of pioneer missionary and working theologian.

In light of these comments, we can see how Bishop John Shelby Spong,[14] and his particular brand of DIY/designer Christianity, is somewhat of a danger to us today. I am not just trying to be needlessly provocative here—this is a real live issue for us. Designer Christianity is a form of diluted, consumerist, and syncretized faith that, in my opinion, has in the context of postmodern pluralism and relativism become a genuine threat to the church in the West *precisely* because it distances us from the real vigor of our original and primary message.[15] In many ways it has always been one of the major functions

14. For those unaware of Spong and his teaching, essentially he is the best-known heretic of our day. Not only is he a syncretistic universalist in the extreme, but he proposes that we abandon any notion of a theistic, interventionist God. The net effect is to use the language of Christianity but to bleach it of its content. He is very popular in the Western media. See his *Here I Stand* (San Francisco: HarperSanFrancisco, 2000) and *A New Christianity for a New World: Why Traditional Faith Is Dying and How a New Faith Is Being Born* (San Francisco: HarperSanFrancisco, 2001).

15. In fact this theological temptation poses one of the most potent threats to the EMC, hence my vehemence. As a late-twentieth-century, early-twenty-first-century phenomenon, the EMC is very susceptible to the postmodern blend of religious pluralism and philosophical relativism. This makes it very hard to stand for issues of truth in the public sphere. Claims of truth are thus pushed into the sphere of private opinion. This creates massive pressure to deny the uniqueness of Christ and his work in our behalf. I have seen many emerging churches suc-

of apostolic ministry to keep the gospel uncontaminated and so preserve its saving God-power for future generations (Rom. 1:16). This is just one of the reasons why such ministry is so vital today. There is no doubt in my mind as to how Paul would handle "Spongianism"; he would see it as a direct assault on the DNA of the gospel and therefore the church.

3. To create the environment in which the other ministries emerge

Ever wondered why, in all the lists of ministries, that of apostle is always explicitly listed first? And why it is considered the most important of the ministries (1 Cor. 12:28 ff.; Eph. 4:11)? Or why in Ephesians 2:20 Paul says that the church is built on the foundation of the apostles and prophets?[16] Not because of some hierarchical organizational conception of leadership, because such ideas of leadership did not exist in the New Testament movement (see below). Rather, it is because apostolic ministry is the foundational gift that provides both the *environment* and the *reference point* for the other ministries mentioned in scripture.

New Covenant Ministries International is a mission operating in Western contexts that bases its ministry squarely on this teaching about the foundational nature of apostolic ministry.[17] They claim that they are not a denomination or grouping of churches; they see themselves simply as a group of people committed to advancing the kingdom of God through mission and networking. They view themselves as a translocal apostolic-prophetic team held together by a common purpose and friendships. But in the process of their ministry, they have planted hundreds of churches, networked with hundreds more, and are currently working in over sixty different countries. And they began only in the early eighties.

Roxburgh rightly says that apostolic ministry is ". . . foundational to all the other functions."[18] That is, it initiates the other ones—it constitutes their

---

cumb to theological liberalism a la Spong and then die off. The adaptive challenge must drive us closer to our original message, not further away from it. This, I believe, is critical.

16. Again, I don't wish to deny the unique role of the original apostles in the founding of the apostolic church. However, I do think that this "founding" aspect can be extended, in a less binding and reflective form, to all genuine apostolic and prophetic ministries.

17. http://www.ncmi.net/

18. Roxburgh, *Missionary Congregation,* 62. Even the office of the bishop, the institutional replacement of the prior apostolic role, serves as a custodian of apostolicity (viewed here as inherent in the church and in the New Testament scriptures) and is viewed as "having in himself all the other ministries," which are in turn conferred to others via ordination. See John McQuarrie, *Principles of Christian Theology* (London: SCM, 1966), 391. In instituting the bishop, Christendom took the pioneer aspect out of the equation, institutionalized apostolicity in church and office, and reshaped it in a distinctly pastoral image to suit the diocesan context, but it did keep *some* authentic aspects of the apostolic role that were useful to it. This *founding* role is one of them, and in it a true function of the apostolic can still be discerned.

foundation. From apostolic ministry, the mDNA is embedded and distributed among the various other ministries that form the fivefold ministry of Ephesians 4—what I will call APEPT (apostolic, prophetic, evangelistic, pastoral, and teaching/didactic). The founding and developing of APEPT is therefore a natural extension of the custodial nature of apostolic ministry. Drawing this out, one could say that the apostolic creates the environment for the prophetic, the prophetic creates the environment for the evangelistic, and so on. Using the most comprehensive statement of ministry structure, that of Ephesians 4:7–11, it would look something like this:

Without apostolic ministry, the rest of the APEPT ministries have no practical reference point and therefore lack legitimacy. As such, the apostolic creates the primary field of NT ministry and is crucial to the recovery of missional church.

Without prophetic ministry the evangelistic can become shallow and God becomes an idol. The prophet ensures that the holiness of God is honored and truth is respected.

Without evangelistic ministry, there is no basis for pastoral ministry. No one to pastor!

Pastoral ministry exposes the disciple to the need for self-awareness and understanding.

Teaching based on the revealed will of God leads to maturity and understanding

teaching
Pastoral ministry creates the environment for development of Christlikeness.

pastoral
The evangelist brings people into relationship with Jesus through the gospel. In doing this it initiates the pastoral function.

evangelistic
Prophetic ministry attends to what God has to say and calls the covenant people to faithfulness. As such, it opens the hearer up to God's call, which is the task of the evangelist.

prophetic
Apostolic ministry creates the environment that gives birth to all the other ministries. This is so because it hosts the mDNA of Jesus's church. It thus forms the reference point for the other fivefold ministries. It "births" the prophetic because it establishes the covenant community. Together with the prophetic, it forms the "foundational ministry" of the church (Eph. 2:20).

apostolic

If this is correct, and this is the only way we can explain why *apostle* is always listed first as the primary calling, it once again highlights why "apostolic environment" is one of the five key elements of mDNA that make up Apostolic Genius. All the five ministries are needed to engender, call forth, and sustain a full ministry in the Jesus movement. In fact, all five ministries in dynamic relation to one another are absolutely essential to vigorous discipleship, healthy churches, and growing movements, as we shall see below.[19] As such, APEPT ministries are delegated ministries born out of the apostolic task as custodian of the mDNA—the apostolic being the foundational one. And it needs to be emphasized: the leadership dynamic is that of a servant-inspirer model and not that of one who "lords it over others."

Field of Dreams

Having defined the functions/roles of the apostolic person, we can now look at how apostolic ministry exerts its influence. Part of the resistance to the reception of apostolic ministry in our churches has been that at times people who claim to be apostles have assumed that it involved a dictatorial approach to the leadership of the church. All too often, this has resulted in a disempowering of God's people, who, instead of maturing and growing in the faith, remain basically childlike and powerless, dependent on the autocratic and overwhelming paternal power of the "apostle." This is both a distortion and a misrepresentation of authentic apostolic ministry. Apostolic ministry is authenticated by suffering and empowerment, not by claims of positional leadership, with its institutional levers.[20]

19. The health and maturity of the church are directly related to the fivefold ministry of Ephesians 4. In fact, this is exactly what Paul means when, following directly on from describing the need for APEPT ministries, he says, "It was he who gave some to be apostles, some to be prophets, some to be evangelists, and some to be pastors and teachers, *to prepare God's people for works of service, so that the body of Christ may be built up until we all reach unity in the faith and in the knowledge of the Son of God and become mature, attaining to the whole measure of the fullness of Christ. Then we will no longer be infants, tossed back and forth by the waves, and blown here and there by every wind of teaching and by the cunning and craftiness of men in their deceitful scheming. Instead, speaking the truth in love, we will in all things grow up into him who is the Head, that is, Christ. From him the whole body, joined and held together by every supporting ligament, grows and builds itself up in love, as each part does its work*" (Eph. 4:11–16). In *The Shaping of Things to Come*, we call a fully functioning APEPT the "maturity mechanism" of the church, because without it we can't mature.

20. "No examination of Paul's missionary career can ignore the reality that his whole life was marked by suffering. On the Damascus road, his apostolic call to take the gospel to the Gentiles and to Israel, was at the same time a call to suffering. Luke records how 'the Lord said to Ananias, "Go! This man is my chosen instrument to carry my name before the Gentiles and their kings and before the people of Israel. I will show him how much he must suffer for my name"' (Acts 9:15–16). Paul was both a chosen instrument and one whom the Lord would show how much he must suffer for his name. The last stage of his mission was marked by a revelation from the Spirit, that prison and hardship awaited him in every city (Acts 20:23). Suffering was so much a part of his experience that he regarded it as the badge of his apostolic authenticity." Addison devotes a whole section to the exploration of this aspect of apostolicity in his thesis, "A Basis for the Continuing Ministry of the Apostle in the Church's Mission."

CEOs

In our day I believe that the predominant, top-down, CEO concept of leadership has co-opted the apostolic, so that many who claim apostolic title actually function like CEOs. In the scriptures the Suffering Servant/Jesus image—not that of the chief executive officer—informs and qualifies the apostolic role. Apostolic ministry draws its authority and power primarily from the idea of service and calling, and from moral, or spiritual, authority, and not from positional authority. Perhaps a useful way of exploring the nature of apostolic authority is to identify the distinctive form of leadership involved and see how this creates authority.

In a relationship based on "inspirational" or "moral" leadership, both leaders and followers raise each other to higher levels of motivation and morality by engaging each other on the basis of shared values, calling, and identity. They are in a relationship in which each influences the other to pursue common objectives, with the aim of inspiring followers to becoming leaders in their own right. In other words, influence runs both ways. Inspirational leadership ultimately becomes genuinely moral when it raises the level of human conduct and ethical aspiration of both leaders and led, thus having a transformational effect on both. In this view, followers are persuaded to take action without being threatened or offered material incentives, but rather by an appeal to their values. This can be clearly seen in the way Jesus develops his disciples as well as in Paul's relationship with Timothy, Titus, and the other members of his apostolic team. It is forms the basis of his letters to the churches.[21]

Perhaps we can best call this type of influence "greatness." To be a great leader in this sense is to inspire, to evoke, and to nurture something correspondingly great out of those who follow. Through an integrated life, great leaders remind their followers of what they can become if they too base their lives on a compassionate notion of humanity framed by a higher moral vision of the world in which we live. We seldom call a leader with significant technical or managerial ability "great." We don't build statues to commemorate great bureaucrats, do we? And it is with understanding in mind that we can identify spiritual "greatness" as the basic substance that provides a genuine apostolic form of leadership with its authority. It is the strongest form of leadership available, because it awakens the

---

21. For the sake of comparison, inspirational leadership can be distinguished from what has been called "transactional leadership," which is built largely on the direct offer of an exchange of value, which most commonly takes the form of money for work. This understanding of leadership generally infuses most non-Christian forms of leadership and necessitates a top-down management approach to staff and resources. This is by far the most common form of leadership in organizations, including most churches and denominations, whether it be the relationship between the board and the senior minister, or the senior minister and his or her ministry staff. There is a real authority established in this relationship, but it is substantially different in its basis of authority from that of the more biblical form of leadership embodied in the inspirational leader.

human spirit, focuses it, and holds it together by managing the shared meaning. As with Uncle L and Brother Shi, it has the power to hold vast movements together without much external structure. It's the kind of leadership mythically reflected in the William Wallace character in the movie *Braveheart*: a man whom the people willingly followed, not because they ought, or because he had some official position (he didn't), but because he reminded them of their right to freedom and would help them obtain it if it cost him his life.

This idea of "greatness" squares with Weber's explorations on leadership: the "charismatic" leader, in Weber's thought, is the person who usually leads in times of mission, crisis, or development and always radically challenges the established practices by going to "the roots of the matter." People follow such a leader because they are carried away by the belief in the manifestation that authenticates him or her, and in so doing they turn away from established ways of doing things and submit to the unprecedented order that the leader proclaims. This type of leadership involves, therefore, a degree of commitment on the part of the disciples that has no parallel in the other types of established leadership.[22] Once again, Jesus is our best example. The following he calls for is so absolute that it is called discipleship—the process of becoming like him.

Consistent with the people movement that it serves, apostolic ministry, based as it is on inspirational-spiritual leadership, involves an organic, relational style of leadership influence that evokes purpose, movement, and response from those who come into its orbit. This is done on the basis of the apostolic person's discernible calling, spiritual gifting, and spiritual authority. And like all great leadership, it creates a *field of influence* wherein certain behaviors take place.

The universe in which we live is filled with fields of influence. While invisible, fields nonetheless assert a definite influence on objects within their orbit. There are gravitational fields, electromagnetic fields, quantum fields, and so forth that form part of the very structure of reality. These unseen influences affect the behavior of atoms, objects, and people. But fields don't just exist in nature and physics; they exist in social systems as well. For example, think about the power of ideas in human affairs—a powerful idea has no substance, but one cannot doubt its influence.

In the last few decades, organizational behaviorists have begun to see that organizations themselves are laced with invisible fields, composed of culture, values, vision, and ethics. "Each of these concepts describes a quality of organizational life that can be observed in behavior yet doesn't

22. R. Bendix, *Max Weber: An Intellectual Portrait* (Berkeley: University of California Press, 1977), ch. 10.

exist anywhere independent of those behaviors."[23] They are invisible forces that affect behavior for good or for ill. We can feel the vibe of an organization, can't we? Sometimes in a group of people, we feel obliged to behave in certain ways, even though no one has told us explicitly how to behave. To learn the impact of such fields, just look at what people are doing. They have picked up the messages, discerned what is truly valued, and shaped their behavior accordingly. So when the organizational field is filled with divergent messages, when contradictions inform the organizational culture, then invisible incongruities become visible through troubling behaviors.

What is remarkable is the entrance of true leadership into such a situation. With inspirational leadership the whole "vibe" changes: things begin to become clearer, competitiveness is diminished, and people feel freer and more empowered to do their tasks; as a result the organization gains focus and energy, becomes healthy. The converse is true and obvious: leadership of a poor quality creates unhealthy organizations. We have only to reach into our own experiences to know the truth of this. Such is the power of people who embody vision and values—they bring inspiration, coherence, and a sense of direction and purpose to the people in their orbit. Leadership is influence. It is a *field* that shapes behaviors. It is the basis of authentic spiritual power and authority. Nelson Mandela is a great leader not because he was president of South Africa, but because long before he was president, he was a deeply moral person who embodied his personal code of freedom in his own life. It is the greatness of his life that gives his leadership substance and impact.

To conceptualize leadership as influence, think of a magnet and its effect on iron filings scattered on a sheet of paper. When the filings come into the orbit of influence of the magnet, they form a certain pattern that we all recognize from our school days. Leadership does exactly the same thing—it creates a *field,* which in turn influences people in a certain way, just like the magnet's influence on the iron filings. The presence of a great leader in a group of people changes the patterning of that group. For instance, Nelson Mandela's appearance among a group of people will impact them in a significant way. His physical presence will be unmistakable and will change the social climate of the room. *Apostolic* leadership qualifies the mood of this influence, but the dynamics of influence operate in the same way.

It is precisely this field, this matrix of *apostolicity* that is critical to the emergence of authentic missional church, because it is the task of apostolic ministry to create environments wherein the apostolic imagination of God's

23. M. Wheatley, *Leadership and the New Science: Discovering Order in a Chaotic World* (San Francisco: Berrett-Koehler, 1999), 54.

people can be evoked, the spiritual gifts and ministries developed, and the love and hope inspired by the gospel be made known.[24] For instance, John Wimber would have exerted just this sort of influence. Within two decades, Wimber altered the shape of evangelicalism and underscored the role of the Holy Spirit in mission and ministry in a way that has changed us forever. We still feel the influence of John Wesley, even though none of us ever met him. Every Nation Churches and Ministries, a missional movement based in the United States, has a vision to plant hundreds of churches in the West. It explicitly uses both the language and the structures of apostolic ministry. One of the stated objectives is to become an apostolic church. Listen to how they describe the effect that this has on associated churches:

> As the [apostolic] focus of reaching out permeates a congregation amazing things happen. God begins to bring in those who have been searching for a way to get involved in his purposes. Families begin to be energized with a sense of excitement because they realize that they can make a difference in history. The youth find a reason to not just "hang on" and try to stay true, but they begin to see the vision that keeps them from perishing.
>
> This is the kind of atmosphere that produces miracles. The local church becomes the doorway to endless possibilities for every Believer. It also takes its place as the primary means through which the world will be reached for Christ.[25]

Here is a description of apostolic influence on a local congregation. In their words, it creates an "atmosphere" of expectation and movement.

It is this more bottom-up, highly relational quality of leadership that characterizes true apostolic influence. We have been so captivated by hierarchical, top-down conceptions of leadership, be it that of bishops, superintendents, pastors, and CEO-type leaders, that we have inadvertently blocked the power latent in the people of God. In Australia we have an amazingly large, spreading tree called the Morton Bay fig. It is a beautiful, very imposing tree. The problem is that nothing grows underneath it, because it casts such a wide shadow. A top-down, more autocratic leadership style can be likened to the Morton Bay fig. It can be magnificent, but it casts such a shadow that no other leadership develops in its shade.

The problem with CEO-type leadership is that it tends to disempower others, and when, for various reasons, that leader should leave the group,

---

24. In living systems theory, this task can be defined as unleashing distributed intelligence. It assumes that the organization has latent intelligence and can, given the right conditions, respond, learn, and develop higher levels of organization and effectiveness.

25. From a strategic vision document, "The 2010 Initiative," available at http://ministries.everynation.org/web_files/The 2010 Initiative.pdf.

the organization tends to be weak and underdeveloped. This is the very thing that apostolic influence is at pains not to do—rather, apostolic ministry calls forth and develops the gifts and callings of all of God's people. It does not create reliance but develops the capacities of the whole people of God based on the dynamics of the gospel. In a word it involves *empowerment*. Jim Collins, in his study of outstanding organizations, actually says that dominant, charismatic leaders are one of the greatest hindrances to an organization moving from being good to becoming great.[26]

Paul doesn't seem to be a charismatic leader in Collins's sense at all. He does not dominate; he is perhaps more parental (he uses images of both father and mother) in the way he works (1 Thess. 2:7ff.; Gal. 4:19). In fact, in 2 Corinthians 10:1[27] and elsewhere, it seems that he actually lacks charismatic "presence" and that he constantly has to affirm his leadership by other means.[28] In their observations about leadership dynamics, Pascale et al. also note that the impact of adaptive catalytic leadership seems to have little to do with personality, charisma, or style. They point to some leaders in large organizations who could hardly have been called charismatic but who managed to move the organization into higher levels of learning and effectiveness in terms of the stated mission. Rather, they suggest that the adaptive leader works with an organization's latent appetites, which are already present in the organization but await articulation. The leader senses the dormant energy and then catalyzes it—like seeding clouds with iodine crystals. An adaptive shift comes into existence, and not because the leader has all the answers and subsequently rolls them out through the organization. Rather, movement and adaptation take place because of the interplay of sympathetic chords in the environment, the issues of the times, the organization's members, and "a leader who can express the challenge in a way that invites others into a dance that is being choreographed as it is performed."[29] It might be useful to recall the impact that John Wesley had on his followers, the church, and the

26. See Jim Collins, *Good to Great: Why Some Companies Make the Leap, and Others Don't* (New York: HarperBusiness, 2001).

27. Second Corinthians 10:1: "By the meekness and gentleness of Christ, I appeal to you—I, Paul, who am 'timid' when face to face with you, but 'bold' when away!"

28. Some at Corinth regarded Paul's trials and apparent weakness as reason to doubt his credentials as an apostle. They were more impressed with those who displayed signs of spiritual power, both through their eloquence and through the miraculous. Paul could match these wonder workers with his own share of signs, wonders, and miracles (2 Cor. 12:11–12), but he regarded his apostolic sufferings as even more important in establishing his credentials. He devotes more space to describing his sufferings than to any other sign of apostleship.

29. R. T. Pascale, M. Millemann, and L. Gioja, *Surfing the Edge of Chaos* (New York: Three Rivers Press, 2000), 75. They go on to summarize, stating that the strange attractor of adaptive leadership is co-generated; strange attractors "arise through the convergence of many factors within the organization and its environment; they materialize when what is already present is expressed in a way that provides shape and substance; they flourish in an environment of adaptive challenge and tend to atrophy when subjugated under the heavy load of operational

broader society around him. He was a classic adaptive leader. Things just seemed to happen, because he awakened dreams and impulses that were already latent in the people he led and impacted.

Likewise, all the elements of Apostolic Genius are already there, latent in the very mDNA coding of the church; all that leadership needs to do is awaken it under the power of the Holy Spirit. The apostolic leader calls this forth; he or she does not create it. Don't get me wrong, there is *real* power and leadership in this, but it is of a different sort than that which the kings of the earth lord over others (Matt. 20:25–28).[30]

In passing, it is worth noting that one important reason why we should be suspicious of the hierarchical top-down notion of leadership is that we know from history and from human nature that institutional systems confer social power and concentrate it at the top. It is precisely because of human nature that we should be very wary of such power in human hands. It almost always corrupts and damages the relational fabric that constitutes the church. Very few people can handle it and not be altered by it—perhaps only the great. History is quite clear about that. At least we should learn this from the *Lord of the Rings* trilogy, where the ring of power exercises a powerfully alluring and corruptive power on those who wield it. Besides, the servant/slave image of leadership (dis)qualifies all forms of top-down leadership and establishes the bottom-up servant approach (Rom. 1:1; Titus 1:1; etc.). Jesus could not be more explicit when he says to his disciples, "The kings of the Gentiles lord it over them; and those who exercise authority over them call themselves Benefactors. *But you are not to be like that.* Instead, the greatest among you should be like the youngest, and the one who rules like the one who serves. For who is greater, the one who is at the table or the one who serves? Is it not the one who is at the table? But I am among you as one who serves" (Luke 22:25–27). Howard Snyder is right when he says that "the New Testament does not teach hierarchy as the principle of either authority or organization in the church" and that "Jesus seems to be opposed to both the abuse of power and the hierarchical structure on which (such) power was based."[31]

But there are powerful metaphors that help us to avoid the alluring notions of top-down coercive power, ones that aid us in understanding our

---

tasks and expectations and; they foster breakthroughs and outcomes that are unforeseen and unimaginable."

30. "Jesus called them together and said, 'You know that the rulers of the **Gentiles lord it** over them, and their high officials exercise authority over them. Not so with you. Instead, whoever wants to become great among you must be your servant, and whoever wants to be first must be your slave—just as the Son of Man did not come to be served, but to serve, and to give his life as a ransom for many."

31. H. A. Snyder, *Decoding the Church: Mapping the DNA of Christ's Body* (Grand Rapids: Baker, 2002).

task of creating environments where missional church can arise. At Forge Mission Training Network, we like to think of ourselves as *midwives to a new dream.* Our stated mission is to "help birth and nurture the missional church in Australia and beyond." And while this describes our own particular calling, the idea of being midwives is both a very biblical and a humane image of leadership, and I recommend it to you here as describing the actual mode of leadership that informs all authentic apostolic influence. A midwife aids and assists in the birth of a child. All that he or she makes sure of is that all the conditions are right for a healthy birth—the birth is the result of things beyond the midwife's influence. It is interesting that Socrates called himself a midwife and that he saw his role as helping others discover the truth for themselves. This he did by the constant use of questions that drove the learner to his own insights and observations. Jesus is very "midwifey" through his use of questions, stories, and parables.

But perhaps one more image of this quality of leadership is needed to pin this concept down in our minds, and this is the image of a farmer. A good farmer creates the conditions for the growth of healthy crops by tilling the soil, replenishing it with nutrients, removing weeds, scattering the seeds, and watering the field. He or she is wide open to natural rhythms of nature, which are out of his or her control, and so the farmer is reliant on God for the sun and rain. The seed itself, if given the right conditions, will flourish in this type of environment and produce good crops. All that the farmer does is to create the right environment for this mysterious process of life to take place.

Apostolic ministry works in precisely the same way. Paul even alludes to similar organic processes in 1 Corinthians 3:5–9 when he says

> What, after all, is Apollos? And what is Paul? Only servants, through whom you came to believe—as the Lord has assigned to each his task. I planted the seed, Apollos watered it, but God made it grow. So neither he who plants nor he who waters is anything, but only God, who makes things grow. The man who plants and the man who waters have one purpose, and each will be rewarded according to his own labor. For we are God's fellow workers; you are God's field.

In fact, the Bible is laced with organic images that engender an "ecological view" of church and leadership (seeds, ground, yeast, body, flock, trees, etc.). If we remodeled our leadership and churches with these organic metaphors in mind, we would develop a more fertile communal life. An organic view of church is much richer because it is truer to, and more consistent with, the inner structure of life and cosmology itself.[32]

---

32. See Fritjof Capra, *The Hidden Connections: A Science for Sustainable Living* (London: Harper-Collins, 2002), and M. Wheatley, *Leadership and the New Science* (San Francisco: Berrett-Koehler, 1999), for this approach.

Creating Webs of Meaning

Encountering apostolic ministry of the sort found in Uncle L is actually quite a disturbing experience because it raises a disquieting question: if he didn't have any centralized organization and the ordinary management resources we seem to need to run organizations, how did he lead a movement of 3 million people? The only conclusion we can come to is that the kind of leadership he embodied is something conferred through the strange combination of personal inspiration, spiritual power, gifting, calling, and character and through the willing love and respect of the various people and organizations within his movement. But a crucial element is that Uncle L is in a real sense the father/initiator of the movement. In other words, leadership and followership were based on a common and shared meaning and purpose held together by spiritual and personal ties, the fabric of which can extend to millions of people.

Similar influence is exercised by apostolic leaders in the West like Mike Breen. As rector and team leader of St. Thomas's church in Sheffield, Mike led this Anglican and Baptist church as it grew to the largest church in the north of England, with more than 2,000 members, 80 percent of whom are under age forty. Mike, with his family, subsequently moved from Sheffield to Phoenix in 2004 to become the superior of The Order of Mission (TOM), founded as a worldwide covenant community of missionary leaders.[33] Established in April, TOM grew out of an understanding that "institutional forms of Christianity are hollow, boring, irrelevant and have little bearing on the real issues in the lives of most unchurched people." Breen focused on the desire among people in their twenties and thirties to belong and to find meaning, value, and purpose. Drawing on the historic English/Roman Minster model and the Celtic pattern of mobile evangelists, Breen birthed what he describes as a global missionary order. Those desiring to join must adopt the rule of TOM, which reinterprets traditional monastic concepts of poverty, chastity, and obedience as devotion to a life of simplicity, purity, and accountability. Full vows are taken after three years and are binding for life. The structure of TOM is built squarely on the fivefold gifting of Ephesians 4, with each ministry represented by a "guardian." Members of TOM meet in clusters and form communities of faith in cafés, pubs, schools, university campuses, and homes, wherever they settle. TOM has become a worldwide movement spanning the United States, the United Kingdom, Europe, and Australasia. What is interesting, though, is that, throughout, membership in the order remains a purely voluntary affair, and Breen himself rejects all notions of top-down leadership. He leads from a position of inspirational influence, with voluntary adherence from all the members.

33. http://www.sttoms.net/modules/wfsection/index.php?category=45

Another great example of apostolic movement is found in Northwood Church in Texas. Northwood is a large 2000+ member church that has birthed almost ninety churches. From the beginning, NorthWood has been outwardly focused, with a clear mission to impact the world both locally and globally. As a result, more than 800 church-planting leaders have been trained, coached, or mentored through NorthWood's Church Multiplication Center. There are clusters of the churches that Northwood has started in nineteen cities throughout the United States. Sixty-two new churches have been planted in the network in 2005. Bob Roberts is the exceptional leader of this movement and has written up the model in his book *Transformation*. Real apostolic stuff![34]

Perhaps another way of looking at how apostolic ministry exercises extensive influence without reliance on centralized forms of organization is to see it in terms of the management of meaning. If Apostolic Genius usually manifests in the form of a movement composed of networks of agencies, churches, and individuals (as we shall see in the mDNA of organic systems), it holds together through a web of meaning created by apostolic influence and environment. Apostolic leadership does this by focusing the network of relations on the meaning and implications of the gospel and on the relationships that are established through it. Each individual, church, or agency relates to the apostolic leader only *because it is meaningful for them to do so,* and not because they have to. It is because the gospel is implanted, and the Holy Spirit is present in every Christian community, that apostolic ministry and leadership are able to hold the network together. So it might look something like this:

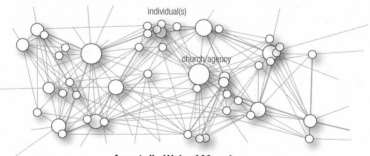

Apostolic Web of Meaning
based on discipling relationships, gospel meaning, and sharing information

Considerable time has been spent on the dynamics of this form of leadership because of the need to emphasize that it is this aspect of leadership that informs true apostolic influence. And it is this type of leadership that creates the context for missional church to arise.

34. http://www.northwoodchurch.org/v2/index.htm and http://www.glocal.net/. See Bob Roberts, *Transformation: How Global Churches Transform Lives and the World* (Grand Rapids: Zondervan, 2006).

A Stroke of (Apostolic) Genius

Missional church requires a missional ministry and leadership system. For the most part, the Christendom church obscured the need for a full-fledged missional leadership system, because the self-understanding of the church became fundamentally nonmissional. Because all citizens were deemed to be Christians, all that was really needed were the pastoral and teaching ministries to care for and teach the congregation. These were eventually instituted as offices in the church and became the principal metaphors for church leadership. The net effect is that the whole system weighted itself in favor of maintenance and pastoral care and that these became hegemonic in practice,[35] and therefore both fragmented and distorted the total mission and ministry of the church in favor of only part of its calling.

A direct consequence of this was that the apostolic, the prophetic, and the evangelistic ministries and leadership styles were marginalized and effectively "exiled" from the church's official ministry and leadership. This is not to say that these ministries have totally disappeared. Far from it: many within current and historical church life have exercised these ministries without specifically being tagged "apostles" or "prophets," but by and large these lacked formal legitimacy and recognition, and they have tended to be exercised outside of the context of the local church, denominational systems, and seminaries.[36] This "exiling" in part gave rise to the development of parachurch agencies and missional orders, each with a somewhat atomized ministry focus. For example, the Navigators arose out of a calling to evangelize and disciple people outside the church structures because the church was not effective (or interested?) in doing so. The Sojourners emerged to represent the social justice concerns that the church by and large ignores. World Vision as an aid and development agency is yet another example. But in these were generally initiated and maintained the apostolic/prophetic/evangelistic (APE)-type leadership styles. This divorce of APE from the pastoral/teaching/didactic (PTD) has been disastrous for the local church and has damaged the cause of Christ and his mission.[37]

35. A hegemony is a form of monopolizing leadership or dominance, especially by one state, ideology, or social group over others.

36. As Addison says. "If the thesis of this paper is correct, the gift of apostle has functioned in every age of the church, at times without recognition. The gift is given by the risen Lord, regardless of the titles we use for our church leaders and regardless of denominational polity and structures. Church history is full of examples of those who have exercised an apostolic ministry without ever receiving the title or acknowledgement. Our challenge is not to reinvent apostolic ministry, it is to recognize and release those who are already functioning as apostles." The same is certainly true for all APEPT ministries. S. Addison, *A Basis for the Continuing Ministry*, 198.

37. In chapter 10 of *The Shaping of Things to Come*, we argued the case for the recognition of these vital ministries from both a biblical-theological and a sociological-organizational perspective. I refer the reader to that book for a more thorough exploration of this topic.

	Definition	Focus/Core Tasks	Impact When in Sync with Other Ministries	Impact When Monopolizing
Apostolic	• essentially the steward of the DNA of the church • as the "sent ones" apostolic ministry and leadership ensures that Christianity is faithfully transmitted from one context to another context and from one era to another era	• extending Christianity • guarding and embedding DNA of the church both theologically and missionally • establishing the church in new contexts • "founding" the other ministries (A→PEPT) • development of leaders and leadership systems • strategic missional perspective • translocal networking	• healthy manifestation of Apostolic Genius • extension of the faith • authentic Christianity • missional mode of church is fostered • healthy translocal networking • growth of church and movement • pioneering mission • experimentation with new forms of (incarnational) church • manifestations of APEPT	• tendency to autocratic styles of leadership • lots of wounded people in the organization due to task and future orientation of the apostle • lots of challenge and change, not enough healthy transition—this requires the pastoral and teaching function
Prophetic	• essentially the person who has an ear toward God, acts as the mouth of God, and therefore speaks for God—often in tension with dominant consciousness • truth-teller to the believer	• discerning and communicating God's will • ensuring the obedience of the covenant community • questioning the status quo	• church's obedience and faithfulness to God • God-oriented faith (less "fear of man") • challenge to prevailing consciousness • countercultural action • social justice	• one-dimensional, "hobby-horse" feel to leadership's conception of church • factiousness • exclusive and even offensive • propensity to be overly activistic and driven • sometimes an overly "spiritual" feel
Evangelistic	• essentially the recruiter, the carrier, and the communicator of the gospel message • truth-teller to the unbeliever • calls for personal response to God's redemption in Jesus	• making clear the offer of salvation so that people might hear and respond in faith • recruiting to the cause	• expansion of the faith through a response to God's personal call • organic numerical growth of the people of God	• loss of overarching vision and communal health • narrow perspectives on faith. limited to "simple gospel"
Pastoral	• essentially the pastor cares for and develops the people of God by leading, nurturing, protecting, and discipling them	• cultivating a loving and spiritually mature network of relationships and community • making disciples	• nurture into the faith and the community • loving relationships • growth in discipleship • sense of connectedness • worship and prayer	• closed, nonmissional community • co-dependency between church & pastor (messiah complex) • don't rock the boat approach to organization • if too "feminine" in expression, males can be alienated from the church
Teaching	• essentially the ministry that clarifies the revealed mind/will of God so that the people of God gain wisdom and understanding	• discernment • guidance • helping the faith community to explore and seek to understand the mind of God	• understanding of God and the faith • truth guides behavior • self-awareness • devotion to learning and integration	• theological dogmatism • Christian gnosticism ("saved" by knowledge of Bible and theology—Bible replaces Holy Spirit) • intellectualism • control through ideas: pharisaism ("is it lawful?")

To understand the different nature of each of these ministries, we need to briefly explore the core tasks/functions of each, the effect when one monopolizes and dominates in isolation from the others, and the effect when it is integrated with the other ministries. The easiest way to do this is within a comparative table.

Some Qualifications about APEPT

First, in *The Shaping of Things to Come,* we articulated that it is important to keep in mind that ministry is different from leadership by matter of degree and function.[38] Ephesians 4:7, 11–12 assigns the APEPT ministries to the entire church, not just to leadership ("to each one of us grace has been given," v. 7; "It was he who gave some to be . . . ," v. 11). All are therefore to be found somewhere in APEPT (apostolic, prophetic, evangelistic, pastoral, teaching/didactic). I would strongly argue that APEPT is in actual fact part of the DNA of all God's people—in the very fabric of what it means to be "church." In other words, it is *latent.* Recognizing this is critical to unlocking the real power of the Pauline teaching and is as such an extension of the New Testament teaching of the priesthood and ministry of all God's people. So much for the generic ministry embodied in Paul's ecclesiology. What of leadership?

Snyder rightly remarks that the central task of leadership is to build an apostolic, charismatically empowered, ministering community based on Ephesians 4:11–12.[39] Leadership in the light of APEPT can be conceived as a "calling within a calling"; it is a distinct task that entails leading and influencing the body of Christ, and not just ministering. Not all ministers are leaders—that much is obvious. As such, leadership embodies a particular APEPT ministry that is given to the believer but extends and reorients it to fit the distinct calling and tasks of leadership.

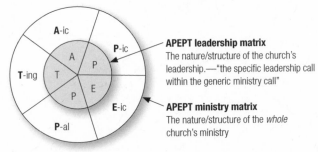

APEPT leadership matrix
The nature/structure of the church's leadership.—"the specific leadership call within the generic ministry call"

APEPT ministry matrix
The nature/structure of the *whole* church's ministry

Second, in my experience, it is rare that a person has only one of these ministries in operation. Rather, our ministry callings seem to be expressed

38. Ibid., 170–73.
39. Snyder, *Decoding the Church,* 91.

more as complex of ministries, though we operate primarily out of one of these, depending on our context. So we can view it this way: we can have primary, secondary, and possibly tertiary ministries all acting in a dynamic way. Each informs and qualifies the primary ministry type. These go to form a certain ministry complex, not dissimilar to personality typing (go to www.theforgottenways.org to do a personal profile of your ministry). For example, a person might be primarily prophetic but have evangelistic and pastoral dimensions as well. That can be diagrammatically represented as follows.

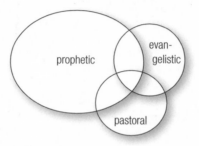

Third, many have asked if the Ephesians text is the definitive and final list of ministries. My answer is that it is definitive but not necessarily final. There could well be others, but these only add to the basic listing found in Ephesians 4 and must not subtract from them.[40] Perhaps the best way to say it is that the nature of the New Testament ministry is *at least fivefold*.

Fourth, how do the spiritual gifts relate to these ministries? My belief is that the ministries draw upon all the various spiritual gifts as needed and as God graces. Clearly, particular ministries draw upon a particular group of spiritual gifts. For instance, the teaching ministry clearly relies on the gift of teaching, wisdom, and other forms of revelatory gifts. The prophetic draws upon a different compound of gifts, but all are available if the situation requires them and the Spirit wills it.

Finally, APEPT is meant to be, and to operate as, a system: a system within the living system that makes up the church. The whole Ephesians 4 text is rich in organic images and perspectives (body, ligaments, head, etc.). Christian ministry is never meant to be onefold or twofold, but *fivefold*, and each leadership style is strengthened and informed by the particular contributions of the others. Let's look at this a little more closely.

40. Clearly, there are other lists, but these are not located in passages that describe the fundamental nature and structure of the church's ministry. Also, I distinguish between spiritual gifts and ministries. The gifts as I understand them are given as the situation demands; the ministries tend to be more stable and relate to vocation and calling. However, ministries draw upon the gifts to fulfill their functions.

One Plus One Equals Three or More

Moving away from the more theological perspectives, let us take a quick look at the church as a social system to explore further the impact of differing leadership styles. When we do this, we discover that Paul's radical plan for the Christian movement is affirmed by current best practice in leadership and management theory and practice.

In most human leadership systems it is acknowledged that there may be one or more of the following leadership styles:

- The entrepreneur, innovator, and ground breaker who initiates a new product, or service, or type of organization
- The questioner or inquirer who probes awareness and fosters questioning of current programming leading to organizational learning (*agent provocateur*)
- The communicator and recruiter to the organizational cause who markets the idea or product and gains loyalty and allegiance to a brand
- The humanizer or people-oriented motivator who fosters a healthy relational system through the management of meaning
- The systematizer and philosopher who is able to clearly articulate the organizational purpose and goals in such a way as to advance corporate understanding.[41]

In *The Shaping of Things to Come*, Michael Frost and I comment that the

various social scientists use different terms for the above categories but recognize that these represent vital contributions that different types of leaders

41. Frost and Hirsch, *Shaping of Things to Come*, 173–74.

bring to an organization. In most leadership management theory it is assumed that the conflicting agendas and motivations of the above leaders pull them in different directions. However, imagine a leadership system in any setting (corporate, government, political, etc.) where the entrepreneurial ground breaker and strategist dynamically interacts with the disturber of the status quo (the questioner). Imagine that both these are in active dialogue and relation with the passionate communicator/recruiter, the person who carries the message beyond organizational borders and sells the idea/s or product/s. These in turn are in constant engagement with the humanizer (HR), the carer, the social cement and the systematizer and articulator of the whole. The synergy in this system would be significant in any context. Clearly the combination of these different leadership styles is greater than the sum of its parts.[42]

Just as the various systems in the human body (e.g., the circulatory, nervous, digestive systems) work together to sustain and enhance life, so too in all living systems the various elements in the system interrelate and serve to augment each other. Dysfunction is the result of a breakdown between various components or agents within the system. When each component operates at peak and harmonizes with the other components, the whole system is enhanced and benefits from synergy—that is, where the result is greater than the sum of the individual parts. So it is with APEPT. When all are present and interrelated in an effective way, the body of Christ will operate at peak. To use Paul's terms in Ephesians 4, it "grows," "matures," "builds itself up," and "reaches unity in the faith."

Furthermore, in living systems theory, moving an organization into adaptive organic mode requires that we (1) develop and enhance relationships, (2) cross-pollinate ideas from different specialties and departments, (3) disturb equilibrium by moving to the edge of chaos, and (4) focus information according to organizational mission. Developing a fully functioning APEPT system in a local church, mission agency, or denomination will go a long way toward achieving these ends.

Around 2000 at South Melbourne Restoration Community, we restructured our leadership team on this principle, and it led to significant movement toward being a missional church. We restructured leadership so that we could ensure that all five ministries were represented on the team, each in turn heading up a team related to the respective APEPT ministries. So we had an apostolic team that focused on the translocal, missional, strategic, and experimental issues facing the church. We had a prophetic team that focused on listening to God and discerning his will for us, paying attention to social justice issues, and questioning the status quo of an increasingly middle-class church. We had an evangelistic team whose task it was to oversee and develop evangelism and outreach. The pastoral team's task was to develop community,

42. Ibid., 174.

cell groups, worship, and counseling, and to enhance the love capacity of the church. The teaching team's task was to create contexts of learning and to develop the love of wisdom and understanding through Bible study, theological and philosophical discussion groups, etc. All were represented by a key leader on the leadership team. While at times it created significant debate on what the key issues facing the church were, it was thoroughly stimulating.

At leadership-team level, we operated this model on the idea of open learning system, which allows the team to "fit and split" and to "contend and transcend."[43] The term *fit* refers to that which binds an organization together (unity). It is the group's common ethos and purpose. *Split* happens when we intentionally allow for a great diversity of expression in the team (diversity). *Contend* refers to leadership permitting, even encouraging, disagreement, debate, and dialogue around core tasks (duality). *Transcend* means that all collectively agree to overcome disagreement in order to find new solutions (vitality, "reaching unity in the faith").

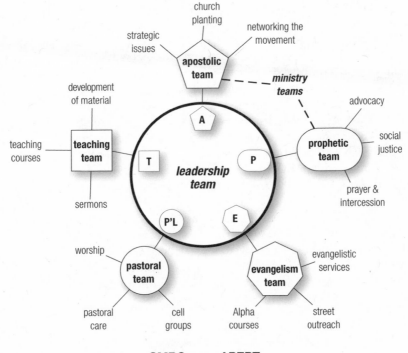

SMRC goes APEPT

43. See Richard T. Pascale, *Managing on the Edge: How Successful Companies Use Conflict to Stay Ahead* (London: Viking, 1990).

So on just about any ministry issue, the leadership team would be pre-committed to the common mission of the group. We were covenanted to do "whatever it takes" to see our mission fulfilled. And given healthy relationships within the team, this meant that we allowed for the divergent opinions of each member without being offended. We had lived together, struggled together, faced issues together, and our bond to Jesus and this particular expression of his people was strong. It was this sense of fit that gave permission for each member to operate out of their own ministry biases and represent their perspectives on the issue at hand. The apostolic person would present or critique in light of the need to galvanize the community around mission. The prophetic types would challenge just about everything and ask irritating questions about how God fit into our grand schemes. The evangelist would always be trying to emphasize the need to bring people to faith and how what we suggested would achieve that. The pastoral type expressed concerns about how the community could healthily engage the issue sustainably, and the theologian would try discerning its validity from scripture and history. The split therefore allowed for significant divergence of interests, and there were many debates, even arguments. But we would not try to resolve debate and disagreement too quickly (this drove the pastoral types nuts). We would sit with the problem until we had assessed all options and had, through dialogue and debate, arrived at the best solution—an outcome that was likely to be more true to calling, more faithful to God, sensitive to the needs of the not-yet-believers, sustainable and mature, and theologically well grounded.[44]

APEPT, if well led and directed, can operate in a very invigorating way indeed. Most churches seem to prefer more hierarchical structures with a chain-of-command approach and are most often led by people gifted as pastors and teachers. Such ministry types can tend to avoid conflict or focus primarily on ideas and not action. The resultant organizational culture struggles to find fit and split, contend and transcend. In the operational model, decisions are made at the top and filter down to the grass roots. There's little room for any real interaction and participation around central tasks and ideas. As a result, in many denominational structures and churches the members at the "bottom" of the system can tend to feel silenced and resentful.

A bottom-up approach to APEPT creates a healthy learning system: the dynamic nature of the whole matrix ensures that an open learning system results from an organization built with such leadership structures. The

44. Let me encourage the reader to try to identify his or her own ministry by creating the online profile provided at the website related to this book (www.theforgottenways.org). This can be done either through filling out the simple personal questionnaire or, preferably, by doing the 360° test. Our ministries are not always defined in the same way we see them, but they are discerned through the impact that we have on others around us—hence the need for feedback from colleagues and friends. I encourage the reader to undertake the online 360° APEPT profiling test to help identify the dynamics of his or her own ministry.

more outward-looking, non-status quo types (in this case A, P, and E) will ensure incoming information from outside the system and guarantee a dynamic engagement and growth with the organization's environment. The more sustaining ministries (like P and T) will ensure that the church is not overextended beyond its capacities. All in all it makes for a good balance of church health and missional fitness.

There seems to be a wonderful "ecology" for healthy ministry at work in a fully functioning APEPT system. It provides us with a theologically rich and organically consistent understanding to help leaders and organizations become more missional and agile. In fact it would be hard *not* to be missional if one intentionally develops this into the life of God's people at the local and/or regional levels. I have been involved in a similar organizational reconstruction around the APEPT idea for my denomination, both at the national and at the international level in the form of an informal, very talented, tri-national body called the International Missional Team (IMT). The IMT has been responsible for significant stimulation of the missional cause in my denomination in the United Kingdom, Australia, and New Zealand, as these ideas have been employed at a strategic level. I say this to assure the reader that these ideas are actually being tested in practice at local, regional, and international levels, and while the full impact has not yet had time to be assessed, there is no doubt that they are creating significant movement in the denominational culture.

The Final Word

This chapter has tried to articulate why the apostolic environment, with all that it means, is a key component of Apostolic Genius. Quite frankly, it is hard to conceive of metabolic, organic, missional movements existing, let alone lasting, without apostolic influence in its varying forms. This is because apostolic ministry is entrusted with the mDNA of Jesus's church, and without this mDNA manifesting itself in its true form, Apostolic Genius cannot fully manifest. Apostolic influence awakens the church to its true calling and identity and as such is irreplaceable. At best, movements and churches without apostolic influence can only pick up aspects of mDNA; they cannot connect them in that cohesive, synergistic whole that constitutes true Apostolic Genius. This is partly the reason for calling the elemental force of the church "Apostolic Genius." There is something essential and irreplaceable in the ministry of the apostle that is critical to the emergence of missional movements like that of the biblical and postbiblical periods and of the underground phenomenon of the Chinese church.

7

organic systems

The main stimulus for the renewal of Christianity will come from the bottom and from the edge, from sectors of the Christian world that are on the margins.

Harvey Cox, *Religion in the Secular City*

... [T]he most probable assumption is that no currently working business theory will be valid 10 years hence. ... And yet few executives accept that turning a business around requires fundamental changes in the assumptions on which the business is run. It requires a *different business*.

Peter Drucker, "A Turnaround Primer"

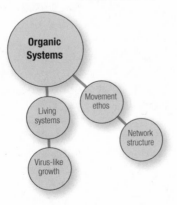

This chapter will explore the next critical element in mDNA, the inner structures and systems that embody Apostolic Genius and thus enable metabolic growth (growth that takes place exponentially and organically). In this chapter we will probe how the church in its most phenomenal form (when it genuinely manifests Apostolic Genius) organizes itself as a living organism that reflects more how God has structured life itself, as opposed to a machine, which is the artificial, inorganic alterative to a living system. And here we are on fertile biblical ground, because organic images of the church and the kingdom abound in the scriptures—images like body, field, yeast, seeds, trees, living temples, vines, animals, etc. These images are not just verbal metaphors that help us describe the theological nature of God's people but actually go to issues of essence. Therefore, they will need to be rediscovered, re-embraced, and relived in order to position us as Jesus's people for the challenges and complexities facing us in the twenty-first century. We must find a new way to experience ourselves, beyond the static, mechanistic, and institutional paradigm that predominates in our ecclesial life.

It should not surprise us that organic images of the church should draw their primary theological funding from the biblical doctrine of creation (cosmology), from an ecological and an intrinsically spiritual view of the world rather than from any of the other disciplines that have conventionally informed leadership and the development of organizations. Cosmology must guide us into a deeper understanding of ourselves and our function in the world.

And why would we not look to creation itself for clues as to how God himself has intended for authentic human life and community to manifest? All of life bears God's creative fingerprints, and he has filled every aspect of it with intrinsic vitality and intelligence. The cosmos itself seems to operate in a profoundly intelligent way; the more we find out about it from science, from the structures of atoms, the patterns of weather, the migration of birds, the human psyche, the more stunningly ingenious it all seems. From quarks to supernovas, the universe seems to vibrate with living potency that causes us to be filled with wonder and awe at the sheer omnipotence and omniscience of the Creator-God.

This Cosmic Creator should be no stranger to us. The scriptures clearly teach that is was the Trinity that was fully involved in the inception of the cosmos and in the maintenance all life. God the Father speaks the cosmos into being with creative words (Genesis 1). As Father, he is the genesis, the source, of all life. Christ is portrayed in the scriptures as the instrument of creation ("by him all things were created," Col. 1:16; "through him all things were made; without him nothing was made that has been made," John 1:3), and is its organizing principle ("in him all things hold together," Col. 1:17; "sustaining all things by his powerful word," Heb. 1:3). The Holy

Spirit is described as the essence of life/spirit: it was he who brooded over the chaos of the preformed universe and brought forth form, and it was he who has filled every atom of it with design and vivacity. From atoms to stars, *every* aspect of creation points to an unbelievably intelligent and utterly powerful Being and looks to him for its ongoing reality and existence (called continuing creation by theologians). The universe declares the glory of God and is a constant stream of knowledge of, and revelation about, God (Ps. 19:1–4).

Furthermore, this triune Creator-God cannot be divided. God's presence is found in every part of his universe. As J. V. Taylor, in his remarkable book *The Christlike God* points out,

> Wherever God exists he exists *wholly*. In his infinitude he cradles the universe, *yet he knows every atom of its structure from within*. The truth of God transcendent and of God immanent, his mystery and his availability, must be held together as a single reality, dialectical to human thought but indivisible in itself. The God who is within things is not secondary or less than the God who is beyond. His unfathomable otherness addresses each of us with an intimacy surpassing all other relationships.[1]

The doctrine of God's transcendence informs us that God is beyond his creation—he is far greater than it, and it exists in him. But the related doctrine of God's immanence reveals to us that he is also *fully* present in even the smallest atom. He fills the universe as well as transcends it. This means that the whole cosmos, and life itself, is directly connected to God and is therefore filled with the sacred mystery of divine life. As a means of revelation, creation can teach us much of the mind of God as to how life ought to be lived. And because it is the Trinity who creates this world, this does not distract one iota from the truth of God and his redemption as revealed in the scriptures. And it is from both creation and scripture that an organic understanding of the God's people is gleaned.

All this is to say that an organic image of church and mission is theologically richer by far than any mechanistic and institutional conceptions of church that we might devise. This is because it is funded by a sense of God's intimate relation and investment in his creation. Followers of Jesus who seek to base their communal life in organic ways find in scripture, as well as creation, a rich theological resource to fund and sustain it. To find a pattern of church closer to life is to move closer to what God intended in creation in the first place. For instance, it turns out that the seemingly obscure and insignificant yeast has much to teach us about the inner workings of God's kingdom (Matt. 13:33).

---

1. J. V. Taylor, *The Christlike God* (London: SCM, 1992), 117 (emphasis mine).

Get a Life: The Church as a Living System

How does this grand cosmology relate to our experience of the local church? One of the reflections arising out of my fifteen years' experience at SMRC is that as we grew and began to operate in the classic church growth mode it became increasingly harder to find God in the midst of the progressively more machinelike apparatus required to "run a church." With numerical growth, it seemed that we were increasingly being drawn away from the natural rhythms of life, from direct ministry, and that our roles seemed to become more managerial than ever before. But this mechanization of ministry was not only felt by the leadership of the church; the people in the church were increasingly being programmed out of life and therefore less engaged in active relationships with those outside of the faith community. Given my broader ministry, I know that this experience is endemic to many contemporary expressions of church. All this led to a personal quest to find a more life-oriented approach to mission, ministry, and community, and eventually led to the discovery of what has been called the *living systems approach* (see addendum "A Crash Course in Chaos").

A living systems approach seeks to structure the common life of an organization around the rhythms and structures that mirror life itself. In this approach we seek to probe the nature of life, we seek to observe how living things tend to organize themselves, and then we try to emulate as closely as possible this innate capacity of living systems to develop higher levels of organization, to adapt to different conditions, and to activate latent intelligence when needed (emergence). This quest for a more sustainable way of life is not just limited to the church. Leading proponents of this view explicitly propose "a science of sustainable living" based on the study of, and respect for, life (Fritjof Capra, Margaret Wheatley, Richard Pascale, et al.)[2] In these books I have found new metaphors and perspectives that have profoundly inspired me in my search for a more life-oriented and organic, less programmatical approach to our task. Some of these include:

- That all living things seem to have innate intelligence. Living systems, whether organic in form (e.g., a virus, a human being) or systemic organizations (e.g., the stock market, a beehive, a city, or a commercial enterprise, even crystal formations), seem to have a life of their own and possess a built-in intelligence that involves an aptitude for survival, adaptation, and reproduction. This capacity for developing higher life forms has been linked with what is called "distributed intelligence" by theorists in the field. When applied to organizational theory, the task

2. See bibliography for details.

of leadership is to unleash, harness, and direct distributed intelligence by creating environments where it can manifest.

- Life seems to be profoundly interconnected. The primary operative idea is that of relationships arranged in a dynamic network—a web of life and meaning. Living systems theory recognizes that we are always part of a larger system; we belong to an ecology composed of internal and external systems with which we are constantly relating. Disturbances in one part of the system set off a chain reaction that affects all the elements in a system. Capra calls this "the web of life." Some of the implications are as follows: (1) Small things can have system-wide consequences, sometimes called "the butterfly effect" (the idea that a butterfly flapping its wings in the Amazon can cause a hurricane in another continent). We should never underestimate the power of seemingly insignificant things to affect a system even if they seem unrelated at first. (2) A system is functional or dysfunctional to the extent that all of its parts are healthy and relating to each other in an organic way. (3) The way to develop a healthy learning/adaptive system is to bring disparate elements into meaningful communication with each other.

- Information brings change: all living systems respond to information. In fact, they seem to be able to sort out information based on what is meaningful or useful to them. Information is therefore critical to intelligence, adaptivity, and growth. The free flow of information in the system is vital to growth and adaptation.

- Adaptive challenges and emergence: by constantly interacting with its environment, the living system will catalyze its built-in capacity to adapt to changing circumstances. Failure to do so results in decline and death. Emergence (new forms of organization) happens when a living system is in adaptive (and therefore learning) mode, all the elements in the system are relating functionally, and distributed intelligence is cultivated and focused through information.

While all this might seem to be a little esoteric and conceptual, just stop for a moment and consider a living systems approach as it relates to Christian community. Following this approach, we first need to assume that any particular group of God's people, if they are truly his people, have everything in themselves (latent mDNA) to be able to adapt and thrive in any setting. We must assume that given the right conditions, the community can discover latent resources and capacities that it never thought it possessed. The task of missional leadership here is simply to unleash the mDNA that is dormant in the system and help guide it to its God-intended purpose.

Second, the task of missional leadership here is to bring the various elements in the system into meaningful interrelationship. This will require the leader to focus on developing a relationally networked, as opposed to an institutional, structure for the church. We must become an effective expression of the "body of Christ" (1 Cor. 12:12–27 is not just a metaphor, after all—it's a description of the church in its interrelationship with each part to its Head). It is critical to share information and ideas and to cross-pollinate in terms of gifts and callings around common tasks (Eph. 4:1ff.). We must bring all necessary parts of the body into the missional equation if we want to truly function as a body. In nonecclesial settings, this would mean getting the various departments and specialists to relate meaningfully and share information functionally around common tasks, thereby bringing diversity into a functioning unity. It seems that in living systems, the real answer is always found in the grander perspective—when diverse gifts and knowledge rub up against each other, new forms of knowledge and possibilities will arise.

Third, we need to move the system toward the edge of chaos; that is, it needs to become highly responsive to its environment. The assumption here is that if it will not deal with real issues facing it, the system will not adapt and will thus perish in the context of any significant adaptive challenge. Burying its head in the sand never did help the ostrich when there was a predator in the area. We need to disturb the system that is in equilibrium in order to activate a learning journey and missional mode. The community needs to become responsive and response-*able*. Aligning elements in a system into a healthy network will inevitably involve dealing with dysfunctions that, due to the fallenness of all things, are inevitably in the system. Failure to deal with dysfunction will always undermine the organization or community's health. Here conflict will arise (I promise), and the task of good leadership in this situation is to manage it and creatively translate it into a significant learning experience.

Fourth, because systems exist in a mass of disordered information, the task of leadership here will be to help select the flow of information and focus the community around it. Not in order to dominate and try to predetermine the outcome, but rather to supply accurate and *meaningful* information to the system so that it can *in-form* itself in response to it. This aspect has sometimes been called the management of meaning, because it is through the engagement with *meaningful* information that systems will respond, change, and thrive. Missional leaders must know how to handle *meaning* in order to motivate a group of people from the inside out. Focusing the flow of information requires a good handle on theology and psychology, as well as sociology, because it will involve focusing information based on the church's primary narratives (the scriptures, and particularly the Gospels), information about the *core* tasks of the church, and essential data about our cultural and social contexts, etc. If we get all these elements right, the whole church is activated, motivated, responsive, and informed, and the mission of God will flow naturally through and out of the mix.

What is most exciting about this approach is that things seem to flow effortlessly, because one is not going against the grain of the universe. The resultant ambience in the Jesus community is one that feels natural and therefore closer to the actual rhythms of life itself—in fact, it is based squarely on these rhythms and relationships—they are its starting point as well as its ongoing substructure. When we look at networks, which are an essential aspect of organic structures, we will see that church must structure itself around the natural ebb and flow of the believer's life. Existing relationships with believers and nonbelievers alike become the very fabric of the church. There ought to be nothing artificial about it. Planting a new church, or remissionalizing an existing one, in this approach isn't primarily about buildings, worship services, size of congregations, and pastoral care, but rather about gearing the whole community around natural discipling friendships, worship as lifestyle, and mission in the context of everyday life. As a living network "in Christ" it can meet anywhere, anytime and still be a viable expression of church. This is a much more organic way to plant a church or to revitalize it.[3]

The Problem of Institutions

A living systems perspective of community and organization is just one aspect of what it means to be a truly organic missional church. To get a clearer perspective of the nature of Apostolic Genius, especially as it expresses itself in the early church and in the Chinese phenomenon, we will need to explore the dynamics of what it means to be and to become a movement.

Let me say up front that in prescribing a recovery of this aspect of organic systems I am not trying to be anarchic and anti-institutional for the sake of it. In fact I think that the anarchist approach to church is misinformed about the nature of living systems in general and Apostolic Genius in particular and is itself loaded with political agendas.[4] Rather than thinking of the early church as noninstitutional, we need to think of it rather as "preinstitutional."

3. For a highly stimulating articulation of the theology and structures of a networked church, see Peter Ward, *Liquid Church* (Peabody, MA: Hendrickson: 2003).

4. Anarchism is a cluster of doctrines and attitudes united in the belief that government is both harmful and unnecessary. It is derived from a Greek root signifying "without a rule." In our day, theological anarchism is associated with the work of the French philosopher Jacques Ellul, and others.

All living systems require some form of structure in order to maintain and perpetuate their existence. And while it is entirely true that structure does not in itself create life (as in a machine), without it life cannot exist for very long. The more complex a living system, the more necessary it is to have a built-in means to maintain it. Our body, for instance, is made up of trillions of cells, which, by reference to its genetic coding, organizes itself into various systems (nervous, digestive, circulative, etc.), all interconnected and interrelated in a common purpose—to preserve and enable human life. The soul cannot fully exist without a body (although I haven't tried this lately). Even a flame, such as that of a candle in a closed room, will maintain a perfectly defined and predictable shape with a fixed boundary and will be sustained by the combination of its organic fuels with oxygen, producing carbon dioxide and water. Life as it appears to even the lay observer is a highly organized phenomenon consisting in the complex interplay between static form and dynamic function. Or as Neil Cole of Church Multiplication Associates says,

> Structures are needed, but they must be simple, reproducible and internal rather than external. Every living thing is made up of structure and systems. Your body has a nervous system, a circulatory system, and even a skeletal system to add structure to the whole. The universe and nature itself teach us that order is possible even when there is no control but God Himself.[5]

Quite clearly there is something "structural" going on in the people movements of the early periods and in China—it's just not the same as what we have experienced. For me the question is about the *right kind* of living structure, or medium, appropriate to the message of the apostolic church.[6] And this looks significantly different from what we have come to know as the top-down, institutional/governance form of church—which is far and away the predominant structural mode of the church in the West.[7]

This should be fair warning to us if we wish to recover Apostolic Genius. Or as Bill Easum in a chapter titled "Christianity as an Organic Movement" says,

> Most theories about congregational life are flawed from the start because they are based on an institutional and mechanical worldview. . . . Such a view is

---

X   5. Neil Cole, "Out-of-Control Order: Simple Structures for a Decentralized Multiplication Movement," from the CMA website, http://www.organicchurchplanting.org/articles/simple_structures.asp, or search at www.cmaresources.org.

6. The function of leadership is to grow structure, not impose it. The process is organic, the work of a gardener, not a mechanic.

7. If aspects of institution can be found in the New Testament and the subsequent church, these are never allowed to bloom into full-grown institutional form as we now know it. We can say, rather, that these expressions of structure are *pre-institutional* and not fully institutional.

not biblical. Instead, it is fatalistic and self-serving because the goal is to fix and preserve the institution for as long a life as possible. Such a worldview allows one to focus on mere organizational and institutional survival rather than following Jesus onto the mission field for the purpose of fulfilling the great commission. However, the Old and New Testaments are based on an organic worldview. They clearly show a bias for "salvation history" rather than institutional viability.[8]

He goes on to suggest that "the key to unfreezing the church to be with Jesus on the mission field is to view our congregations and denominations as the roots and shoots of an 'organic movement' that goes far beyond organizational survival."[9] In other words, we need to move away from institutional forms of organization and recover a movement ethos if we are going to become truly missional.

Perhaps a further exploration of what is meant by *institutionalism* is needed here. Institutions are organizations initially set up in order to fill a necessary religious and social function and to provide some sort of structural support for whatever that function requires. In many ways they fulfill the very purpose of structure; organization is needed if we seek to act collectively for a common cause. All movements start this way, but in the initial stages structure exists *solely to support the grass roots*. The problem happens when the newly instituted structures move beyond being simply structural support to become a governing body of sorts—structure becomes centralized governance. So religious institutionalism happens when in the name of some convenience we set up a system to do what we must do ourselves so that over time the structures we create take on a life of their own. A classic example is churches outsourcing education to external organizations. Initially, these training organizations exist to fully serve the grass roots. However, over time they increase in authority, eventually becoming ordaining bodies whose imprimatur is needed to minister. As the provider of degrees, they become increasingly more accountable to the government bodies than they do to the mission of the church. But the net result for the local community is that not only do they become dependent on an increasingly powerful and cloistered institution, they also lose the ancient art of discipling and educating for life in the local setting. The local church as a learning and theologizing community is degraded as a result.

But something else begins to happen: as we outsource to the structure what is essential to the function, there is a transfer of responsibility and power/authority to the newly established centralized body. In this situation it inevitably becomes the locus of power, which uses some of that

8. Easum, *Unfreezing Moves*, 17.
9. Ibid., 18.

power to sanction behaviors of its members that are out of keeping with the institution. Instead of serving the mission, institutions begin to have a life of their own, and they can become blockers, not "blessers." One of the most tragic examples of the conformist impulse in institutions was seen in the effective hobbling of the remarkable, organic Celtic Mission by the more centralist Roman Catholic Church in Britain in that fateful meeting at the Abbey of Whitby in 664. The Celtic movement was never the same again.[10] But centralized coercion and conformity surely climaxed in the Inquisition (which began in 1231), which burned and killed hundreds of thousands of people in the name of compliance and control.

The tragedy these examples serve to highlight is that when power is entrenched in the religious institution it creates a dangerous culture of restraint. No one intends it; it just appears to be a part of our fallen condition—genuine gospel freedom, it seems, is very difficult to maintain over the long haul, and one cannot bind it down in well-meaning structures. But when organizations enshrine this culture of restraint, they are extremely hard to change. As far as I am aware, no historical denomination has ever been able to fully recover its earlier, more fluid and dynamic movement ethos again. That's why it is the network structure, where power and responsibility is diffused throughout the organization and not concentrated at the center, that more approximates our real nature and calling as the body of Christ. A network structure thus guards us from the dangerous creep of religious institutionalism.

So it should be no surprise to us that genuine Jesus movements are essentially networks. Curtis Sergeant, an expert on the Chinese underground church, notes that

> In regard to church-planting patterns, external human control over the new converts and churches is inversely proportional to the potential growth and rate of growth in terms of both maturity and size. If a church planter or agency or denomination or other entity seeks to exercise authority to a great extent, then the new church and its members will tend to be dependent and not take responsibility for their own growth or for reaching others. Every time you are tempted to micro-manage, remember this principle.[11]

10. The main issue at the synod was ostensibly to set the correct date for celebrating Easter and to address the issue of the hairstyle of the monks (called a tonsure). The Roman party thought the Celtic calculation, which differed from their own by only a few days, and the different form of tonsure were tantamount to heresy. It was over these trivia that the Roman party was able to tame the most remarkable missionary movement in Western history. See, for instance, Thomas Cahill, *How the Irish Saved Civilization: The Untold Story of Ireland's Heroic Role from the Fall of Rome to the Rise of Medieval Europe* (New York: Anchor, 1995).

11. Taken from notes on church planting movements given to me in the course of my research. Curtis's work is exceptional because he has lived in China for much of his adult life and has grasped some of the inner workings of the Chinese phenomenon.

As church-planting movement researcher David Garrison says, in all truly vigorous Jesus movements leadership authority is decentralized.

> Denominations and church structures that impose a hierarchy of authority or require bureaucratic decision-making are ill-suited to handle the dynamism of a Church Planting Movement. It is important that every cell or house church leader has all the authority required to do whatever needs to be done in terms of evangelism, ministry and new church planting without seeking approval from a church hierarchy.[12]

To illustrate this with a bit of living irony, a friend of mine, Michael Frost, was, in 2005, privy to a meeting with three Chinese leaders from the underground church who were smuggled out to a group of Western leaders. When they were asked what they wanted people to pray for, they asked for three things: While acknowledging that the government has become more lenient, they were still not allowed to gather in groups of more than fifteen people, and when they grew beyond that they had to split and start a new church. Could the Westerners please pray about that? The second issue they addressed was that they were not allowed to have church buildings and were thus forced to meet in homes, cafés, karaoke bars, and social clubs. Could the Westerners please pray that they could build churches as well? The third thing they felt they needed a breakthrough with was that they were forbidden to develop separate organizations where they could collectively train leaders; they were forced to train leaders in the local church. Michael, himself a vice president of a seminary, has often said that in all good conscience he simply could not pray for them in this way, because he and the group gathered there realized that in many ways the Communist state was forcing the church to remain more true to itself. Philip Yancey likewise reports on his life-changing trip to China. He says, "Before going to China I met with one of the missionaries who had been expelled in 1950. 'We felt so sorry for the church we left behind,' he said. 'They had no one to teach them, no printing presses, no seminaries, no one to run their clinics and orphanages. No resources, really, except the Holy Spirit.'" Yancey wryly concludes, "It appears the Holy Spirit is doing just fine."[13]

These stories highlight how reliance on buildings and external institutions can seriously distort our experience of God, our understanding of church, and our experience of Apostolic Genius. History has amply shown us that we are actually at our very best when we have very little of these.

12. David Garrison, *Church Planting Movements*, chapter 4, online resource booklet on church planting movements, available at http://www.imb.org/CPM/Chapter4.htm.

13. Philip Yancey, *Christianity Today*, July 2004, vol. 48, no. 7, 72.

A Movement Ethos

As previously mentioned, maintaining a movement ethos is one sure antidote to the dangers of increasing institutionalism. The goal of awakening a dormant movement ethos was one of the strategic cornerstones of my ministry in my denomination. I believed then, as I do now, that we somehow had to recover the lost dynamics of movements if we were to avert inevitable decline and eventual closure. And while my denomination might still use the terminology of movement to describe itself, like most denominations we do not exhibit a movement *culture*. If we were to become a movement again, we first needed to know what movements actually look and feel like. What is clear is that movements have a very different composition and feel to that of the denominational institutions we had become. The differences are nothing less than paradigmatic. H. R. Niebuhr noted that "there are essential differences between an institution and a movement: The one is conservative, the other progressive; the one is more or less passive yielding to influences from the outside, the other is active in influencing rather than being influenced; the one looks to the past, the other to the future. In addition the one is anxious, the other is prepared to take risks; the one guards boundaries, the other crosses them."[14] Studies over the years have only further highlighted these differences and in so doing shown how far we have really moved from our own roots.

Christian Associates International is a grassroots church-planting movement in Europe.[15] In 1999 CAI set a long-range goal: to identify and develop 500 missionaries sent out to establish one or more missional churches in fifty major cities in Europe by the year 2010—and they are well on the way to achieving this. By explicitly adopting a movement ethos, CAI sees its core task is to initiate a chain reaction of church-planting movements. As they see it, "a church-planting movement is characterized by habitual (organic, natural) church planting."[16]

What is absolutely critical to CAI's thinking is the central importance of generating a genuine grassroots movement. This they see as critical for the re-evangelization of post-Christian, and post-Christendom, Europe. And while they couch it in simple, visionary language of grassroots communities of faith, in invoking movement imagery they are definitely onto something significant, something that harks back to the dynamic of Apostolic Genius. The Jesus movements of history can only be understood, as well as socio-

14. Quoted in Bosch, *Transforming Mission*, 51.
15. http://www.christianassociates.org/index.asp.
16. To inculcate this ethos they have adopted the following approach: initiating (facilitating the process of initiating a new church community); establishing (facilitating the process of community development); maturing (facilitating the maturing process of community); reproducing (facilitating the church planting process within a church community).

logically categorized, as grassroots people movements. There is much to be learned about Christianity from the dynamics of people movements.

"It is perfectly true to say that most groups that have impact on either a local, national, or international level almost always begin with a form that sociologists call a *movement*. That is, there are some common characteristics that mark off the early phase of dynamic social movements that are distinct from the social structures of the later institutions that arise from them."[17] This is as true for ecclesial, parachurch, and mission agencies, as it is of corporations, community projects, political parties and many other secular organizations. Most transformational organizations, religious or otherwise, are launched with a certain ethos and energy that starts with a seminal vision/idea and swells like a wave to impact society around it. Take the Celtic Christians, the Moravians, early Pentecostalism, and closer to our time, the Vineyard, for examples of dynamic movements that have changed the world.

In seeking to recover Apostolic Genius it is therefore critical to study the dynamic nature of movements, because "in the movement's form, with all its fluidity, vision, chaos and dynamism, lies one of the most significant clues to transforming our world for Jesus."[18] So, for our purposes, a working definition of a movement will be as follows:

> a group of people organized for, ideologically motivated by, and committed to a purpose which implements some form of personal or social change; who are actively engaged in the recruitment of others; and whose influence is spreading in opposition to the established order within which it originated.[19]

This definition, however technical it may sound, accurately describes not only all socially impacting movements, but also the New Testament people of God. From what you know of the church in Acts, try to discern the elements of this definition in these early communities. You will find that it does fit. Not only does it describe the early Christian movement, this definition is

17. Hirsch and Frost, *Shaping of Things to Come*, 202. The following description of movements follows closely the work that I did with Michael there.

18. Ibid.

19. Ibid. A brief comment on the final phrase is necessary: this opposition to established order seems to be a universal characteristic of movements. What is clear is that genuine Christianity, wherever it expresses itself, is always in tension with significant aspects of the surrounding culture, because it always seeks to transform it. Movements are transformative by nature, so they do not accept the status quo. On the other hand, theologically liberal Christianity, while sincere, seeks to minimize this tension—that is why liberalism is often called cultural Christianity. And that is why it is just about impossible to find a liberal movement that has made any significant missional impact on the world. Liberalism comes later in the life of a movement and usually is a clear signal of decline (see the place of ideological doubt in the diagram on life cycle in the section on movements).

also consistent with the situations where Apostolic Genius manifests. Try using the definition for what you know of the church in China or in parts of South America and Africa.

If we interplay movement dynamics against the concept the organizational life cycles (below), by comparing the two sides of the growth curve we can discern what movements might actually *look and feel* like. Observe the dynamics that make for the early growth phases of the organization (the foundation and growth periods). What's going on here? What kind of leadership is required? What is the focus of the organization? What makes for its growth?[20] These are questions of fundamental importance for the missionary and church planter who is all about trying to pioneer some form of movement in varying contexts. Ask yourself these questions. Try asking the same questions of the historical movements you admire, of your heroes, and learn from them what makes for dynamic missional impact.

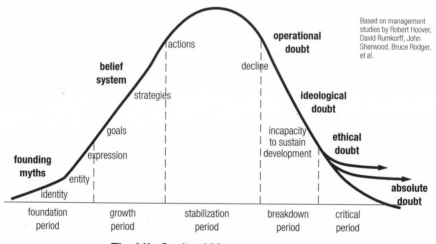

The Life Cycle of Movements

Following the logic of the bell curve above, similar questions could be asked of the decline phase. Whereas in the early phases of movements, vision and mission are in the driving seat, now programming and administration tend to replace and sideline vision and mission. Here decline is directly related to the institutionalization, and the eventual demise, of the movement. What's going on in these stages? What mode of leadership is involved? What is the organization focusing on? What is it missing? What kind of theology undergirds it? These are significant questions relating to the revitalization of churches and denominations, but are also important for new mission work,

20. Ibid.

as it is critical to have the right mix of leadership and structure that makes movements such powerful agents of transformational change.[21]

To clarify our understanding of the ethos of movements as it relates to Apostolic Genius, it is important to identify some of the signature characteristics of movements. For this we turn to Howard Snyder's important book *Signs of the Spirit,* where he identifies the following as characteristics of movements:

- *A thirst for renewal:* A holy discontent with what exists precipitates a recovery of the vitality and patterns of the early church.
- *A new stress on the work of the Spirit:* The work of the Spirit is seen not only as important in the past but also as an experience in the present.
- *An institutional–charismatic tension:* In almost every case of renewal, tensions within existing structures will arise (this raises the issue of wineskins).
- *A concern for being a countercultural community:* Movements call the church to a more radical commitment and a more active tension with the world.
- *Nontraditional or nonordained leadership:* Renewal movements are often led by people with no recognized formal leadership status in the church. Spiritual authority is the key. Furthermore, women are noticeably more active in movements.
- *Ministry to the poor:* Movements almost always involve people at the grassroots level. They actively involve the masses (the uneducated or socially outcast) and often start as mission on the edges and among the poor (St. Francis, the Wesleys, Salvation Army, etc.).[22]
- *Energy and dynamism:* New movements have the ability to excite and enlist others as leaders and participants.[23]

Now we will compare Snyder's distinctly Wesleyan perspective with that of Gerlach and Hine, sociologists whose research on movements indicates that movements are characterized by the following elements:[24]

21. Ibid.

22. Renewal movements show us that deep renewal often begins at the periphery, or the margins, of the church (Snyder, *Decoding the Church,* 81).

23. Howard A. Snyder, *New Wineskins: Changing the Man-Made Structures of the Church* (London: Marshall, Morgan and Scott, 1978).

24. L. P. Gerlach and V. H. Hine, *People, Power, Change: Movements of Social Transformation* (Indianapolis: Bobbs-Merrill, 1970). Again, this has been referred to in *The Shaping of Things to Come,* 204–5. The similarities of Snyder's theological approach to Gerlach and Hine's sociological one are evident. While using different language, they describe a similar phenomenon that is common to all human movements and social forces.

- A segmented, cellular organization composed of units held together by various personal, structural, and ideological ties. In other words, a group of small faith communities (e.g., house churches or cell groups) gathered around Jesus and his mission.
- Face-to-face recruitment by committed individuals using their own preexisting, significant social relationships. Friendships and organic relationships are the primary means of recruiting people to the cause.
- Personal commitment generated by an act or experience that separates a convert in some way from the established order, identifies him or her with a new set of values, and commits him or her to changed patterns of behavior. This is what believers have always called *conversion*—a radical reorientation of life and lifestyle.
- An ideology of articulated values and goals, which provides a conceptual framework for life, motivates and provides a rationale for change, defines the opposition, and forms the basis for the unity among the segmented networks of groups in the movement.
- Real or perceived opposition from the society at large or from that segment of the established order within which the movement has arisen.[25] This has occurred in almost every instance of the emergence of movements that we are aware of. Wesley was shunned by the Anglican Church, as was Booth. Martin Luther King Jr. was rejected by the hegemonic Christianity of his day, etc. Dynamic movements always have a transformative vision for society, and that puts them in tension with it.

An aspect worth adding to the above lists is that new missional movements almost always begin on the edges of society/culture and among the common people. They are nonelitist. And they have the ability to excite and enlist others as leaders and participants.[26]

What is clear is that the ethos of a movement remains somewhat different from the feel of almost any established denomination or church because these are mostly on the decline side of the lifecycle. In order to remain truly missional, established organizations need to be very aware of the dangers of institutionalization. Harvard's David K. Hurst talks about the shifts in emphasis that take place in institutionalization in the metaphor of moving

25. "History is absolutely clear about this: most established institutions will resist a movement ethos. It's just too chaotic and uncontrollable for institutions to handle. That is why most movements are ejected from the host organization. This needn't be the case, but it does require a significant permission-giving at high levels of denominational or established organization leadership to ensure that they are not" *Shaping of Things to Come*, 206.

26. As Harvey Cox has similarly noted, the main stimulus for the renewal of Christianity will come from the bottom and from the edge, from sectors of the Christian world that are on the margins.

from being hunters to becoming herders.[27] In his analysis the marks identifying this transition are that

- Mission becomes Strategy
- Roles become Tasks
- Teams become Structure
- Networks become Organization[28]
- Recognition becomes Compensation

But more important than just being *aware* of institutionalism, we have to be extremely wary of it, because if what we can learn from the phenomenal Jesus movements is correct, it keeps us from ever fully becoming ourselves as the people of God. It is truly remarkable, for instance, that the Chinese church was only truly activated in a powerful way when all institutional reference points were forcibly removed. We need to constantly remind ourselves that the way of Jesus, the kingdom of God, is in fact what Jacques Ellul called "anti-religion." We must constantly subject our institutions to prophetic critique, because it is the prophet, in his or her simple call to faithfulness to God alone, that is most aware of the dangers of the claims that institutions make on faith. It is the heart of the prophetic ministry to constantly call us to unadorned covenantal faithfulness; this is summed up in Micah 6:8 "He has showed you, O man, what is good. And what does the LORD require of you? To act justly and to love mercy and to walk humbly with your God." In relation to institutionalism, the simple prophetic vision always poses a threat and a challenge. The sheer simplicity of its message undermines the ever increasing clutter of the institutional message and fixes sole loyalty to God. It therefore undermines the false claims of all human authorities.

In order to recover the missional vitality of the early church, we have to reawaken a virile *movement ethos* in so many of the organizations we inhabit. And to do that we need to "shed all that which does not matter" and get back to the uncluttered way of Jesus. The reader is wise to take these elements seriously when establishing pioneering missional activities or in remissionalizing established ones.

Using a table of comparison, we can now distill, isolate, and contrast the differences between institutionalized religion and movement ethos as follows:[29]

27. David K. Hurst, *Crisis and Renewal* (Cambridge: Harvard Business School Press, 2002).

28. He uses the word *system* here but means by it "centralized structures of organization." I didn't want to confuse this with what I have previously stated in living systems theory, which is not what he is referring to . . . hence, the change.

29. Significantly adapted and developed from Easum, *Unfreezing Moves*, 18.

Organic Missional Movement	Institutional Religion
Has pioneering missional leadership as its central role	Avoids leadership based on personality and is often led by an "aristocratic class" who inherit leadership based on loyalty
Seeks to embody the way of life of the Founder	Represents a more codified belief system
Based on internal operational principles (mDNA)	Based increasingly on external legislating policies/ governance
Has a cause	Is "the cause"
The mission is to change the future	The mission shifts to preserving the past
Tends be to mobile and dynamic	Tends to be more static and fixed
Decentralized network built on relationships	Centralized organization built on loyalty
Appeals to the common person	Tends to become more and more elitist and therefore exclusive
Inspirational/transformational leadership dominant; spiritual authority tends to be the primary basis of influence	Transactional leadership dominant; institutional authorizing tends to be the primary basis of influence
People of the Way	People of the Book
Centered-set dynamic	Closed-set dynamic[30]

As an exercise to pin down the learning up to this point, the reader should try to test this table against what he or she knows of movements versus institutions. Try adding or subtracting elements that you think do or do not fit. Try and measure your experience of church against this table.

Networked Structures

If Apostolic Genius expresses itself in a movement ethos, it forms itself around a network structure. And once again this tends to be very different from what we have come to expect from our general concept of church. When we use the word *church* it is very hard to get the image of some kind of building out of our minds. But this is not the way that phenomenal expressions of Christian movements experience it. This is due partly to the fact that the early church didn't have such buildings; the Chinese had all their church buildings taken away from them. But it is also because buildings are not what is meant in any of the theological images of church in the scriptures. Since Constantine, it seems that we have simply got it all mixed up. On comparison, the Chinese church is much closer to what the New Testament intends, as well as more consistent with the New Testament

30. For a description of closed and open sets, see Frost and Hirsch, *Shaping of Things to Come*, 206–10.

experience of church. It is we who are inconsistent in this regard—it's that simple. So what do networks look like?

Liquid vs. Solid Church

Peter Ward has written an excellent book exploring the theological, ecclesiological, and sociological dimensions of networks. Following Zygmunt Bauman's analysis of culture in terms of liquid and solid modernity, he uses the term *liquid church* to describe the essence of what a truly networked church would look like—a church responsive to that increasing fluid dimension of our culture that Bauman called *liquid modernity*.[31] He contrasts liquid church with what he calls *solid church*. To simplify this, solid church is roughly equivalent to what I have here described as institutional church. Because of the continuing existence of solid modernity, he does not counsel the total abandonment of solid church, but he does suggest that it is one of decreasing effectiveness. Solid church is related to solid modernity. And solid church has generally mutated from its original basis into becoming communities of heritage (that embody the inherited tradition), communities of refuge (a safe place from the world), and communities of nostalgia (living in past successes). He suggests that almost all manifestations of solid church fall into one or more of these categories.

He says that "the mutation of solid church into heritage, refuge, and nostalgic communities has seriously decreased its ability to engage in genuine mission in liquid modernity."[32] This is so because the church finds itself increasingly stranded from its surrounding culture. He remarks that this has seriously damaged the gospel genetic code of the church because the church cannot truly be and become itself in such a condition. Solid church has mutated the gospel code because it has by and large ignored cultural change and found itself changed in ways that are less than planned or perfect. In catering to the religious needs of some (largely the insiders) it has as a consequence failed to respond to the wider spiritual hunger of not-yet-Christians. What is more, "the mutant genetic code within these kinds of churches means that they are a poor starting point for a new kind of church that connects with the flow of spiritual hunger evident in our societies."[33] This highlights the need to engage liquid modernity with a liquid form of church. Liquid church is essential because it takes the present culture seriously and seeks to express the fullness of the Christian gospel within that culture. The defining element of this is church as a living, adaptive network

31. Bauman maintains that our current situation is a mixture of the modern and postmodern and feels that rather than opting for one or the other, we should see ourselves in a fluid situation that he calls "liquid modernity."

32. Ward, *Liquid Church*, 29.

33. Ibid., 30.

highly responsive to the deep spiritual needs and hunger expressed in surrounding society.

Make no mistake; liquid church as Ward defines it is theologically much
closer to the conception of church advocated in the New Testament teachings, not only because it is missional and responsive to the surrounding
context, not only because it is structurally more consistent with biblical
ecclesiology, but because it takes the twin doctrines of what it means to be
"in Christ" and the "body of Christ" with utmost seriousness and reworks
them in light of the missional situation. It is clear that the church in Corinth
was distinctly different in structure and ethos from the church in Jerusalem,
and yet they were both legitimate expressions of the body of Christ. There
is little by way of uniformity of structure in the NT church.

The reality of the church is to be found only "in Christ." "Christ is our
origin and our truth. To be a Christian is to be joined to Christ and to be
joined to Christ is to be joined to his church."[34] This is what constitutes the
body of Christ. It is this primal connection with Jesus that defines what it
means to be a Christian and to be in his church. How this expresses itself
will depend largely on missional context. In a liquid culture, Ward says,
we need a liquid form of church that can express truly what it means to be
"in Christ."

> To be joined to Christ is to be joined to the body of Christ. This corporate and
> corporeal expression of Christ is fundamental to any theology of the church.
> The idea of the body of Christ goes very deep into people's minds. Yet it is
> worth reflecting on *how* we express this truth, for to say that the body of Christ
> is the church is not the same as saying that the church is the body of Christ.
> The implication of my reading of Paul's theology is that we should place
> significantly more emphasis upon the way our connection to Christ makes
> us part of the body, rather than the other way around.[35]

Our problem, it seems, is that we too quickly identify the concrete-
historical expressions of church as the body of Christ. And while there is a
truth to this, for the *church is the body of Christ,* perhaps the greater truth is
that the *body of Christ is the church.* When we say that the church *is* the body
of Christ, it claims a certain authority for a particular expression of church.
To say that the body of Christ is the church is to open up possibilities as
to how it might physically and organizationally express itself. This doesn't
just localize it to *one* particular expression of church.[36] The body can express
itself in many different ways and forms. The distinction is paradigmatic. To
restate it in these terms enables us to escape the monopolizing grip that the

34. Ibid., 33.
35. Ibid., 37.
36. Ibid., 38

institutional image of church holds over our theological imaginations, and allows us to undertake a journey of reimagining what it means to be God's people in our own day and in our own situations.

So how can liquid church express itself? Ward points out that all liquids are characterized by flow.[37] In contrast, solids are located and firm. Shape or solidity, to use Bauman again, is the equivalent of "fixing space" and "binding time," and therefore there is no need for change or movement. However, if we are to envisage a liquid church, then like liquids themselves, movement and change must be part of its basic characteristic. "We need to let go of a static model of church that is based primarily on congregation, programs, and buildings. In its place we need to develop a notion of Christian community, worship, mission, and organization which, like the NT *ecclesia,* is more flexible, adaptive, and responsive to change."[38] Instead of the centralist and more "solid" hierarchical structure of the later church, we observe the more fluid network in the NT church.

What eventually became known as DOVE Christian Fellowship International (DCFI) had its roots in a Bible study involving young people coming to faith in the Jesus People phenomenon in the early 1970s.[39] Larry Kreider, the leader of the group, had became increasingly frustrated with the cultural mismatch of the prevailing church and the people they were reaching, and so began to develop what he called "an underground church model." Gaining inspiration from the house churches in the book of Acts and around the world, they structured themselves as a movement that met regularly in cells across the city. And so began the story of DCFI. When the new movement officially started in 1980, there were twenty-five people meeting in one house church. By adopting the networked structures of Apostolic Genius, the movement had swelled to about 2,500 believers meeting in over 125 cell groups all over south-central Pennsylvania by 1992. During this period they also began planting churches in Scotland, Brazil, Kenya, and New Zealand.

In spite of this significant growth, they felt that they had reached a growth barrier because they had become somewhat reliant on centralized structures to manage the growth. They decided that they "needed to adjust [their] church government and 'give the church away.'" They felt that the vision God had given them was "to build a relationship with Jesus, with one another, and reach the world from house to house, city to city and nation to nation," and this simply could not be fulfilled with their prevailing church structure at the time. Thus, they self-consciously began to transition into what they called an "apostolic movement." Unlike a denomination or association of churches, which confers ordination and provides general accountability to

37. Ibid., 40ff.

38. Ibid., 41.

39. This and the following information regarding DCFI were taken from http://www .dcfi.org/About3.htm.

church leaders through centralized structure, they conceived an "apostolic movement" as being a networked family of churches with a common focus, minus the restrictive structures of a denomination.

They soon found that "apostolic ministry provides a safe environment for each congregation and ministry partnering with DCFI to flourish and reproduce themselves [because the new model created space for growth by emphasizing] leading by relationship and influence rather than hands-on-management." As a cell-based church-planting movement, they soon recognized the strategic need to train church planters and leaders with a missionary heart and spirit. They felt called to "mobilize and empower God's people (individuals, families, cells and congregations) at the grassroots level to fulfill His purposes. Every cell group should have a vision to plant new cells. Every church should have a God-given vision to plant new churches." The new network structure combined with the apostolic movement ethos and leadership has allowed them to grow from the initial eight congregations to around a hundred networks involving exponentially more people in fifteen countries around the world.

More about Networks

Not surprisingly, as we move closer to a network structure, we will not only find ourselves closer to the structures of the NT people of God but also more aligned with the dynamics of Apostolic Genius. It is therefore critical to explore the nature and forms of networks. In doing so, we need to realize that this is closer to our truest expression of *ecclesia*, even though it might at first seem somewhat strange to us. We should also note that in this we explore things that relate not just to issues of reactivating missional church, but to much of what we experience in God's world. Albert-Laszlo Barabasi, the guru of network thinking, says it this way:

> Network thinking is poised to invade all domains of human activity and most fields of human inquiry. It is more than another useful perspective or tool. Networks are by their very nature the fabric of most complex systems, and nodes and links deeply infuse all strategies aimed at approaching our interlocked universe.[40]

So what are the networks and how do they help us in our task? In the literature describing and analyzing networks and networking, networks come in basically three types:[41]

40. Albert-Laszlo Barabasi, *Linked: The New Science of Networks* (Cambridge, MA: Perseus, 2002), 222.
41. Slightly adapted from John Arquilla and David Ronfeldt, *Networks and Netwars: The Future of Terror, Crime, and Militancy* (downloadable online resource http://www.rand.org/publications/MR/MR1382/), 7ff.

- the chain or line network, as in a chain where people, goods, or information move along a line of separated contacts, and where end-to-end communication must travel through the intermediate nodes;
- the hub, star, or wheel network, as in a franchise or a cartel where the agents are tied to a central (but not hierarchical) node or actor and must go through that node to communicate and coordinate with each other;
- the all-channel or full-matrix network, as in a collaborative network of green groups and activists where everybody is independent but connected to everybody else.

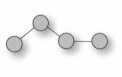
chain network

star or hub network

all-channel network

Each node in the diagrams may refer to an individual, a group, an organization, part of a group or organization, or even a state. The nodes may be large or small, tightly or loosely coupled, and inclusive or exclusive in membership. . . . They may look alike and engage in similar activities, or they may undertake a division of labor based on specialization. The boundaries of the network, or of any node included in it, may be well defined, or they may be blurred and porous in relation to the outside environment. Many variations are possible.[42]

It might be clear to see that of the three network types, the all-channel form has traditionally been the most difficult to organize and sustain. This is so partly because it requires lots of communication. But it is precisely this form of network that maximizes potential for collaborative undertakings without centralized organization.[43] And this all-channel form is gaining new strength and legitimacy from the information revolution—for instance, in open source programming and online business and networking. In networks of this kind, the organizational system generally tends to be flat (as opposed to hierarchical).[44] Also, in its purer form, there is no single, central leadership, command, or headquarters—no precise heart or head that can readily be identified. "The network as a whole (but not necessarily each node) has little to no hierarchy; there may be multiple leaders. Decision-making and operations are decentralized, allowing for local initiative and autonomy. Thus

42. Ibid., 8.
43. Ibid., 9.
44. Ibid.

the design may sometimes appear acephalous (headless), and at other times polycephalous (Hydra-headed)."[45] The structure will tend to be comprised of small units or cells. However, the presence of "cells" does not necessarily mean a network exists—a hierarchy can also be made up of cells, as is the case with most churches with an active cell group program. It is the *way* in which the cells organize and relate that makes them a network.[46]

What is particularly instructive for Christian movements and organizations is how networks hold together. The effective performance of a network over time and distance will depend to a large degree on the cultivation of shared beliefs, principles, interests, and goals—perhaps articulated in an overarching ideology. This combination of beliefs and principles forms the cultural glue, or reference point, that holds the nodes together and to which the members subscribe in a deep way. "Such a set of principles, shaped through mutual consultation and consensus-building, can enable members to be 'all of one mind' even though they are dispersed and devoted to different tasks."[47] Dee Hock, the brilliant philosopher-businessman who founded the trillion-dollar Visa Corporation squarely on the network model, makes this point well when he notes that

> Purpose and principle, clearly understood and articulated, and commonly shared, are the genetic code of any healthy organization. To the degree that you hold purpose and principles in common among you, you can dispense with command and control. People will know how to behave in accordance with them, and they'll do it in thousands of unimaginable, creative ways. The organization will become a vital, living set of beliefs.[48]

Remember the reference to "fit and split" in the chapter on Apostolic Environment? These overarching beliefs provide a central ideological and operational coherence (fit) that allows for wide tactical decentralization (split). This culture or ideology "also sets the boundaries and provides guidelines for decisions and actions so that the members do not have to resort to a hierarchy, because 'they know what they have to do.'"[49] This

---

45. Ibid.
46. Ibid.
47. Ibid.
48. Quoted from http://en.wikipedia.org/wiki/Command_and_control. From Hock's book *The Birth of the Chaordic Age* (San Francisco: Berrett-Koehler, 1999). He says elsewhere that "all organizations are merely conceptual embodiments of a very old, very basic idea—the idea of community. They can be no more or less than the sum of the beliefs of the people drawn to them; of their character, judgments, acts, and efforts. An organization's success has enormously more to do with clarity of a shared purpose, common principles and strength of belief in them than to assets, expertise, operating ability, or management competence, important as they may be" (M. Mitchell Waldrop, "Dee Hock on Organizations," *Fast Company* 5 (October/November 1996), 84. Online article at http://www.fastcompany.com/online/05/dee3.html.
49. Arquilla and Ronfeldt, *Networks and Netwars*, 9.

is analogous to what the best military practice refers to as "commander's intent" and "rules of engagement": these set the guidelines for the scope of individual decision making. Through these, the solider knows *what* to do and *what* the limitations are, but *how* they do it remains up to them.

It is worth reflecting here on what Hock says are keys to developing networked organization:[50]

- The organization must be adaptable and responsive to changing conditions, while preserving overall cohesion and unity of purpose.
- The trick is to find the delicate balance that allows the system to avoid turf fights and back-stabbing on the one hand, and authoritarian micromanagement on the other.
- The organization must cultivate equity, autonomy, and individual opportunity.
- The organization's governing structure must distribute power and function to the lowest level possible.[51]   *subsidiarity*
- The governing structure must not be a chain of command, but rather a framework for dialogue, deliberation, and coordination among equals.

But all this organic networking requires significant or "dense" communications to hold it all together. Arquilla and Ronfeldt note, "The network design may depend on having an infrastructure for the concentrated communication of information. But this does not mean that all nodes must be in constant communication. But when communication is needed, the network's members must be able to disseminate information as promptly and broadly as desired within the network as well as to outside audiences."[52]

This lines up exactly with what popular writer on networks Manuel Castells[53] describes as the dynamics of a network. In his view they are made up not only of nodes but also of hubs. The hubs are places where the lines of

50. Waldrop, "Hock on Organizations."

51. It is worth elaborating this point in light of the problem of institutionalism inherent in centralizing functions. He goes on to say, "No function should be performed by any part of the whole that could reasonably be done by any more peripheral part and no power should be vested in any part that might reasonably be exercised by any lesser part" (Waldrop, "Hock on Organizations").

52. In many respects, then, the archetypal design corresponds to what sociologists of movements Gerlach and Hine called a "segmented, polycentric, ideologically integrated network" (SPIN): "By segmentary I mean that it is cellular, composed of many different groups.... By polycentric I mean that it has many different leaders or centers of direction.... By networked I mean that the segments and the leaders are integrated into reticulated systems or networks through various structural, personal, and ideological ties. Networks are usually unbounded and expanding.... This acronym [SPIN] helps us picture this organization as a fluid, dynamic, expanding one, spinning out into mainstream society." See Aquilla and Ronfelt, *Networks and Netwars*, 10.

53. See Manual Castells, *The Rise of the Network Society*, 2nd ed. (Oxford: Blackwell, 2000).

communication connect. A node may be just about anything: a media outlet, a website, an organization, or an individual. Over time some nodes in the network may emerge as being more important than others depending on geographical, political, historical, or personal circumstances. For example: a company that offers a particular service or product will be connected to various other outlets and customers because it is useful to them. It serves their purposes to be linked. With a growing importance in the network, certain sites may become major nodes or hubs where other nodes connect and intersect. This can be diagrammatically represented as follows:

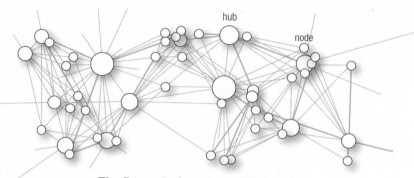

The Dynamic Structure of Networks

Having described all these characteristics of networks, it is not hard to see that this is exactly how the early church and the Chinese church operated. Look at the diagram again. The hubs would have been places like Antioch, Jerusalem, or Rome, or people like Paul. The nodes could be house churches and clumps of people involved in various dimensions of life. Nodes could become hubs, depending on their relative importance in the network. Antioch and Jerusalem were certainly hubs in this view. When the New Testament writers articulated the foundational doctrine of *ecclesia,* this is what they meant—not buildings and institutions, but a fluid body of Christ dynamically involved in all spheres of life.[54] It is within this structure that Apostolic Genius seems to manifest most fully. And due to the missional situation of our era, the time has come to rediscover the church as a dynamic network beyond the institution and in every arena of life and creation.

Stadia is a network-based, organic church multiplication movement in the United States. Its mission is to find, train, deploy, and network church multiplication leaders. In turn, these leaders build regional networks of

54. See James Thwaites, *The Church beyond the Congregation: The Strategic Role of the Church in the Postmodern Era* (Milton Keynes: Paternoster, 2002) for a fascinating articulation of the biblical idea of *ecclesia.*

planters, multiplying churches, and support personnel, who together build a church multiplication movement that is sustainable and reproducible. Their goal is to establish 5,500 new churches across the United States.[55]

Another remarkable organic movement that follows these approaches has been evolving in California and around the world: Church Multiplication Associates. This network is led by Neil Cole, a pioneer in developing organic church planting and someone who has clearly articulated a movement based on movement dynamics, multichannel networking, and organic reproducibility, although their language is somewhat different. This has been translated into a leadership training system called Greenhouse, which coaches leaders from various contexts in organic methodology.[56] The movement has grown exponentially as new expressions of incarnational church break out in car parks, cafés, houses, clubs, etc. The Korean movement associated with Paul Yonggi Cho is built on similar principles—Cho always maintained that the real church existed in the cells and that the rest was frills. These are just some examples of many such movements being generated around the world.

An Australian expression of this is in a new Pentecostal movement called The Junction, led by Kim and Maria Hammond.[57] This network has incarnated deeply into their local area. They meet in the neighborhood school, where they have become part of the actual functioning of the school, and in the local pubs and cafés, and they are involved in many of the projects their contextual community is engaged in, including walks-against-want, mentoring disadvantaged kids in their area, and feeding the poor. There is no center and no circumference—it just exists in nodes, hubs, and enriching relationships and is built squarely on the fabric of friendships. Third Place Communities in Tasmania operates on the same principles and looks remarkably like the network diagram above. All these new missions demonstrate a recovery of a latent potency that bodes well for the future of the church in the West. We do well to give thanks.

Networks and Netwars: What We Can Learn about Ourselves from Al Qaeda

As shocking as it seems at first, it's not hard to see the striking similarities between the structures of international terrorist networks like Al Qaeda and that of the early church, or the Chinese church for that matter. And while the agenda of each is entirely different, it is partly the *structure* that makes both so effective and just about impossible to "take out." How is it that all

55. http://www.stadia.cc/
56. Go to www.cmaresources.org and check out the various aspects of the movement.
57. http://www.thejunction.info

the legitimate governments of the world are, together, spending hundreds of billions of dollars trying to stamp out a relatively small movement and have largely failed to make even a dent?! The most powerful armies in the world are dedicated to the purpose of destroying it and have yet to get close to fulfilling that mission. Putting aside its political agenda, what is it about this vile movement that makes it so hard to snuff out?

Al Qaeda has all the elements of a movement as defined in this chapter; it also exhibits all the features of an all-channel network, consisting as it does of decentralized nodes and multiple energy centers. It is made up of small, self-contained units, or cells, which can easily recruit and multiply. Furthermore, the DNA of its message and ideology is embedded in every terrorist cell through the development of a simple "sneezable" message that can be reproduced in any given context. The geopolitical conditions are ripe for its message. And it has a seemingly built-in capacity to spread and then swarm around issues and places where its mission potential has the maximum possibility of greatest impact. It then seemingly disappears into the air, making it just about impossible to destroy.

I make this comparison not to be needlessly provocative (I am totally opposed to what Al Qaeda stands for), but because we can learn so much about the nature of mDNA from it—at least as far as structures are concerned. So, it appears that the church in its most exceptional form (including the early and Chinese churches) appears to be more like Al Qaeda than it does what we have generally come to know as church. So much so that most of us (including the vast majority of church leaders) would simply not recognize these remarkable expressions of church as *church* if we stumbled upon them—they simply don't fit our criteria of church, influenced as it is by buildings, professional clergy, institutional structures, and so forth.

But there is more to consider still. As mentioned above, each Al Qaeda cell has in it the complete DNA of the whole movement. That is why it can replicate itself and still remain true to its cause. When we consider Apostolic Genius and the church, this is exactly the same. Just like a seed or a cutting, each Jesus community has the full and complete quotient of mDNA embedded in it, and if it is true to its own calling, and given the right conditions, it can become the beginning of a whole new apostolic movement.[58] In the seed the whole tree lies coiled, and in the tree, there lies the potential for the production of countless other seeds. In the tree is the full potential of the forest.

It is interesting to note in passing that in the natural world of organisms similar patterns of organized spread can be observed. Some species maximize their chances of survival by massive spread (e.g., bacteria or ants). Others

---

58. Again, as Easum said, we must view each church as the roots and shoots of a new movement (*Unfreezing Moves*, 18).

seek survival by the concentration of cells into one indivisible unit but in doing so bear greater risk in terms of extinction. For example, it is just about impossible to wipe out a bacteria strain, because of massive spread and because each bacterium has that darn DNA that can replicate and develop. Likewise, plants, when their system senses that their survival is threatened, use all their energies to produce more seeds to maximize survival. This is what happens when we prune plants or trees—they produce more flowers, which in turn produce more fruit, which contains seeds. I have come to conclude that in times of serious adaptive challenge, the church too will maximize its survival by decentralizing, spreading, and multiplying. This is exactly what happened in the early church and in China. And strangely enough, it is certainly beginning to happen in the context of the twenty-first century.

Viruslike Growth

This idea of replication leads us to consider the issues of patterns of growth. One of the most powerful elements of organic systems is their capacity to reproduce spontaneously and hyperbolically. It is this aspect of organic multiplication at a remarkable rate that makes the missional-incarnational impulse described in a previous chapter so very powerful. And here's where it gets really interesting.

Pay It Forward: Hyperbolic Growth and Organic Systems

A few years ago there was a wonderful movie called *Pay It Forward* that illustrated the power of hyperbolic growth in social systems perfectly. Young Trevor McKinney (played by Haley Joel Osment), troubled by his mother's alcoholism and fears of his abusive but absent father, is caught up by an intriguing assignment from his new social studies teacher, Mr. Simonet (Kevin Spacey). The assignment: think of something to change the world and put it into action. Trevor conjures the notion of paying a favor not back, but forward—repaying good deeds not with payback, but with new good deeds "paid forward" to two new people. Eventually this becomes known as the "pay-it-forward" phenomenon, and it becomes a movement that spans the United States. The story picks up when a journalist from a state on the other side of America is given a Jaguar car in a pay-it-forward incident. Totally intrigued, he sets out to trace where this whole movement came from, eventually tracing it back to Trevor. Trevor's efforts to make good on his idea bring a revolution not only in the lives of himself, his mother, and his physically and emotionally scarred teacher, but in those of an ever widening circle of people completely unknown to him. This is what it looks like graphically:

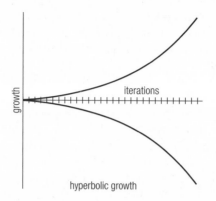

Imagine that every one in your community took a pay-it-forward approach to mission. It might go like this: each of us covenants to bring two people to the Lord in our lifetimes; we commit ourselves to disciple them, and give them the challenge to do exactly the same. But there are more implications. What if every church covenanted to pay it forward by planting two others and committing them in turn to pay it forward by planting two others and so on? So, here's the deal: apply this to (1) evangelism, (2) discipleship, and (3) church planting, and we would get the job done in no time. All we need to do is stick to the method and the principle of metabolic growth and see where it goes. And this is *precisely* how the early church grew from 25,000 to 20,000,000 in two hundred years and precisely how the Chinese church grew from 2,000,000 to 60,000,000 or more in forty years. It's as simple and complicated as that.

If you are still not convinced, consider this: you may be familiar with the story of the inventor of the chess game. As a reward for his invention he was offered one free wish as his reward by the king of India. As a most "modest" reward, he wished just for a kernel of rice on the first square of the chess board to be squared (multiplied by itself) for every section of the chess board—64 sections in all. That will mean two kernels on the second square, four on the third, sixteen on the forth, and so on. The king, who had initially smiled on it, thinking that he would get off lightly, simply could not grant the wish. He would have to produce 2^{63} kernels of rice, which is 2,223,372,036,000,000,000 kernels, or 153 billion tons of rice—more than the world can harvest for the next thousand years. This is what is meant by hyperbolic growth. Simply pay it forward.

Ideaviruses and Memes

Walter Henrichsen points out that "the reason that the church of Jesus Christ finds it so hard to stay on top of the great commission is that the population of the world is multiplying while the church is merely adding. Addition can never keep pace with multiplication."[59] As a bit of a representative of, and spokesperson for, the emerging missional church, I'm often hounded with the issue of numbers and the relatively small sizes of the churches in the EMC. My response is that not only is it happening and flying under the radar of church growth enthusiasts (see the figures in ch. 2), but given the right conditions, and if Apostolic Genius can be recovered and applied, I promise its critics that things will be different soon. If the EMC in the West can truly activate Apostolic Genius, then all means of measurement that we currently use will pale in comparison. Church-growth-style addition can never even hope to match a truly missional-incarnational movement manifesting Apostolic Genius for impact. Not a hope!

And if we doubt the power of organic growth, we are wise to remember that each one of us started as a sperm fusing with an egg. And here we are, over significant time, with trillions of cells hanging out together. Organic multiplication begins a whole lot slower than addition, but in the end it is infinitely more effective. Epidemiologists understand this all too well. When the SARS virus broke out a few years ago, there were only about a thousand cases reported worldwide. Why, then, did it distress the world economy and almost bankrupt many international airlines? It is because that given the right conditions for contagion, it could have killed 20 percent of the world's population. We were right to fear it. And yet ideas travel just like the SARS virus. They start small and, given the right conditions, spread like mad.

Without going into this in a deep way, the cybernetic concept of memes provides us with an extremely useful theory about the genesis, reproduction, and development of ideas.[60] Essentially, a meme is to the world of ideas what genes are to the world of biology—they encode ideas in easily reproducible form. In this theory, a memeplex is a complex of memes (ideas) that constitute the inner structure of an ideology or belief system. And like DNA, they seek to replicate themselves by mutation into evolving forms of ideas by adding, developing, or shedding memes as the situation requires.[61] Why this idea is so valuable is that the memeplex has the capacity to reproduce itself by embedding itself in the receiver's brain, whence it passes itself on to other brains via human communication. Sounds rather strange at first, doesn't it? But actually we experience this every day. We all know the feeling of being "captivated by an idea," don't we? We get caught

59. Walter Henrichsen, quoted in N. Cole, *Cultivating a Life for God* (Elgin, IL: Brethren Press, 1999), 22.

60. The initiative for the idea of memes came from biologist Richard Dawkins in his provocative book *The Selfish Gene* (Oxford: Oxford University Press, 1976), ch. 11.

61. To further explore these ideas, I suggest that the reader do a Web search on "memes," and see where that leads. A good place to start is Principia Cybernetica at http://pespmc1 .vub.ac.be/.

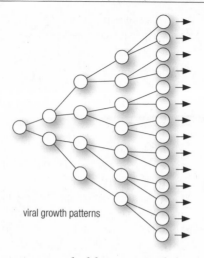

viral growth patterns

up into its life. It seems to get a hold on us. And then, if it is a particularly compelling idea, we pass it onto other people. In some way that is exactly the way we all got caught up into the gospel and thus adopted a biblical worldview/memeplex.

The gospel itself can be viewed as a very powerful memeplex that can travel just like a viral epidemic if it is given the right conditions. But especially important here is that Apostolic Genius, the memeplex of the Christian church, is actually latent in the gospel itself. As such, it feels that when we as Christians come across the ideas that are part of Apostolic Genius, we feel like we "remember" them. I ask the reader to be attentive to the phenomena as presented in this book and to test in yourself if you did not already "know" that they were true but lacked words for them. On hearing about Apostolic Genius, many people have said, "I feel that I already know this but have somehow forgotten it." I believe this is exactly how churches in extreme adaptive challenges, like the church in Communist China, actually rediscover Apostolic Genius. It was already there "in them" as part of the gospel and the work of the Spirit.

Seth Godin, a marketing guru, building on the theory of memes, coined the phrase *ideaviruses* to try and articulate hyperbolic growth in relation to marketing and ideas in general.[62] In Godin's conception, "an ideavirus is a big idea that runs amok across the target audience."[63] It's a fashionable idea that captures the thinking and imagination of a section of the population, teaching and influencing and changing everyone it touches. Godin claims that in our rapidly/instantly changing world, the art and science of

---

62. Download Seth Godin's material for free at www.ideavirus.com.

63. Seth Godin, *Unleashing the Ideavirus,* at http://www.sethgodin.com/ideavirus/01-getit .html, 14.

building, launching, and profiting from ideaviruses is the next frontier. He asks, "Have you ever heard of Hotmail? Ever used it? If so, it's not because Hotmail ran a lot of TV ads (they didn't). It's because the manifesto of free email got to you. It turned into an ideavirus. Someone you know and trust probably infected you with it."[64] Have you ever watched how a computer virus can spread through the Internet and jam the world's computers in one week? So an ideavirus is simply the notion that an idea can become contagious, in precisely the same way that a virus does.[65]

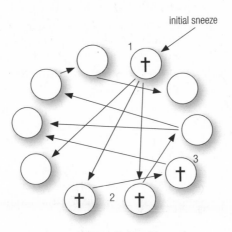

"Sneezing" the Gospel

In this sense the gospel, too, travels just like a virus. It is "sneezed" and then passed on through further sneezing from one person to the other. All that is needed are the right conditions and the appropriate relationships into which we can "sneeze." These conditions might arise from a complex interrelationship between our communication with culturally resonant ideas through meaningful relationships, using new media, understanding human need for the gospel, engaging the existential search that is going on, and facing the adaptive challenge of the twenty-first century.

Strangely, it appears we can learn not only from Al Qaeda, but from the SARS virus as well.

64. Ibid.

65. A message's capacity to transform en masse depends largely on the right kind of people in the mix, the currency of our message, the audiences' receptivity to its meaning, and the correct social conditions. At some point we reach a tipping point, a critical mass, and things can take off. Malcolm Gladwell explores social epidemics in his outstanding book *The Tipping Point: How Little Things Can Make a Big Difference* (New York: Back Bay Books, 2002).

When you add all this to the idea that the whole world is profoundly interconnected, you can see the sheer power of ideaviruses. Six degrees of separation is the theory that any one person is connected to any other person on the planet through a chain of acquaintances that has no more than five intermediaries. "American sociologist Stanley Milgram devised a way to test the theory. . . . He randomly selected people in the mid-West to send packages to a stranger located in Massachusetts. The senders knew the recipient's name, occupation, and general location but not the specific address. They were instructed to send the package to a person they knew on a first-name basis who they thought was most likely, out of all their friends, to know the target personally. That person would do the same, and so on, until the package was personally delivered to its target recipient. Although the participants expected the chain to include at least a hundred intermediaries," [66] to get it package delivered, it averaged only six. Hence the popular phrase "six degrees of separation."

Following metabolic viral patterns, it would not take long to get the job done. The critical factor is that *we consistently stick at it* all the way through. This gospel, or mission, as ideavirus is hyperbolic growth in action, and missional leaders cannot afford to ignore it. In fact, to ignore it is to quite possibly miss the chance of truly evangelizing our world, because through mere addition the task is simply impossible. With the dawn of the network and the age of new technology and media, we have a great opportunity to relearn how to do mission organically, traversing the rhythms of life, memes, and relationships.

Let's Talk about Sex

One more thing needs to be noted before we conclude this chapter, and that is the issue of reproduction and reproduce-*ability*. All organic life seeks to reproduce and perpetuate itself through reproduction. In the case of bio-logical life, it is specifically through sexual reproduction and not cloning or replication. This distinction is significant, because generally when churches and denominations have undertaken church-planting strategies and pro-grams, their approaches have been more consistent with the procedures of cloning than with those of sexual reproduction. The result is that of merely duplicating and copying the original model or system from which it came. The "daughter" church is, in effect, an attempt at an exact replica of the

66. R. Todd Stephens, "Knowledge: The Essence of Meta Data: Six Degrees of Separation of Our Assets," *DM Review Online*, Sept. 2004, at http://www.dmreview.com/editorial/dmreview /print_action.cfm?articleId=1010448. See also ibid., 47ff., for a great exploration of this idea as it relates to the adoption of ideas.

"mother" church. This practice not only seeds Constantinian DNA into the new church community, but it also minimizes the internal missional variety that is needed to ensure maximum impact in a different missional setting.

But why reproduction and not cloning? Not only because it is more pleasurable but because "(c)omplex adaptive systems become more vulnerable as they become more homogenous. To thwart homogeneity, nature relies on the rich structural recombination triggered by sexual reproduction. . . . Sexual reproduction maximizes diversity."[67] Chromosome combinations are randomly matched in variant pairings, thereby generating more permutations and variety in the offspring. And this permutation also enriches and strengthens the organism against enemies (e.g., harmful diseases and parasites) and arms the offspring with novel DNA combinations while maintaining the species. We all know what happens in a closed genetic pool. Serious deformities and weaknesses result from inbreeding. Healthy reproduction therefore draws upon a much larger gene pool and thereby invigorates the living system by giving rise to more possibilities in the genetic makeup. It is also what makes us unique. Cloning cannot do this:

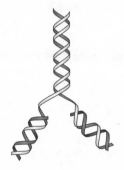

But there is another factor that we need to consider here and that is the issue of reproduce-*ability*: the capacity of living systems to be able to perpetuate themselves through simple, reproducible mechanisms. Deeply associated with living systems, movements, and networks, *reproducibility* needs to be built into the initiating model through the embedding of a simple guiding system that ensures that the organization will continue and evolve through a process akin to sexual reproduction, whereby we share new genetic information and yet remain the same species. The answer is again found in the idea of mDNA. This has to be the simple, reproducible, guiding agent of any new endeavor, and it needs to encode all that is required for healthy expressions of church. Garrison is right in saying that that we will probably accomplish exactly what we set out to accomplish. "'If you want to see

67. Pascale, Millemann, and Gioja, *Surfing the Edge of Chaos*, 28–29.

churches planted, then you must set out to plant churches.' The same axiom can be taken a step further to say, 'If you want to see *reproducing* churches planted, then you must set out to plant *reproducing* churches.'"[68] He is, here, onto the insight of innate reproducibility in the initiating DNA.

The new church must itself be adaptable enough to be enriched by the gene pool of other systems (other movements and social forces) while maintaining the original charism, or founding gift. After all, this is how we reproduce. Our offspring are unique but retain some of our individual characteristics but also all the characteristics that make us *human*. It is reproduction that ensures uniqueness, development, and variety, in order to maximize survivability in various conditions. Curtis Sergeant suggests that the way the Chinese underground church has maximized internal (genetic) variety is that new converts are not incorporated and absorbed into existing churches. Instead they form the basis of a new church and create a form of ecclesial genetic variety geared around reproduction.

But there is more for us to consider here: when one looks again to the phenomenal movements of the early church and China, one discovers that they were driven to the idea, and practice, of simplicity. As one Russian Baptist pastor in the time of Stalin remarked, after their buildings were confiscated and their religion outlawed, they were driven to *"eliminate all that which does not matter."* They had to rediscover the faith in utter, uncluttered simplicity. And this was perhaps a great gift to the Russian church. Gone were the beloved institutions of the church, gone were the buildings and public worship services, and in this situation the church was forced to discover itself anew. Amazingly, this small Baptist church went underground and emerged sixty years later as an underground movement numbering around 20,000 people. Again, it was driven to discover Apostolic Genius embedded within itself, latent but forgotten, and filled with apostolic potency and life.

If we are to recover our latent Apostolic Genius in the West, we need to ask exactly the same question of ourselves. What is the irreducible minimum of the faith? What can be done away with? What is too complex and heavy to carry into a new missional situation and an adaptive challenge? We too need to eliminate the things that don't matter. But why is this so? Because so many of these institutions that have encrusted the faith weigh us down and are themselves *irreproducible*. Recall the introduction to chapter 3, where one of the "gifts" that persecution bestows on the church is to minimize the theological clutter that so easily obscures the essential gospel. This theological distillation that takes place in a context of adaptive challenge allows the whole movement to access its essential message and then reproduce it in an easily "sneezed" form. This applies not only to the gospel itself, but to the whole idea of church. It becomes quite "simple."

68. Garrison, *Church Planting Movements*, 181.

Take for instance the predominant idea of attractional church in the church growth mode. If we wished to start a church plant on the assumption that we need to look like the local megachurch, with all its polished professionalism, great worship bands, exceptional communication, fully staffed children and youth ministry, effective cell programs, and all around attractive appeal, then for the most part, it is *simply not reproducible*—at least not by the vast majority of average Christians. Whether we intend it or not, the implicit message of this medium says that if you want to start a church, then you will need all these things if you wish to be effective. Well, the fact is that most people can't put together a show like that—and it is a fact that we have had church growth and megachurch for well over thirty years now and the overwhelming majority of the 485,000 churches in the United States remain under eighty per congregation, while laboring under the guilt of failure to perform like the bigger churches. Let's face it squarely: it is darn hard to reproduce a Saddleback or a Willow Creek, as remarkable as those churches are. A church like that, with all its professional departments, charismatic leaders, large staffing, and financial resources, simply cannot be easily reproduced. If we put this up as the sole model of effective church, the net effect will be to marginalize most people from ministry and church planting, and it will effectively put a contraceptive on the reproductive mechanism of the church. It will certainly stifle genuine people movements, because it necessitates a professional concept of ministry with massive buildings and resources.

Once again, I don't wish to be heard as being unnecessarily critical of church growth or question the sincerity of those who operate by its lights. The point here is that it simply must not be the only arrow in our quiver. And it has been that for far too long; as a result we have become more than a little inbred. Even where some megachurches in the West have undertaken church-planting approaches, the offspring seem to be clones of the attractional parent church and don't have the built-in genetic variety to cope; the vast majority of these fail. Strangely enough, there are very few examples in which a megachurch has successfully started a church planting movement. We need diversity for healthy reproduction. The hegemonic sway of mechanistic church growth theory over our imaginations must be challenged if we are to be able to adapt to missional conditions in the twenty-first century. It has been said that if the only tool you have is a hammer, then everything begins to look like a nail. We need other tools. And my particular point in this section is to say that, by and large, successful church growth models aren't readily reproducible. That is why that, apart from some contexts in the United States, in Western contexts successful megachurches are few and far between, even though they exert an overwhelming influence.

And before a whole lot of academics say, "I told you so," let me say that exactly the same critique must be laid on the seminary. It too is innately irreproducible for exactly the same reasons. In the historical expressions of Apostolic Genius, leadership and theological development are built-in tasks of grassroots movements themselves. Theologizing, intellectual engagement, and leadership development are an integral part of the movement's discipleship in relation to God's calling and gifting. If in our practice we separate it and outsource it to professional, highly funded institutions, then it will not be long before we will not only become dependent on them, but will be unable to easily reproduce them in situations that require responsiveness and adaptability. They are generally too unwieldy and heavily institutionalized. This is not to say that we must do away with them at all. What is being said is that the critical functions that these were created to serve need to be recovered as part of the simple, internal, and reproducible function of the local church or grassroots movement.

Clearly, neither the seminary as we know it nor the attractional megachurch as we now experience it were part of the phenomenal people movements of the first few centuries. Neither of these were irreducible aspects of the significant people movements in history (think China again if this is too shocking to hear). And yet these movements are a great deal more effective than we can dream to be in our current context, in spite of our resources, institutions, and buildings. This must sound a clear warning to us as we attempt to negotiate the missional complexities of the twenty-first century. As indicated above, we need to get it right from the start—in the stem cell of the church, so to speak. Or as organizational architect Bill Broussard puts it, "revitalization is all in the setup."[69] Very hard to correct it later on—mDNA purity is vital, especially in the beginning of things.

Finally

When organic/living systems meet a genuine movement ethos that expresses itself in networked structures, if it is given the right conditions for reproducibility and exponential growth, then history is in the making. This is not to say that we can exclude the other four elements of phenomenal mDNA, but one can see that this is in itself an extremely powerful element in the equation. Even if left unguided by the other elements of Apostolic Genius, it can be used for good or evil (as in Al Qaeda and network marketing). The living system is one way in which Apostolic Genius expresses itself in the phenomenal movements of God and gospel. It is my contention that it is a fundamental part of mDNA embedded at the core of the church of Jesus Christ, against which, we must be reminded, the gates of hell will not prevail (Matt. 16:18).

69. Quoted in Pascale, Millemann, and Gioja, *Surfing the Edge of Chaos*, 209.

8

communitas, not community

That which does not kill you will make you stronger.

Friedrich Nietzsche

The ship is safest when it is in port. But that's not what ships were made for.

Paulo Coelho

It is the unknown that defines our existence. We are constantly seeking, not just for answers to our questions, but for new questions. We are explorers . . .

Cmdr. Benjamin Sisko, *Star Trek: Deep Space Nine*

In December 2004 something both dreadful and remarkable happened—the Asian tsunami that killed about 250,000 people provoked what was undoubtedly one of the most amazing explosions of worldwide generosity and compassion in recent history. Never before had so much international aid been given in any crisis. In and through the sheer horror and ordeal of the tsunami, people not only found their own humanity, but found each other in a new and remarkable way. Exactly the same phenomenon was experienced in New York on that fateful day of September 11, 2001, only to be repeated two years later when all the lights on the eastern seaboard went out. The events of 9/11 changed the world, but New York particularly underwent an elemental transformation: it shed its brash, no-nonsense persona and became a city filled with kindness and largesse.

These were manifestations of *communitas*, and it is *exactly* this aspect of the human situation that will be explored in this chapter. *Communitas*, as we shall see, takes many forms, but whatever the form, it describes accurately the type of communality or comradeship that was and is experienced in the phenomenal Jesus movements, and so is an essential element of Apostolic Genius. The persecuted church in both the early Christian movement and in China experience each other in the context of a shared ordeal that binds them together in a much deeper form of community than the one we have generally become accustomed to.

In the introduction to this section of the book, some meaning and definition was given to the concept of missional church.[1] Coming to grips with *communitas* requires that we try to work out *why* mission is indeed so central to the church's identity, purpose, and function, and *why* it seems to form one of the central aspects of mDNA and therefore Apostolic Genius.

"The Community for Me"? or "Me for the Community"?

The explorations of these questions took on a very personal form in my own experience as leader of South Melbourne Restoration Community, the story of which is conveyed in the first chapter of this book. When I look back to the early dynamics of that vibrant community, especially as it was still forming, we were functioning as missional church in a very naïve, precognitive, and instinctive kind of way. All we did was set out to build a community that was radically open and engaged with all kinds of people on the edges and fringes of society. Things happened. It was exciting—the community was focused and sharpened by a sense of destiny and mission,

---

1. The basic idea is that the church's mission is inextricably linked to the mission of God—that God is a missionary and the church is the principal historical agent of that mission in the world. What this means is that the redemptive purposes of God therefore flow right through every Christian community into all the world.

and as a result we grew in a strange and wonderful kind of way. *We were missional*, even though at the time this was as yet largely unarticulated, and because of this we experienced a remarkable form of community.

But something seemed to change as we grew and self-consciously became a more trendy, pomo, Gen-X church. For understandable reasons lots of grounded middle-class Christians from Melbourne's Bible belt moved to the inner city to be part of what God was doing—and we welcomed the newfound stability in what was to that point a very chaotic experience of *ecclesia*. They were established Christians who weren't needy. That was a wonderful change for us, and we basked in a period of sublime stability. But something shifted as we became more stable. And while we gained a lot from the participation of those wonderful people, nonetheless something significant was inadvertently lost as the church culture changed and became more middle-class and steady.

There is something about middle-class culture that seems to be contrary to authentic gospel values. And this is not a statement about middle-class people per se—I myself am from a very middle-class family—but rather to isolate some of the values and assumptions that seem to just come along as part of the deal. In a previous chapter, I noted that much of what goes by the name "middle-class" involves a preoccupation with *safety* and *security*, developed mostly in pursuit of what seems to be best for our children. And this is understandable as long as it does not become obsessive. But when these impulses of middle-class culture fuse with consumerism, as they most often do, we can add the obsession with *comfort* and *convenience* to the list. And this is not a good mix—at least as far as the gospel and missional church are concerned.[2]

Operating under the influence of these "bugs" in our middle-class software, our community became a marketer of particularly zesty religious goods and services, vying for the attention of discerning spiritual consum-

2. Robert Inchausti relates that Nikolai Berdyaev saw middle-classness at its most debased level as "a state of the soul characterized by a degrading clutching after security and a small-mindedness incapable of imagining a world much larger than one's own. [For him] the bourgeois didn't worship money per se, but they were addicted to personal success, security, and happiness. For these things, they willingly compromised their honor, ignored injustice, and betrayed truth, replacing these high values with trite moralisms and facile bromides that blur important distinctions and justify selfish actions. . . . The word *bourgeois* became synonymous with mean-spirited wealth, narrow-minded technological know-how, and a preoccupation with worldly success. The cultural ideals of the knight, the monk, the philosopher, and the poet were all superseded by the cultural ideal of the businessman. The will to power had been usurped by the 'will to well-being.' . . . The bourgeois did not repudiate religion but reinterpreted its value in terms of utility. The love of the poor moved to the periphery of the faith and was embraced only insofar as its didn't clash with one's own personal economic interests" (Robert Inchausti, *Subversive Orthodoxy: Rebels, Revolutionaries, and Other Christians in Disguise* [Grand Rapids: Brazos Press, 2005]), 42–43.

ers. Flattered by the numerical growth, and driven by our own middle-class agendas, we thoughtlessly followed the "gather and amuse" impulse implicit in church growth theory, and so we grew in numbers—but something primal and indispensable was lost in the bargain. We got more transfers from other churches, but the flow of conversion slowed down to a trickle and then ran completely dry. Paradoxically, we became busier than ever before, but with less and less real missional impact. We had moved from the missional idea of "me for the community and the community for the world" to the more consumptive "the community for me" and it just about destroyed us. We recovered only by recalibrating the community along fundamentally missional lines, and this was not achieved without pain and numerical loss. But in doing so, we moved from an experience of church as community to that of *communitas*.

Liminality and *Communitas*

To really come to grips with the dynamics of these primal shifts in community dynamics, I have found the anthropologist Victor Turner's ideas of *liminality* and *communitas* particularly useful.[3] Turner was an anthropologist who studied various rites of passage among African people groups and came up with the term *liminality* to describe the transition process accompanying a fundamental change of state or social position. Situations of liminality in this context can be extreme, where the participant is cast out of the normal structures of life, is humbled, disoriented, and subjected to various rites of passage, which together constitute a form of test as to whether the participant will be allowed back into society and to transition to the next level in the prevailing social structure. *Liminality* therefore applies to that situation where people find themselves in an in-between, marginal state in relation to the surrounding society, a place that could involve significant danger and disorientation, but not necessarily so.[4]

For example, in some tribes younger boys are kept under the care of the women until initiation age—around thirteen. At the appropriate time the men sneak into the female compound of the village at night and "kidnap" the lads. The boys are blindfolded, then roughed up, and herded out of the village and taken into the bush. They are then circumcised and left to

3. See Victor Turner, *The Ritual Process* (Cornell University Press, 1969), and Victor Turner, "Passages, Margins, and Poverty: Religious Symbols of Communitas," part 1, *Worship* 46 (1972).

4. And contrary to what we might think, danger can be good for us. As Corbin Carnell rightly notes, "Danger does highlight the paradoxical nature of good and evil—at least as to how we experience it. It highlights goodness and gives it a wholesome aspect that evil in itself denies" (*Bright Shadow of Reality* [Grand Rapids: Eerdmans, 1974], 109).

fend for themselves in the wild African bush for a period lasting up to six months. Once a month the elders of the tribe go to meet them to help debrief and mentor them. But on the whole they have to find both inner and outer resources to cope with the ordeal pretty much by themselves. During this shared ordeal, the initiates move from being disoriented and individualistic to developing a bond of comradeship and communality forged in the testing conditions of liminality. This sense Turner calls *communitas*. *Communitas* in his view *happens* in situations where individuals are driven to find each other through a common experience of ordeal, humbling, transition, and marginalization. It involves intense feelings of social togetherness and belonging brought about by having to rely on each other in order to survive. If the boys emerge from these experiences, they are reintroduced into the tribe as men. They are thus accorded the full status of manhood—they are no longer considered boys.

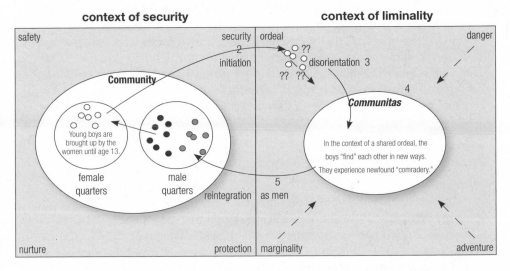

So the related ideas of liminality and *communitas* describe the dynamics of the Christian community inspired to overcome their instincts to "huddle and cuddle" and to instead form themselves around a common mission that calls them onto a dangerous journey to unknown places—a mission that calls the church to shake off its collective securities and to plunge into the world of action, where its members will experience disorientation and marginalization but also where they encounter God and one another in a new way. *Communitas* is therefore always linked with the experience of liminality. It involves adventure and movement, and it describes that unique experience of *togetherness* that only really happens among a group of people inspired by the vision of a better world who actually attempt to do something about it. (Remember the response to the tsunami.) It is here where the safe, middle-class, consumerist captivity of the church is so very problematic. And it is here where the adaptive challenge of the twenty-first century could be God's invitation to the church to rediscover itself as a missional *communitas*.

While some missiologists use this idea to describe the experience of transition the church in the West is currently experiencing in moving from one state (Christendom) or mode of church to another (missional),[5] the emphasis has generally been on the new state of the church at the end of the process, and so liminality and *communitas* are viewed as temporary experiences. From my perspective, significant manifestations of Apostolic Genius teach us that liminality and *communitas* are more *the normative situation and condition* of the pilgrim people of God. This is certainly the case for the phenomenal Jesus movements in view; it is in the conditions of shared ordeal that these Jesus movements thrive and are driven to the activation of Apostolic Genius. What is clear is that both the early Christian movements and the Chinese underground church experienced liminality through being outlawed and persecuted.

In this perspective, the phenomenal Jesus movements were/are expressions of *communitas*, and not community as we normally conceive it. As far as I can discern, *communitas* is always a normative element of Apostolic Genius. The loss of it leads to a diminution of the total phenomenon of Apostolic Genius—the life force of the authentic Christian movement wherever it truly manifests.

The Bible and *Communitas*

This claim that *communitas* and liminality are normative for God's people stirred up a bit of a storm in a recent speaking tour. Some people in the audience responded with some vehemence when Michael Frost and I proposed this way of understanding Christian community. This negative response forced a deep reflection on the validity of these ideas, but after much searching I have to say that I have not fundamentally changed my mind. On the contrary, this clash of conceptions in relation to the purpose of the church has forced me to conclude that for many of our critics Christian community has become little more than a quiet and reflective soul-space (as in Alt Worship circles) or a spiritual buzz (as in charismatic circles) for people trying to recuperate from an overly busy, consumerist lifestyle. But is this really what the church is meant to be about? Is this our grand purpose—to be a sort of refuge for recovering work addicts and experience junkies? A sort of spiritual hospital or entertainment center? I believe that the reason for the strong response in our critics is that they actually did "get the message"

5. Roxburgh, *Missionary Congregation*, ch. 2.

about missional church but didn't like it because, in this case, it called them out of a religion of quiet moments in quiet places (or passive entertainment) and into liminality and engagement.

But the primary reason for not changing my mind is not because I simply disagree about their sense of the purpose of God's people (I do), but rather because I have come to believe that *communitas* is thoroughly biblical and is inextricably linked to Apostolic Genius. When we survey scripture with liminality and *communitas* in mind, we must conclude that the theologically most fertile sections were in those times of extremity, when people were well out of their comfort zones. The main clusters of revelation seem to come in times of liminality (e.g., patriarchs, the Torah, the prophets, Jesus, Paul, John, etc.), and most of the miracles in the Bible are recorded in situations of liminality (e.g., the exodus, exile, the Gospels, and Acts). And when we consider the stories that have inspired the people of God throughout the ages, we find that they are stories involving adventures of the spirit in the context of challenge. In fact, that is *exactly why* they inspire (e.g., Hebrews 11).

Take Abram for instance, who with his entire extended family (estimated to be about seventy people) is called by God to leave house and home and all that is familiar, to undertake a very risky journey to a land that at that stage remained a mere promise by an invisible God. And when we look at the various experiences they have along the way, stories that have shaped all subsequent faith (e.g., the offering of Isaac), we see that they are not safe little bedtime stories. Rather they call us to a dangerous form of faithfulness that echoes the faithfulness of Abraham (Gal. 3:15ff.; Heb. 11:9–13). Or when we explore the profoundly liminal exodus experience, we find that this very tricky journey permanently shaped the people of God, and continues to do so to this very day. It was also the context of the substantial revelation of God in his covenant with his people. The same can be said of the exile into Babylon many centuries later—this was an extreme situation that changed the whole way Israel related to its God, and still does. The prophets spoke the Word of God into such contexts of extremity, and it was precisely when the people of God settled down and forgot the Lord (Deut. 4:23–31) that they had to be spiritually disturbed once again by the prophets. To awaken the people to their lost calling, the prophets recalled the dangerous memories about fires on the mountain and pursuing armies and a God who lovingly redeems a people to himself and enters into a sacred and eternal covenant with them. This sounds pretty liminal to me.

When we consider the lives and ministries of Samuel, Elijah, Samson, and David and his band and ask what conditions they encountered, we come up with the consistent themes of liminality and *communitas*. And when we come to the New Testament, we need look only to the life of Jesus, who had nowhere to rest or lay his head, and who discipled his followers *on the road* in the dangerous conditions of an occupied land and against a hostile and dodgy religious elite.

To find these themes in abundance, look at the life of Paul. He describes it pretty vividly for us in 2 Corinthians. Whippings, beatings, imprisonment, and shipwrecks can hardly be called safe, secure, comfortable, and convenient, and yet through these experiences he and his apostolic band totally realign the course of history around the gospel of Jesus Christ. The book of Acts is so brimful with *communitas* and liminality that it reads like a rollicking adventure story.

And the point of all this is that these are prescriptive descriptions for the church because it seems that liminality and *communitas* are normative for the pilgrim people of God in the Bible and in the Jesus movements of history. It is so deeply "there" that I am simply at a loss to explain how we lost this perspective. I have come to the conclusion that the clash of images of the church experienced in the recent ministry trip just serves to highlight how far we have moved from the biblical imagination and experience of church.

It's Everywhere! It's Everywhere!

Having seen *communitas* for what it is, it is hard not to spot this type of communal experience in so many aspects of our lives. Already mentioned are those times of great social upheaval and disaster that awaken something in us and call us to find ourselves in a new way: the tsunami, as tragic as it was, called something really good out of us. But *communitas* can be found in far more common and less hazardous situations, like sports teams, where a group of otherwise individualistic people band together to achieve a common task. They become a team around a common challenge. This is mirrored in common work practices where a group of people in a corporate situation are called together to do something that they could not do alone. The deadline in this situation creates the ordeal wherein people working together can become truly good colleagues. The same dynamic is at work in adventure camps and in short-term missions in which people are taken out of their normal safe environments and put in situations of disorientation and marginalization. So many people who go to visit the slums of Mexico are deeply and profoundly changed through that experience.

The devotees of the Burning Man phenomenon that takes place annually in Black Rock, Nevada, experience the mystical joy of liminality and *communitas* that binds them together as they share radically in what they call a "gift economy."[6] Burning Man, they claim, "is a community, that although

6. www.burningman.com/whatisburningman/

temporary for six days each year, remains connected during the rest of the year to keep the fire burning."

> There are no rules about how one must behave or express oneself at this event (save the rules that serve to protect the health, safety, and experience of the community at large); rather, it is up to each participant to decide how they will contribute and what they will give to this community. The event takes place on an ancient lakebed, known as the playa. By the time the event is completed and the volunteers leave, sometimes nearly a month after the event has ended, there will be no trace of the city that was, for a short time, the most populous town in the entire county. Art is an unavoidable part of this experience, and in fact, is such a part of the experience that Larry Harvey, founder of the Burning Man project, gives a theme to it each year, to encourage a common bond to help tie each individual's contribution together in a meaningful way. Participants are encouraged to find a way to help make the theme come alive, whether it is through a large-scale art installation, a theme camp, gifts brought to be given to other individuals, costumes, or any other medium that one comes up with. The Burning Man project has grown from a small group of people gathering spontaneously to a community of over 25,000 people. The impact of the Burning Man experience has been so profound that a culture has formed around it. This culture pushes the limits of Burning Man and has led to people banding together nationwide (even internationally) and putting on their own events, in attempt to rekindle that magic feeling that only being part of this community can provide.[7]

We will explore some the mythic dimensions of *communitas* in specific movies and literature below, but note here that while not actually using the language of liminality and *communitas*, a great many movies are actually built around these themes. We all know the storyline so well, don't we? A man is on the run from rogue elements in the CIA. In a situation of desperation he gets assistance from a bystander, who also happens to be a beautiful woman, and so she gets implicated by association with him. They hit the road together. Dodging bullets and keeping one step ahead of their pursuers, the man and woman, in having to rely on each other, actually get to "find each other" and in doing so eventually resolve the situation. In fact, most adventure stories involve a group of disparate people who have to work together to overcome danger, from *The Bourne Supremacy* (with Matt Damon) to the heart-wrenching *Saving Private Ryan*, from Russell Crowe's great performance in *Master and Commander* to Zion's courageous stand against the machines in the *Matrix* series. *Communitas* features in just about every adventure movie. These stories have real power over us, because they awaken something very deep inside us—the abiding human need for adventure, journey, and comradeship. What this teaches us is that in contexts

7. Ibid.

where people face a common evil threat and potential obliteration, people can and do find new depths of their own humanity. This is true not only in the movies. It is true there because it is true to life. Liminality can bring out the very best in us because danger highlights the paradoxical nature of good and evil—at least as to how we experience it. It highlights goodness and gives it a wholesome aspect that evil in itself denies. Or as the ever insightful C. S. Lewis said, "I do not think the forest would be so bright, nor the water so warm, nor love so sweet, if there were no danger in the lakes."[8]

While danger and crisis necessarily expose a person or a group to the possibility of destruction or failure, they also provide an opportunity for people to find the inner resources to overcome evil and enrich themselves as a result. And relationships develop into comradeships in such situations.[9] Without using the word *liminality*, David Bosch rightly notes that

> strictly speaking one ought to say that the Church is always in a state of crisis and that its greatest shortcoming is that it is only occasionally aware of it. This ought to be the case because of the abiding tension between the church's essential nature and its empirical condition. . . . That there were so many centuries of crisis-free existence for the Church was therefore an abnormality. . . . And if the atmosphere of crisislessness still lingers on in many parts of the West, this is simply the result of a dangerous delusion. Let us also know that to encounter crisis is to encounter the possibility of truly being the Church.[10]

But it's not all about danger and crisis. There are more chilled versions of *communitas* that have real potency for missional restructuring of communities. Mark Scandrette is an amazing urban missionary in bohemian San Francisco. One of the projects he has helped initiate is a mural art cooperative that has come together to paint walls that the city council gives them for a mural piece. This is how it goes: they secure the project with the council. They then bring the cooperative (made up largely of non-Christian people) together to decide what they want to say through their art. After much discussion about politics, religion, meaning, etc., they decide on a theme. Then they divvy up the mural so that each member of the co-op gets a section. It is their task to design their part of the mural and then make it fit in with both the general theme and the work of the other members of the team. Having done the conceptual design, they then take their Saturdays off, and armed with stepladders and paint, they spend their whole day going up and down the ladder, painting, chatting to each other, sharing lunch and a few beers at the end of the day. The project could take three months

8. C. S. Lewis, quoted in Corbin Carnell, *Bright Shadow of Reality*, 109.
9. Winston Churchill was reported to have said that it is an exhilarating thing to be shot at, and *missed!*
10. Bosch, *Transforming Mission*, 2.

to complete, but by the end of it, they have delved deeply into each other's lives, explored many themes that relate to life, God, and spirituality, and have become friends.[11]

Other versions of this might be a communal vegetable garden, political activism, building houses together with a group of friends for the needy (as in Habitat for Humanity), or just cleaning up the city with a group of other people interested in the environment. It's not all that hard. Here are wonderful examples of how we might, together with others, take a learning journey and enter into a host of marvelous conversations. Here is *communitas* in everyday life.

The Mythos of *Communitas*

To try and bed this concept down, let me return briefly to literature and film, where we can probe the potential of missional *communitas* in the light of its mythic depiction in some of the powerful stories and movies that have captured our imagination and inspired us.[12]

The Fellowship of the Ring

Let us consider the mythic truth in J. R. R. Tolkien's remarkable story *The Lord of the Rings*. The story begins with a young Hobbit called Frodo, who through circumstance (or is it something much deeper than that?) comes into possession of the Ring of Power. This magic ring was made by Sauron the Dark Lord, and he made it to rule the other Rings of Power that he deviously distributed to the various people of Middle-earth. The Ring

11. Turner did a study on the role of artists in society. He saw these clear examples of liminality and *communitas*. In a quote ascribed to him, he says, "Prophets and artists tend to be liminal and marginal people, 'edgemen,' who strive with a passionate sincerity to rid themselves of the clichés associated with status and role-playing and to enter into vital relations with other men in fact or imagination."

12. To say that a story is mythic is not to say that it is mere fantasy. Quite the opposite: by appealing to the power of myth, we give ordinary, everyday things new life and meaning. This is because myth reaches into the innermost levels of human consciousness. And it resonates with us because of its universal and fundamental truth. Listen to C. S. Lewis, the story-telling genius, about the meaning of myth: "The value of the myth is that it takes all the things we know and restores to them the rich significance which has been hidden by the 'veil of familiarity.' The child enjoys his cold meats (otherwise dull to him) by pretending it is a buffalo, just killed with his own bow and arrow. And the child is wise. The real meat comes back to him far tastier for having been dipped in a story: you might say that only then is it the real meat. If you are tired of the old real landscape, look at it in a mirror. By putting bread, gold, horse, apple, or the very roads into a myth [Lewis is here referring to Tolkien's *Lord of the Rings*], we do not retreat from reality, we rediscover it" (C. S. Lewis, "Tolkien's Lord of the Rings," in *Essay Collection and Other Short Pieces* [London: HarperCollins, 2000], 525–26).

was thus made to assemble all the powers under the supreme influence of evil and concentrate them under Sauron himself. It has a very alluring but corrosive influence, and none can handle it without being deeply changed by it. In all Middle-earth, perhaps only Hobbits are innocent enough to not be entirely destroyed by the lure of its coercive power, and even they come under its power and are eventually tainted by it.

Anyhow, the task falls to Frodo to get this ring to the house of Elrond, and against all his innate hobbitish instincts for safety and security, he agrees to undertake the adventure. You need to know that Hobbits rarely, if ever, travel out of the Shire. They are a quaint village folk who like six meals a day and live in burrowlike homes. They are not an adventurous folk. Samwise Gamgee insinuates himself into the journey, and the two set off. Eventually they are joined by Frodo's cousins, the mischievous pair Merry and Pippin. On the road they encounter a dreadful and overpowering evil in the form of the powerful Ringwraiths, Black Riders who are sent by Sauron to recover the Ring.

Eventually, through mortal danger (another horrid encounter with the Ringwraiths), they do make it to the Council of Elrond, the Elf king. And there at the council it is decided that none dare touch the Ring for fear of being corrupted by it. And Frodo, having recently recovered from being poisoned by a Ringwraith's sword, and following his Hobbit-like sense of duty, agrees to take the Ring to Mount Doom, to the black heart of Mordor, Sauron's realm. This is a seemingly impossible task, and the prospect of success is very slim. But it is decided that against the odds, they will undertake the task. At the council, the Fellowship of the Ring is formed. It is made up of the Hobbits, Aragorn (the exiled king), Boromir (an honorable but desperate human prince who is lured to the power of the Ring), Gimli the Dwarf, Legolas the Elf, and Gandalf the wizard. It is also important to note that this is a rather unlikely "fellowship," because Dwarves and Elves traditionally do not get on at all. The humans are as divided as their kingdoms, and the Hobbits are not warriors by any stretch of the imagination. However, against all odds, eventually the combined skills and sheer willpower of this strange *fellowship* wins the day.

The point for this brief retelling of this great story is to highlight the fact that the "Fellowship of the Ring" actually becomes a *real* fellowship, a comradeship, only as it undergoes great struggle and hardship in the face of overwhelming evil. By undertaking this seemingly impossible task, and by facing hardships *together*, the group actually becomes a *communitas*. They discover each other in a way they would not, or could not, in any other circumstance. Here is the mythic representation of mission (nothing less than the destruction of evil in the world), discipleship (constantly choosing goodness in the face of overwhelming opposition), and *communitas* (becoming a great community together in pursuit of a mission). The Elf and the Dwarf become inseparable friends, and the Hobbits become something they never could have been if they remained in the safety of the Shire. They are bound to each other, and they truly *find* each other, in the context of an arduous but common mission.

Artificial Environments and the Church

Hopefully, by now you have got the idea. But how does chaos theory highlight the role of *communitas* and liminality in shaping the church's life and structure?[13] We know from living systems theory that all living systems will tend toward equilibrium (and thus closer to death) if they fail to respond adequately to their environments. The law of requisite variety, an important law of cybernetics, states that "the survival of any living system depends on its capacity to *cultivate* (not just tolerate) adaptability and diversity in its internal structure."[14] The system in equilibrium simply hasn't developed the internal resources or mechanisms to respond adequately to adaptive challenges when they come along and therefore faces potential demise. Hence, we can say that the survival of living systems favors heightened adrenaline levels, attentiveness, and experimentation.

For example, "fish in an aquarium can swim, breed, obtain food with minimal effort, and remain safe from predators. But as all aquarium owners know, such fish are excruciatingly sensitive to even the slightest disturbances in the fishbowl." Owners have to regularly clean the fish tank, monitor the temperature, watch the pH, and feed the fish. This is because there is no natural ecosystem in the fishbowl—it is an artificial environment. "On the other hand, fish in the sea have to work much harder to sustain themselves and they are subject to many more threats. But because they have learned how to cope with more variation" (temperatures, food supplies, predators, etc.), "they are more much more robust when faced with challenge."[15]

Many of us have enjoyed the movie *Finding Nemo*, where young Nemo is captured by a fish collector, and Marlin, his ever fretful dad, sets out to find and rescue him. Buoyed by the companionship of a friendly but forgetful fish named Dory, the overly cautious father embarks on a dangerous trek and finds himself the unlikely hero of an epic journey to rescue his son—who hatches a few daring plans of his own to return safely home. *Finding Nemo* is itself a great story of *communitas*, because many creatures join together to aid in the rescue of the young fish, but my focus here is more on the artificial environment that Nemo has been taken to. Let's examine for a

13. See addendum for an overview on the perspectives of chaos theory as it relates to mission.
14. Pascale, Millemann, and Gioja, *Surfing the Edge of Chaos*, 20.
15. Ibid.

moment the action of the other creatures when Nemo is first introduced from the ocean into the aquarium—they all recoil from him, fearing that he will bring diseases from the dangerous ocean and infect the fish tank. Unscrubbed, he is a danger to the fish in the tank, because living in the safe environment of the tank they can no longer adapt to variation and danger, including normal bugs that their sea cousins cope with very well. So Pierre the Prawn is called forth from his hideaway and subjects Nemo to a thorough cleanup. Only then will the other fish dare to come close and chat with the disoriented youngster. Life in the fish tank is secure, except when the nasty dentist forgets to clean the tank or to feed them, but on the whole life just goes on, even though it is a bit sterile and boring. But some fish dream of escape and long to face the risky freedom of the ocean again.

Finding Nemo contains some lessons for us: without any real engagement with the "outside world," churches quickly become sheltered artificial environments, ecclesial fish tanks that are safeguarded from the danger and disturbances in the surrounding environment. They become closed systems with their own peculiar cultures that have little relational, social, and cultural associations to the world outside (and we call this holiness). People coming in are perceived to be introducing worldly bugs into the church. So they "clean them up" quick. To push the metaphor just a little further, these closed systems are generally maintained by people, themselves significantly cloistered from the world, who feed the insiders and keep things stable, nice, clean, and free from disturbances. I don't intend to be mean and cynical here, but does this not at least sound like more than a hint of the average church? Honestly? My own experience says it does. And once again this does not imply that God is not to be found in such places—clearly he is. But it does seem that he is more often found in these places by the "found" and not by the "lost," because the "lost" can't seem to find their way to it.

Want to test this? I heard recently that research in New Zealand indicated that 80 percent of the kids brought up in Christian youth groups who then go on to university lose their faith in the first year! When this was mentioned to youth workers in America on a recent trip there, they confirmed that the attrition rate was similar in the United States. These are startling figures. And even if the statistics vary from country to country, we know this to be true. In youth groups we entertain the kids with loud music and games and teach them variations of "Jesus loves me this I know for the Bible tells me so" and then wonder why they can't cope in the more caustic environment of the university. Talk about an artificial environment.

The problem is that when a system is closed and artificial, and has generally not cultivated adaptability and internal variety, it will ultimately deteriorate toward equilibrium. And in living systems total equilibrium means death—if your body is in perfect equilibrium you are officially . . .

kaput. Contrary to what we might feel, danger and risk can be good, even necessary, for us. Liminality can either create *communitas* or it can destroy us. Risk is the price we pay for genuine adventure, and it was Alfred North Whitehead who once remarked that without adventure, civilization is in full decay.[16] The same is equally true for the church. And once again, it is largely because we have structured community in isolation from any real engagement with the world. We are missing a *communitas* experience because we are missing the missional component that takes us out of our safety zones into risky engagement with the world.

Thriving in the Ocean

There is much to learn from chaos and living systems theory in relation to *communitas* because these disciplines teach us that engaging outside the fishbowl is actually essential to organizational health. Living systems theory says that:

1. *Equilibrium is a precursor to death.* "When a living system is in a state of equilibrium, it is less responsive to changes occurring around it. This places it at maximum risk."[17] This correlates to the situation in the organizational lifecycle when organizations tend to overregulate, lose dynamism, inhabit unresponsive structures, and degenerate in terms of output. In this state, they are in effect moving *toward* equilibrium. When the Christendom mode of church fails to respond to outside stimuli by disengaging from the liminal experience and becomes purely self-referential, then you can be sure it is on its way out. In other words, it has lost its missional focus, which should drive it outside its own boundaries. In so many churches the mission of the church has actually become the maintenance of the institution itself. This was never Jesus's intention. Our goal in organizing as a people is not to set up, preserve, and maximize an institution over its life cycle, but to extend God's mission to the world. Our primary aim is not to perpetuate the church as an institution, but to follow Jesus into his mission in the world. "Christianity is concerned with the unfolding of the Kingdom of God in this world, not the longevity of organizations."[18] When we keep the mission in mind, the organic ideas about Christianity and church life will flow quite easily. When we have the institution of the church in mind, machinelike approaches are bound to follow, because its innate mechanism of responsiveness (mission)

16. Quoted in ibid., 21.
17. Ibid., 6.
18. Easum, *Unfreezing Moves*, 17.

is effectively taken out of the equation. *Mission is, and must be, the organizing principle of the church.*

2. *"In the face of a threat, or when galvanized by compelling opportunity, living things move toward the edge of chaos."*[19] That is, they move away from stability and equilibrium toward a condition of openness and creativity. This condition evokes higher levels of mutation and experimentation, and in that state fresh new solutions are more likely to be found, because that is exactly how nature advances and ensures survival in the face of threat. We are facing significant threats to our survival. What we are finding now is that we are beginning to move toward the edge of chaos and to begin experimenting with new modes of church. This is precisely why the missional church paradigm is being taken seriously at this point in time and probably why you are reading this book. It is part of the adaptive-learning process and a key indicator that the system is beginning to respond. The reason is that the mission context all around us does not afford us the luxury of stability, location, status quo, and familiarity. Nor does it allow us to maintain the false distinction between sacred and secular and therefore to focus on the sacred.[20] When we engage genuinely with this mission context, we move toward the edge of chaos, and this results in all sorts of experimentations and innovations. Hence, we are in our day seeing a flourishing of new forms of church and new ways of engaging people in mission. Exciting!

3. When this excitation takes place, and is held in that state long enough for the system to respond to outside conditions (be they threat or opportunity), the components of living systems *self-organize,* and as a result new forms and repertoires *emerge* from the turmoil.[21] It is the genius that God has built into life itself: the ability to organize at higher levels of intelligence given the right conditions. In life creativity and adaptability express themselves through the spontaneous emergence of novelty at critical points of instability. War is a good example—as horrific as it is, it is an adaptive challenge that usually spawns new innovations in technology and human learning.

4. "Living systems cannot be *directed* along a linear path. Unforeseen consequences are inevitable."[22] Try herding cats or butterflies. Human nature itself is profoundly unpredictable—that is the meaning of history or why we watch the news every night. It is because we simply do not know what each day will bring. The challenge is not to direct living systems, but to *disturb* them in a manner that approximates the

19. Pascale, Millemann, and Gioja, *Surfing the Edge of Chaos,* 6.
20. Easum, *Unfreezing Moves,* 21.
21. Pascale, Millemann, and Gioja, *Surfing the Edge of Chaos,* 6.
22. Ibid.

desired outcome and then for leadership to try and focus the intention by the use of meaning and vision. This process of disturbing the system is a critical function of leadership. It is about creating conditions in which change, adaptation, and innovation will take place.

In addition to holding a clear vision, missional leadership involves facilitating the emergence of novelty by building and nurturing networks of communications; creating a learning culture in which questioning is encouraged and innovation is rewarded; creating a climate of trust and mutual support; and recognizing viable novelty when it emerges, while allowing the freedom to make mistakes. It is for this reason that Roxburgh and Romanuk can say that the *role of leadership within the church is to cultivate environments wherein the Spirit of God might call forth and unleash the missional imagination of the people of God.*[23]

The Future and the Shaping of Things to Come

Cultivating a vigorous transformative vision can also create liminality along with the resultant *communitas*. Fritz Roethlisberger, late professor at Harvard Business School and a pioneer in the field of organizational behavior, observed: "Most people think of the future as the ends and the present as the means, whereas in fact, the present is the ends and the future the means."[24] Translated, Roethlisberger is telling us that holding a definite sense of vision (a preferred future) and mission informs and alters how people think and how they will behave in the present. Viewed this way, the future is a means to alter behavior. The new behavior shapes the ends, which in turn alter the future, and the spiral continues.

One does not creep up on a big future. Rather, the future is boldly declared in a vision and serves as the catalyst for all that follows. "When President Kennedy announced his famous moonwalk vision, there were no solutions to the problems that lay ahead: Congressional approval, appropriation of funds, technological breakthroughs, and the rejuvenation of NASA were still needed to fulfill the vision."[25] Kennedy's moonwalk vision, acting as a catalyst, gathered up a collection of emotions and aspirations, desire and excitement, curiosity, power, a quest for knowledge, a competitive wish to be the first country to walk on the moon, and imperialistic lust, and focused all these disparate forces to trigger unified action.[26] The same is true for Martin

23. Part of ongoing discussions and consultation.
24. Quoted in Pascale, Millemann, and Gioja, *Surfing the Edge of Chaos*, 72.
25. Ibid.
26. Ibid., 72–73.

Luther King Jr.'s "I have a dream" speech. It acted as a strange attractor to provoke and initiate action on behalf of that vision.

We look back on such events as inevitable—things that just seemed to happen. But it is not so at all. We seem to lose perspective on the missional *communitas* that visions like these evoke. The authors of *Surfing the Edge of Chaos* profoundly note that "*enactment on behalf of a powerful goal alters the structure of reality.*"[27] We, the people of God, are carried forward by a vision of the future that constitutes our mission. When we are caught up into it, and pursue it, we are changed, and we go on to enact history.

This is exactly what the authors mean when they say that we must "manage from the future."[28] Managing from the future—establishing a compelling goal that draws the organization out of its comfort zone—is a key discipline in moving us to the edge of chaos and therefore is important in developing missional church. This means placing ourselves in the new future and then taking a series of steps, not in order to get there someday, but as if you are there, or almost there, *now*. This is exactly the perspective of the kingdom of God in the New Testament. In saying that the future (eschatological) kingdom of God is already present in our midst, we are called to act in the knowledge that it is already here *now* and yet will be completed *then*. And so we are drawn up into God's future for the world. This "now" and "not yet" tension of the kingdom defines our reality and keeps us moving, growing, and adapting. It is in the language of living systems, our ever present strange attractor (innate guiding mechanism.)

This concept of planning from the future is not just some obscure theological principle, but one of the key activators of mission in our lives and organizations and therefore a direct function of missional leadership. Leaders of God's people need to make it a discipline in the way we do church and lead God's people into mission. Here is an example of how it might work in developing organizations.

> In 1987, inspired by a church service, a real estate lawyer, Billy Payne, set his sights on achieving a very large goal—he wanted to bring the 1996 Olympics to his hometown, Atlanta. As it turned out, he would receive no direct financial support from the city or the state. What is more, Atlanta had very few facilities suitable for the logistics of Olympic competition. Public debate and media criticism constituted a skeptical chorus during the start-up years. But piece-by-piece, Payne stitched the Atlanta games together like a patchwork quilt. He succeeded in part because his goal of bringing the Olympics to Atlanta was tangible and it connected with the strange attractor of southern pride and hospitality.[29]

27. Ibid., 73.
28. Ibid., 240.
29. Ibid., 240–41.

"With Coca-Cola's commitment to sponsorship in 1992, Payne received his first seed money—$540 million. He solved the problem of too few facilities by spreading events as far as Washington, D.C., and Orlando, Florida. He had to create a $1.7 billion temporary organization, oversee projects involving 82,500 workers and 42,000 volunteers."[30] And he pulled it off with money to spare, which he donated to his city. It was a truly remarkable feat, born of a vision for his city. The thing about Billy Payne is that he understood what it means to manage from the future. He says, "I have always thought the way to engage life—in business and personally—is to set enormously high goals that seem absolutely unattainable, and work from the conviction that ~~BHAG~~ you're going to pull it off. By doing that I'm convinced that you are going to reach half of them. As for the others, you're going to go further than you would have otherwise."[31]

But the same dynamic exists in all great visionaries. They speak from the future. No less in the founding of the Urban Neighbors of Hope, a missionary order to the poorest of the poor in Melbourne, or a local church plant with a vision to see people come to Jesus, than in Martin Luther King Jr. The real power is this: that a compelling vision of the future is one way of generating genuine *communitas* by developing a corporate sense of mission that in turn "creates" the future.[32]

Mission as Organizing Principle

In a remark ascribed to Gordon Cosby, the pioneering leader of that remarkable community Church of the Savior in Washington, D.C., he noted that in over sixty years of significant ministry, he had observed that no groups that came together around a non-missional purpose (e.g., prayer, worship, study, etc.) ever ended up becoming missional. It was only those groups that set out to be missional (while embracing prayer, worship, study, etc., in the process) that actually got to doing it. This observation fits with all the research done by Carl George[33] and others that indicates that the vast majority of church activities and groups, even in a healthy church, are aimed at the insiders and fail to address the missional issues facing the church in any situation.

If evangelizing and discipling the nations lie at the heart of the church's purpose in the world, then it is mission, and not ministry, that is the true organizing

30. Ibid., 241.

31. Billy Payne, quoted in ibid., 240–41.

32. As Martin Buber once noted, "Whoever can no longer desire the impossible will be able to achieve nothing more than the all-too-probable. M. Buber, *On Judaism* (New York: Schocken Books), 35. Or as Cesar Pavese once remarked "To know the world, one must construct it."

33. Carl George is the creator of the meta-church model, which was initially based on his observation of the Korean movement associated with Paul Yonggi Cho.

principle of the church. *Mission* is being used in a narrow sense here to suggest the church's orientation to the "outsiders," and *ministry* as the orientation to the "insiders." Experience tells us that a church that aims at ministry seldom gets to mission even if it sincerely intends to do so. But the church that aims at mission will have to do ministry, because *ministry is the means* to do mission. Our services, our ministries, need a greater cause to keep them alive and give them their broader meaning. By planting the flag outside the walls and boundaries of the church, so to speak, the church discovers itself by rallying to it—this is mission. And in pursuing it we discover ourselves, and God, in a new way, and the nations both "see" and hear the gospel and are saved.

An organizing principle is that around which an organization structures its life and activities. It's hard to imagine a sports team surviving long if it forgets its primary mission to compete and win each game and eventually to win the grand final contest in its league. Winning the prized cup, medal, or award keeps the team focused and integrated. Its mission is its organizing principle; comradeship takes place along the way. The team experiences *communitas* as it engages in its core task—when it faces physical challenge and risks failure in order to succeed.

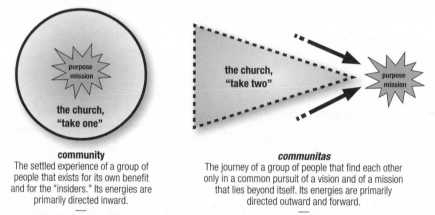

community
The settled experience of a group of people that exists for its own benefit and for the "insiders." Its energies are primarily directed inward.

"The Community for Me"

communitas
The journey of a group of people that find each other only in a common pursuit of a vision and of a mission that lies beyond itself. Its energies are primarily directed outward and forward.

"Me for the Community and the Community for the World"

How Mission and Vision Can Form Communities

Another example of organizing principles: a country's constitution is basically the organizing principle of the state and its associated public and political life. For instance, the constitution of the United States preserves the basic freedoms and democracy that have marked this nation as unique. Similarly, mission is our constitution, or at least a central part of it. To preserve the movement ethos of God's people, it is fundamental that the church keeps mission at the center of its self-understanding. Without mission there is no movement, and the community dies a death of the spirit long before it dies a physical death. To forget mission is to forget ourselves; to forget mission is to lose our *raison d' être* and leads to our eventual demise. Our sense of mission not only flows from an understanding of the mission of God and missional church, but forms the orienting inspiration of the church of Jesus Christ, keeping it constantly moving forward and outward.

Beyond the Either-Or Church

Recall briefly the sterile fish tank, and the terrible statistics about young people in universities falling away from faith. It is partly the way that we actually *do* church that is the problem.[34] As we observed in chapter 3, Platonic dualism is the belief that the world is separated into spiritual and nonspiritual, sacred and secular realms. This worldview, largely foreign to the Hebraic mind, became the predominant one in the church by the late fourth century, largely through the influence of Augustine and other early church theologians. The issue of dualism is raised here because, although we now reject this philosophy intellectually, we still tend to practically embody this belief in the very structures and activities of the church in a way that precludes any life-affirming message we might wish to portray verbally. The result of the dualistic understanding of life and faith is that of the artificial environment of the fishbowl, because it separates in practice what is essential to a holistic biblical worldview and spirituality: an all-of-life-under-God approach.

In a diagram that reworks a diagram previously depicted in chapter 3, we can illustrate what this dualistic structure of church might look like. It would be something like this:

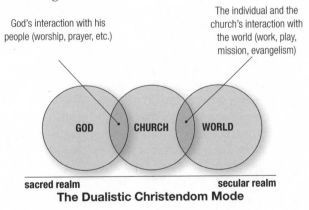

The Dualistic Christendom Mode

34. In this section I have borrowed from my previous work in *The Shaping of Things to Come*, 157–59, but used it in a different way.

Let's play this out: Jane is an average churchgoer. She loves God and wants to grow in him. But her problem is how to bring all the aspects of her life together so that it makes sense of her faith. How does she experience church?

She spends most of her time in the "Godless" secular space called the world. On Sunday she goes to church (the middle circle). Church fellowship offers her a neutral kind of space filled with like-minded believers. She feels safe and reassured when she is around them, because the tension she normally feels when "in the world" is temporarily alleviated. After a bit of "fellowship," she goes into the chapel area (symbolized by the interface between the "God" and "church" circles) in response to the call to worship. The music kicks in, the worship starts, and she is drawn up into a form of ecstasy as she begins to engage her heart in the worship of God. And all of a sudden it is as if God "bungee jumps" into the deal. The worship rocks and Jane begins to feel that she is really connecting with God. After the praise and worship, Jane is then exposed to the Word of God in the sermon. Pastor Bill is a great preacher, and she feels that the sermon really "fed her." So in taking Communion she recommits herself to Jesus as personal Savior. The church then sings a few more rousing songs, and the pastor pronounces the benediction, and whoooop! It is if the bungee cord draws God up again, returning him to heaven. And Jane finds herself back in the middle circle having a coffee or a soda with her Christian friends. But then she has go out into the world (symbolized by the "world" circle). Laboring as she is under a dualistic worldview and experience, this space in Jane's perception is a somewhat caustic context for Christians, because God is not perceived as being "in the world." And so it is a somewhat harrowing experience, and she barely makes it to mid-week cell group, where she undergoes a similar experience to that of Sunday (but not on the same scale). Yes, she has her quiet times when sometimes God "turns up," but other than that she feels that she is rather alone in a spiritually precarious place.

If you'll forgive the slightly satirical oversimplification, I'm sure that many of us can recognize ourselves in this story. The tragedy is that everything in this medium of church sets Jane up to experience her life as fundamentally dualistic and therefore divided between the sacred and the secular. No one has necessarily intended it to be this way; it's just as if a virus somehow got into the system, a nasty sucker that has lodged itself in the fundamental programming that underlies the Christendom software. So no matter how "seeker friendly" one might wish to make the service, it still "communicates" this sacred-secular dualism that has plagued the church. The net result of this way of doing church is that God is experienced as a church-god and not the God of all of life, including church.

Because of the way that church life is conceived and structured, there is no real missional edge in this community—it is cut off from missional engagement with the world. Its institutional message always works against, and thus cancels out, its overt verbal messages. Furthermore its built-in dualistic spirituality sets people up to fail in seeing their work, play, study etc., as ministry or mission. Ministry tends to be seen as a churchy thing done by the experts.

But there is another way to configure these three elements of the diagram in a way that makes more sense and is much more integrated and biblical. This will simply involve reconfiguring the relation of God, world, and the church. In the phraseology of this book, this will mean to become missional-incarnational, which in turn will engender *communitas*. Consider the following diagram:

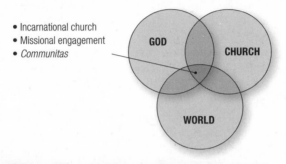

- Incarnational church
- Missional engagement
- *Communitas*

Missional-Incarnational *Communitas* Approach

By reorienting the three circles, we can think of the Christian experience in an altogether different way. When we can conceive of all three circles intersecting at the center, there we have a church that is truly missional, is deeply incarnational, and is acting in a way that extends the ministry of Jesus into the world. In this model our worship of God is always done in the context of our engagement with the world, and because of this it is forced to be culturally meaningful to outsiders. It also has definite missional edges, because it is open to all. Church is not something that is done in abstract from the world. Our evangelism and social action are communal, we join with God in redeeming the world (he's already there), and our spirituality is of the all-of-life variety.

This is exactly what we sought to achieve through Elevation, the café project described in chapter 1. It was all about this convergence of God, his people, mission, spirituality, and community in an organic incarnational way that has the potential to transform whole districts. Another example previously mentioned is Third Place Communities in Tasmania, Australia. This group of Jesus's people refuse to gather as God's people in sacred, isolated spaces. Rather they exist to incarnate and do mission in "third places," where people hang out in their spare time. So they gather in pubs, sports clubs, play groups, interest groups, subcultures, etc., and people look in at what they are doing. By deliberately choosing to hang out and "be church" in public spaces, the group has to be constantly attentive to its missional context. And so the worship and the whole of the church's life is incarnational and culturally sensitive. The missional potency of this is easily tested: try singing ecstatic choruses in a café or pub. In most cases it will just alienate the customers and the owner, and you will not be allowed back—at least when other customers are around. But can we worship in the public space? Of course, but we are going to have to find ways to connect with God that, rather than alienating, attract people and spark their curiosity. The very missional nature of the third place demands a contextualization of the church's cultural life and expression. One of the most missional things that a church community could do is simply to get out of their buildings and go to where the people are—and be God's redeemed people in that place in a way that invites people into the equation! When the three circles intersect, aspects of Apostolic Genius begins to emerge. It always amazes me that in the "church" gatherings of Third Place Communities, about 60 percent of the average attendees are very curious non-Christians.

This is what we try to engender in the interns of Forge Mission Training Network, and one of the most rewarding things about working with them is seeing the lights go on as it dawns on them that they really can bring all the disparate elements of their lives together under the name *church*. Church needn't be something excluded from the rest of life. It is really true to its purpose only when it ties together all the loose ends under the one God—this is the true meaning of monotheism, as we saw in the third chapter. The fact is that God is everywhere. He is already deeply involved in human history and in all people's lives. The conceptual leverage in transitioning to this model is in the circle named church. The church needs to adjust its position in relation to God and the world. And to do this we must break the bondage of dualism. One of the best ways to achieve this is by becoming missional, by directly engaging the various contexts we find ourselves in.

So, Follow the Yellow Brick Road

One of the things that the story of Abraham, the fellowship of sports teams, the desperate comradeship of war veterans, and the Fellowship of the *Lord of the Rings* teach us is that the journey itself is important—that maturity and self-actualization require movement and risk, and that adventure is actually very good for the soul. They all teach that a deep form of togetherness and love is found when we embark on a common mission of discovery, when we encounter danger together and have to find each other in the process in order to survive. We find all these elements in the way Jesus formed his disciples as together they embarked on a journey that took them away from their homes, family, and securities (be they social or religious) and set out on an adventure that involved liminality, risk, action-reflection learning, *communitas*, and spiritual discovery. On the way their fears of inadequacy and lack of provision faded, only to be replaced by a courageous faith that went on to change the world forever.

And what makes phenomenal Jesus movements so dynamic is that they actually involve movement; this does not just describe the organizational structure and system, but the fact that there is real *motion*. This is not to say that every Christian literally left home and family to follow Jesus, but that the foundational spiritual transaction of laying down all in the name of Jesus was at the very base of all of their subsequent following. In this way they had made an abiding decision to enter into the liminality of leaving securities and comforts when they first became Christians and so didn't have to try and factor it in later. This meant that they remained a liquid people, constantly adapting and evolving, depending on context. This was to continue until Constantine gave us buildings and an institution and a bond between church and state that was to put Apostolic Genius to sleep for a long, long, time.

We need to hit the road again. We are the people of the Way, and our path lies before us, inviting us into a new future in which we are permitted to shape and participate. In trying to rearticulate the nature of authentic Christian community, that of a *communitas* formed around a mission and undertaken by a group of uncertain but brave comrades, by evoking mythic imagery from great stories and calling to mind how Jesus and the early church went about spreading the message, we evoke that yearning and that willingness to undertake an adventurous journey of rediscovery of that ancient force called Apostolic Genius.

conclusion

> . . . we shall not cease from exploration
> And the end of all our exploring
> Will be to arrive where we started
> And know the place for the first time
>
> T. S. Eliot, "Little Gidding"

In many ways it is appropriate to end this exploration into Apostolic Genius with Eliot's potent insight into the nature of journeys of exploration. By returning to the primal roots of Christian mission and church, we uncover something long forgotten and only vaguely remembered in our myths, in the stories of the martyrs, and fleetingly embodied in the lives of our saints and heroes. It's as if we have stumbled upon a vitally important treasure that was somehow buried, hidden in the dark recesses of densely cluttered ecclesial archives. And in regaining this treasure, in a very real sense we rediscover ourselves in a new and vital way.[1]

1. To this end I have tried to develop practical tools that will help you and your community in the application of the ideas of this book. This one has to do with trying to identify where you are in terms of APEPT. I have been working with an organizational psychologist to try to develop the profiles based on primary and secondary ministries. By undertaking the questionnaire at www.theforgottenways.org you can either take a personal test or undergo a 360° profile that involves feedback from others in your ministry world and how they perceive your unique contribution. This will be useful for both individuals and ministry teams.

The other primary tool is a test for what I have called "missional fitness." This test is designed to assess the level of Apostolic Genius that manifests in your community by trying to evaluate the levels of the individual mDNA present in them. So, for instance, it will involve delving into how well the community follows missional-incarnational impulses, allows for apostolic influence, focuses on disciple making, develops organic structures, and shapes itself in forms that approximate *communitas*. As such it will provide insights into where you can target your

Apostolic Genius (and its composite elements of mDNA) holds a powerful mirror up to our own practices and conceptions of church, and in doing so affords us that dangerous comparison between ourselves and the remarkable Jesus movements of history. It is dangerous because it awakens in us our deepest instincts, stirs our latent potentials, and calls us to radical, paradigmatic change. It is subversive because it requires a thorough recalibration of our lives and our communities, for it involves a return to the place where it all started—going back to that wild and revolutionary Messiah and the radical movements his life and teachings have inspired through the ages.

For many of us it will feel like it involves an almost impossible leap to get from where we now stand to even approximate the vitality of the Jesus movements we have studied. This is so because much of what we have explored in relation to the various elements of mDNA is thoroughly paradigmatic in substance and nature. My great hope for the church is that in actual fact Apostolic Genius is not something that we have to impose on the church, as if it were something alien to us, but rather is something that already exists in us. It *is* us! It is our truest expression as Jesus's people. And because this is so, we simply need to awaken and cultivate it. I am completely convinced that Apostolic Genius is as available to us today as it is for our remarkable Chinese brothers and sisters. It is the common heritage of the whole people of God, and it is a direct link to our own destiny as we face the daunting challenges of the twenty-first century.

But this challenge of constant adaptation and reshaping along missional lines remains a fundamental part of what it means to be faithful to the idea of church as Jesus intended it in the first place. This is no alien work; rather, it forms a fundamental part of our witness in the world in which we live. The great theologian Karl Barth fully recognized this when he gave guidance to an anxious pastor in then Marxist East Germany who was struggling with how the church could continue to express the traditional form of church that they had inherited while having to go underground in order to maintain community witness. I quote his words at length here because of their sheer relevance for our situation as well.

> I am not now saying anything new to you in reference to this question. It was indeed one of your most renowned and ablest men, General Superintendent Gunther Jacob in Cottbus, who not long ago announced the "end of the Constantinian era." Because I have certain wariness about all theoretical formulation of a philosophy of history, I hesitate to make this expression my own. However, it is certain that something resembling this approaching end begins to show itself simply everywhere, but very sharply in your part of

---

efforts in becoming missional. If you resonate with the central theses of this book, and wish to develop your community (or start one) with Apostolic Genius in mind, then this will be a very useful tool in your hands. Go to www.theforgottenways.org and check it out.

the world. It is certain that we all have reason to ask ourselves each of these questions and in every case quickly and clearly to give the answer:

No, the church's existence does not always have to possess the same form in the future that it possessed in the past as though this were the only possible pattern.

No, the continuance and victory of the cause of God, which the Christian Church is to serve with her witness, is not unconditionally linked with the forms of existence which it has had until now.

Yes, the hour may strike, and perhaps has already struck, when God, to our discomfiture, but to his glory and for the salvation of mankind, will put an end to this mode of existence because it lacks integrity.

Yes, it could be our duty to free ourselves inwardly from our dependency on that mode of existence even while it still lasts. Indeed, on the assumption that it may one day entirely disappear, we definitely should look about us for new ventures in new directions.

Yes, as the Church of God we may depend on it that if only we are attentive, God will show us such new ways as we can hardly anticipate now. And as the people who are bound to God, we may even now claim unconquerably security for ourselves through him. For his name is above all names . . .[2]

The discovery of great truths brings a certain responsibility to live by them. This book has been about bringing to light a lost potential that has lain hidden at the very heart of God's people for much too long. Yes, it will mean change, and it will take us on an adventure where we must risk being overwhelmed. But herein dwells our hope, because it remains the ever potent gospel that has the power to both save and transform our world. It remains our deepest heritage. And it is incumbent on us who follow the way of the gospel to act in ways that unlock its marvelous power. As it was for Paul, the early church, and all throughout the ages, so it will be for us—it will require a hopeful, trusting faith in the One who saves.

2. Karl Barth, "Letter to a Pastor in the German Democratic Republic," in *How to Serve God in a Marxist Land* (New York: Association Press, 1959) 45–80.

addendum and glossary

a crash course in chaos

> Management expertise has become the creation and control of constants, uniformity, and efficiency, while the need has become the understanding and coordination of variability, complexity, and effectiveness.
>
> Dee Hock, *Birth of the Chaordic Age*

> There are two ways to live your life. One is as though nothing is a miracle. The other is as though everything is a miracle.
>
> Albert Einstein

In the somewhat strange but evocative language of living systems, the church in the West is facing what is called an *adaptive challenge.* According to the theory, adaptive challenges are situations in which the organism (or organization) is challenged to change and adapt in order to improve its chance of survival. Adaptive challenges come from two possible sources: (1) a situation of significant threat or (2) a situation of compelling opportunity; or both. The threat scenario poses an "adapt or die" situation to the organism or organization. The compelling opportunity scenario might simply present itself in the promise that the food source is far better in the next valley, an opportunity that galvanizes the organism or organization into movement and action. For the church, both forms of adaptive challenge present very real issues for us in our day. Threat to the existence of the institutional church comes in the form of *rapid discontinuous change,* and compelling opportunity comes in the form of a massive, almost unprecedented *openness to issues of God, spirituality, community, and meaning.* Both are good reasons to change, and the signs are that we are only just beginning to respond.

In terms of the threat, the nature of our challenge in the West is not from overt, state-sponsored persecution, as it was for the phenomenal Jesus movements in the early Christian period or in China. In fact, the lack of this has probably contributed to the malaise in which we find ourselves, because we got all institutional and mainstream and were subverted to being just good middle-class folk. As mentioned in chapter 2, the threat for us is much more from politico-socio-cultural forces and takes the form of *rapid discontinuous change* (including sociopolitical, environmental, biological, technological, religious, philosophical, and cultural threats *and* opportunities).

Only fifty years ago, based on what we knew from the past and a thorough assessment of current conditions, we could forecast future with high levels of predictability. We would then develop a strategic plan, with milestones along the way, and expect that, all things being equal, we could achieve the desired result. It was called strategic planning, and it was based on the idea of slow continuous change. The future was just a projection of the past with some adjustments. Now, because of constant innovations in technology and the resultant redundancies of whole industries, hypersensitive global markets that react to the slightest disturbances across the globe, terrorism, the shift of geopolitical forces, etc., we are living in an age where it is just about impossible to predict what will happen in three years' time, let alone twenty. In other words, change for us is *discontinuous,* and it is increasingly rapid. And it is a real threat to the institutional church, which doesn't normally respond well even to slow continuous change.

Listen to some key thinkers in the area of missions and missional organizations.

North American culture is . . . moving through a period of a highly volatile, discontinuous change. This kind of change is a paradigm of change not experienced through all points in history, but it has become our norm. It is present and pervasive during those periods of history marked by events that *transform* societies and cultures forever. Such periods can be seen in events like that of the *Exodus,* where God forms Israel as a people, or the advent of the *printing press,* which placed the Bible into the hands of ordinary people and led to the transformation not just of the church but the very imagination of the European mind, or the ascendence of the new technologies like the computer and the Internet and the emerging marriage of biology with microchips.[1]

Paradigmatic readjustments are demanded of us in this situation. Peering ahead in the twenty-first century, there is little doubt we are teetering at the edge of chaos. As we will see, this is a good thing because at the edge of chaos is the sweet spot where innovation takes place if handled correctly.

1. A. Roxburgh and F. Romanuk, "Christendom Thinking to Missional Imagination, Leading the Cultivation of Missional Congregations," unpublished manuscript, 2004, 11.

Getting in Touch with the Future: An Exercise

Check out some of these websites that focus on trends in the future. This list was provided to me by a friend and Forge colleague, a talented young futurist called Wayne Petherick.

Some pieces of advice

Consider the "filters" that you are using to read these sites, i.e., What's my angle? Is there another angle? Knowing about emerging issues/events is one thing; acting upon them is another. Challenge yourself to map out possible implications (for good or bad) and whether your conclusions are something worthy of action. Also ask what will the church look and feel like in these contexts.

- **EurekAlert** (http://www.eurekalert.org/)—Comprehensive summary of scientific breakthroughs, research press releases
- **New Scientist** (http://www.newscientist.com/)—Another decent summary of things as they happen
- **Wired** (http://www.wired.com/)—A pop-tech smorgasbord
- **Fast Company Magazine** (http://www.fastcompany.com/homepage/)—"Next big thing" type of business magazine.
- **The Futures Lab** (http://futures-lab.com/news.htm)—Page of emerging issues and the like
- **Salon.com** (http://www.salon.com/)—Opinion on the intersection of society and culture with politics, technology, business
- **Disinformation** (http://www.disinfo.com)—Offers sometimes edgy information on current affairs, politics, new science, and the "hidden information" that seems to slip through the cracks of the corporate-owned media conglomerates
- **Ethics in the News** (http://www.ethics.org.au/things_to_read/ethics_in_ the_news/index.htm)—Operated by the St James Ethics Centre, an NFP based in Sydney
- **Red Herring** (http://www.redherring.com/IndexArticle.aspx)—As the site says, the business of technology
- **Financial Times** (http://news.ft.com/home/asia)—Although sometimes a little staid, a pretty solid survey of economic happenings
- **Signs and Wonders** (http://www.wnrf.org/news/blogger.html)—Monitors trends and events affecting the future of religion; affiliated with the **World Network of Religious Futurists** (http://www.wnrf.org/cms/index.shtml)
- **Arts & Letters Daily** (http://www.aldaily.com/)—A look at philosophy, aesthetics, literature, language, trends, history, music, art, culture, criticism, disputes, and gossip

We Just Got a New Set of Spectacles

So many of our ways of conceptualizing organizations and leadership are derived from what can be called a Newtonian perspective. As inheritors of the modern worldview, framed largely by the perspective generated by the sciences, we have shaped our notions of the world and, particularly in this case, of organizations and leadership on what has aptly been called the mechanistic view of the world. Under Newton's influence, a significant paradigmatic advance for its time, we have tended to view the universe as a giant, highly complex machine based on the ideas of cause and effect. Simplified, it assumes that if we do action X, then Y is sure to result. It assumes strict predictability. It was one of the fundamental tasks of science to match all the causes with their reciprocal effects—a colossal challenge, which resulted in a massively increased knowledge of the world and its workings.

All things were going fine until the advent of the famous Einsteinian theories of relativity and the subsequent study of quantum physics, which tried to probe the nature of subatomic reality. What the researchers found there initially stunned them, because it flatly contradicted the findings of the standard physics of its time, based as it was on Newtonian assumptions of predictability. They found that the very basic structure of reality, the atom, behaved in a totally different way from what was expected. The atom's behavior completely defied the predictability expected by Newtonian physics and initiated a crisis in the prevailing scientific paradigms, ushering in the quantum age, with its nonlinear dynamics. This caused a massive revolution in the theory of science, one that is unfolding to this very day. One of the side effects of this paradigm shift was the study of living systems, which in some real way also defy the determinism of cause and effect and tend to act in unpredictable ways. This science includes, among others, the study of cybernetics, the study of chaos and complexity, and the science of emergent structures.[2] And these are of massive significance for us as we continue into the twenty-first century, with all its challenges.

Changing the Story

One of the foremost signs of present-day society is the presence of increasingly complex systems that permeate just about every aspect of our lives.

2. At this stage I wish to refer the reader to a book that for me was a book to define a decade. It is Margaret Wheatley's book on this subject cited above. Also highly significant in this regard is the work of Fritjof Capra, *The Hidden Connections: A Science for Sustainable Living* (London: Harper Collins, 2002) and his earlier book *The Web of Life: A New Synthesis of Mind and Matter* (London: Flamingo, 1997). They are well worth the read, and I found myself worshiping God through engaging the ideas. For some Christian efforts at applying chaos theory to church dynamics, see Easum, *Unfreezing Moves*, and Snyder, *Decoding the Church*. Both are good books; Easum's is a popular rendition of chaos theory applied to church organizations and is very accessible.

The admiration we feel in contemplating the wonders of new technologies is tinged by an increasing sense of uneasiness, if not outright discomfort. Though these complex systems are hailed for their growing sophistication, there is a growing recognition that they have also ushered in a social, commercial, and organizational environment that is almost unrecognizable from the perspective of standard church leadership theory and practice.[3]

Although we often hear about successful attempts to revitalize existing churches, the overall track record is very poor. Ministers report again and again that their efforts at organizational change did not yield the promised results. Instead of managing new, revitalized, organizations, they ended up managing the unwanted side effects of their efforts. At first glance, this situation seems paradoxical. When we observe our natural environment, we see continuous change, adaptation, and creativity; yet our church organizations seem to be largely incapable of dealing with change.

The movie *Adaptation* dealt wonderfully with this exact issue. Charlie Kaufman (Nicolas Cage) is a confused L.A. screenwriter overwhelmed by feelings of inadequacy, sexual frustration, self-loathing, and the screenwriting ambitions of his freeloading twin brother, Donald. He is commissioned to do a screenplay for a book on flowers called *The Orchid Thief,* written by Susan Orlean (Meryl Streep). This captivating book details the remarkable adaptability nature seems to display. But this only frustrates him all the more, because when Charlie looks at his own life, he feels trapped by the dictates of his own constricted and self-loathing nature. This being the case, he can't seem to translate the ideas of the book into the movie script, let alone alter the miserable dynamics of his own nature. Through some tragic experiences, including the death of his brother, he eventually does change. But the pathos of the movie thus highlights how versatile and responsive nature is in comparison with the determinism of personality, character, and the human condition. This analysis can equally apply to how so many churches feel about their state.

The understanding of human organizations in terms of complex living systems is likely to lead to new insights into the nature of adaptability, and thus to help us deal with the complexities of church and mission in this vastly changed scenario. Moreover, it will help us create organizations that are sustainable, since the principles of organization of ecosystems, which are the basis of sustainability, are identical to the principles of organization of all living systems.

We need a different lens with which to view organizations and leadership if we wish to move beyond the captivity of the mechanistic paradigm that clearly dominates our approach to leadership and church. It is the

3. See Alan Roxburgh, *Crossing the Bridge: Church Leadership in a Time of Change* (Costa Mesa, CA: Percept Group, 2000), for an analysis of the impact of change on the church.

actual paradigm that is being addressed here, not the incidentals. This relates directly to what has been said previously regarding the paradigm of Christendom, but here we will explore the nature of organizations and leadership per se.

A paradigm, or systems story, "is the set of core beliefs which result from the multiplicity of conversations and which maintains the unity of the culture."[4] The "petals" in this diagram are "the manifestations of culture which result from the influence of the paradigm."[5] Most change programs concentrate on the petals; that is, they try to effect change by looking at structures, systems, and processes. Experience shows us that these initiatives usually have limited success. Church consultant Bill Easum is right when he notes that "following Jesus into the mission field is either impossible or extremely difficult for the vast majority of congregations in the Western world because of one thing: They have a systems story that will not allow them to take the first step out of the institution into the mission field, even though the mission field is just outside the door of the congregation."[6]

He goes on to note that every organization is built upon on what he calls "an underlying systems story." He points out that

> this is not a belief system. It is the continually repeated life story that determines how an organization thinks and thus acts. This systems story determines the way an organization behaves, no matter how the organizational chart is drawn. Restructure the organization and leave the systems story in place and nothing changes within the organization. It's futile trying to revitalize the church, or a denomination, without first changing the system.[7]

Drilling down into this systems story, the paradigm, or mode of church, is, he suggests, one of the keys to change and constant innovation.

A lot of energy (and money) is put into the change program, with all the usual communication exercises, consultations, workshops, and so on. In the first few months, things seem to be changing, but gradually the novelty and impetus wear off and the organization settles back into something like its previous configuration. The reason for this is simple, though often overlooked—unless the paradigm at the heart of the culture is changed there will be no lasting change.

I discovered this time and again while working with my denomination. My aim was to try to cheat history by recovering a missional mind-set and a movement ethos as the central paradigm of the denomination. On reflection, we managed to get the missional part of the equation into the center, but we

4. Richard Seel, "Culture and Complexity," 2.
5. Ibid.
6. Easum, *Unfreezing Moves*, 31.
7. Ibid.

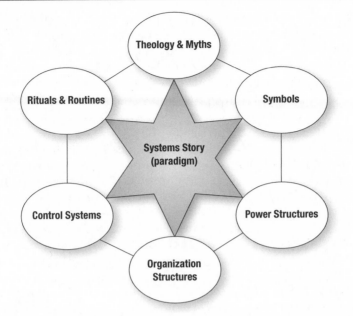

were not able to instill a <u>movement ethos</u> because of a deeply entrenched <u>institutional paradigm</u> at the heart of the organization. The problem is that most people see the church as an institution and not an organic movement (a living system), in spite of the fact that the Bible is replete with organic images of church and kingdom (body, field, vine, soil, etc.). In such a situation, all efforts at other changes are doomed to failure. The structures just revert back to default once the pressure of change is alleviated. The fact remains that for this very reason the vast majority of Christian institutions throughout history never renew and change. The institutional systems story informs so much of what we do. Machiavelli was right: "Nothing is more difficult to carry out, nor more doubtful of success, nor more dangerous to handle, than achieving a new order of things."[8]

This is what is meant in the previous chapters by the *modes* of the church. Easum is right when he says that most theories about congregational life are flawed from the start because they are based on an institutional and mechanical worldview. Or what Easum calls the "Command and Control, Stifling Story."[9] This is particularly marked when you recognize how different the predominant forms of church are from the apostolic modes. The early church was an organic *missional* movement, not a religious institution. Just make a mental comparison between the modes described

8. Quoted in Pascale, Millemann, and Gioja, *Surfing the Edge of Chaos*, 156.
9. Easum, *Unfreezing Moves*, 17.

in the comparative table in chapter 2 to see how different they really are. What we need to do is to allow the organic image of church to seep into the very center of the paradigm above and then reinterpret things from that perspective. We must allow a new systems story to reinform all our practices. Try this: in the diagram above, put the phrase *Christendom Institution* at the center, and then ponder the impact on the "petals." Now put the phrase *Organic Jesus Movement* in the center. What happens to the "petals"?

Ivan Illich was once asked what the most radical way to change society was; was it violent revolution or gradual reform? He gave a careful answer. Neither. Rather, he suggested, if one wanted to change society, then one must tell an alternative story. How true. We need to retell the story of the church and mission in light of the organic living systems perspective if we are to evolve into a genuinely missional church. And believe me, it is a different imagination (a different story) of church that is being presented in the dangerous stories of the phenomenal movements as well as those of the EMC. A new understanding of organization is emerging in our time, born out of quantum physics, chaos theory, and a return to organic biblical principles of organization. "The new understanding can best be described as a Permission-giving, Innovative Story."[10]

It is outside both my expertise and my task in writing this book to write a text on the theories of chaos, complexity, and emergence, and I will leave that to people far more able than myself. However, I do want to extract some of the insights that go to the heart of the issue of paradigm and will thus have bearing on issues of missional church and leadership. And to do this I am going to lean on, in fact I am going to get close to summarizing (with lots of reinterpretation in relation to church with other cross-references), a truly excellent book that seems to me to brilliantly capture the heart of the paradigm and give us some ways forward. The book is by authors Richard T. Pascale, Mark Millemann, and Linda Gioja and is called *Surfing the Edge of Chaos: The Laws of Nature and the New Laws of Business*. I can't recommend it more highly if you want to really get to grips with the paradigm of living systems. As we go, I will try and interpret their work for the issues that face the church. Toward the end of this chapter, I will present a case study that illustrates the process that I am just about to describe.

Survival Is Not Enough

The authors begin with a comparison of two types of leadership. The comparison is between operational and adaptive leadership. Essentially,

10. Ibid., 32.

operational leadership is suited for organizations that are in relatively stable environments where maintenance and development of current programming are the core tasks of leadership. This form of leadership, the authors maintain, is built on the assumptions of social engineering and is thus built squarely on a mechanistic view of the world. It does work, and it is appropriate for *some* organizations. Adaptive leadership, on the other hand, is displayed by the type of leader who develops learning organizations and manages to help the organization transition into different forms of expression where agility, responsiveness, innovation, and entrepreneurship are needed. Adaptive leaders are needed in times of significant threat or considerable new opportunity, or both. This has direct relevance to our situation at the dawn of the twenty-first century.

Adaptive vs. Operational Leadership

It was Harvard's Ronald Heifetz who initially made the distinction between "technical (i.e., operational) leadership" and "adaptive leadership." He noted that

> The former entails the exercise of authority and is an entirely appropriate response in conditions of relative equilibrium. Operational leadership works best when the problems faced can be dealt with by drawing upon a pre-existing repertoire. Operational leadership goes hand in hand with the tenets of social engineering. A solution is devised from above and rolled out through the ranks. If an organization is in crisis; if downsizing, restructuring, or reducing costs is called for; if sharpened execution is the key to success then operational leadership *is* probably the best bet.[11]

Operational leadership describes well the predominant approach to church leadership, with its emphasis on pastoral care and nurture in the faith, and church growth, with its strong emphasis on management, technique, and programs. In many cases it works. But as Pascale and colleagues recognize

> In living systems problems arise, however, when a species (or organization) misapplies a traditional solution to an adaptive problem. In this situation, the current repertoire of solutions is inadequate or just plain wrong. In nature, the alpha male silverback mountain gorilla draws its troop together in a tight circle and behaves aggressively toward rival males or other natural threats. This traditional solution works effectively—*unless* the troop is facing poachers armed with guns, tranquilizer darts and capture nets.[12]

11. Pascale, Millemann, and Gioja, *Surfing the Edge of Chaos,* 39.
12. Ibid.

All the apelike bravado in the world will not stop a bullet. Now the gorillas face a genuine adaptive challenge, and unless they learn to adapt to the new threat and find new responses, they are history. It's not hard to see the relevance for us as we face the challenges of the twenty-first century.

We saw in chapter 2 how the *come-to-us* Christendom mode worked well in a society where all were considered Christians and church attendance was kind of compulsory, but it doesn't quite work in situations that require a *go-to-them* missional approach. It also highlights the different kind of leadership that is needed to drive the different paradigms of church. This is a classical example of operative versus adaptive leadership and organization.

According to the authors of *Surfing the Edge of Chaos*, the central assumptions of operative leadership are:

"The Leaders Are the Head, the Organization Is the Body."[13] In this view corporate intelligence is concentrated at the top of the organizational structure. (In contrast, the living systems approach recognizes that every living system has what is called "distributed intelligence" throughout the organization. The aim of leadership in the new paradigm is to identify, cultivate, and unleash that distributed intelligence. This is precisely what I mean when I suggest that our task is to unleash Apostolic Genius, which is "already there" in the *ecclesia*).

"A Promise of Predictable Change. Implementation plans are scripted on the assumption of a reasonable degree of predictability and control during the time span of the change effort."[14] In contrast, the organic approach asserts that life is unpredictable (watch the atom or a swarm of bees at work) and that at best you can disturb, and generally direct, but cannot fully predict the outcome of a living system.

"An Assumption of Cascading Intention. This simply means that once a course of action is determined by leadership, *initiative flows from the top down.* When a program is defined, it is communicated and rolled out through the ranks. Often, this includes a veneer of participation to engender buy-in."[15] In contrast, the organic approach says that real change, especially lasting change, comes from the bottom up and that it is the task of leadership to create the conditions that foster imagination, initiative, and creativity.

It is easy to see these assumptions about organization working in the way we generally operate in leading and managing churches and related organizations. But that these assumptions are not compatible with the way living systems generally work becomes self-evident the more we grapple with the way God has structured life itself. This is not to say that the more

13. Ibid., 13.
14. Ibid.
15. Ibid.

mechanistic, operational form of leadership does not have its place. But we must recognize that the tools and methods generally associated with this type of leadership work well "*only when the solution is known in advance and an established repertoire of choices exists to implement it*.[16] They are not appropriate for situations of unpredictability, which require innovative thinking and adaptive forms of leadership.

A note of warning for those leading in established churches: what Western Christianity desperately needs at the moment is adaptive leadership—people who can help us transition to a different, more agile, mode of church. Such leaders don't necessarily have to be highly creative innovators themselves, but rather people who can move the church into adaptive modes—people who can disturb the stifling equilibrium and create the conditions for change and innovation. By and large, many leaders in church organizations, particularly those with strong caring and teaching gifts, can exhibit a tendency to avoid conflict and too easily soothe tensions. Left unchecked, this can be lethal, because it caters to equilibrium and therefore ultimately to death.

A lesson from history: Heifetz warns us that adaptive leaders can be frozen out when followers don't want to face bad news. He cites an example of Churchill's warnings to the British public about Hitler prior to World War II. At the time, the British people would rather listen to Neville Chamberlain's disastrous "peace in our time" policy than face Churchill's chilling prophecy of impending conflict or even war if nothing was done to preempt the rise of Hitler. Heifetz notes that "followers often turn to authority as a bulwark against the associated uncertainty and risk. The essential work of adaptive leadership is to resist these appeals. Instead, they must

hold the collective feet to the fire,

regulate distress such that the system is drawn out of its comfort zone (yet contain stress so it does not become dysfunctional), and

manage avoidance mechanisms that inevitably surface (such as scapegoating, looking to authority for the answer, and so forth)."[17]

---

16. Ibid. These conditions do apply in many situations, and it is not my intent to minimize them. Many churches find themselves in relatively stable situations. The American Midwest and South, for instance, are still bastions of conservative society, and operative approaches will still be viable there. However, even in such situations ownership of any initiative is a prerequisite for success, regarding each person as an intelligent "node" in a living system and involving them as such does improve implementation of change programs. Pascale, Millemann, and Gioja don't reject all the *methods* of social engineering out of hand but advocate the termination of it as the primary paradigm of organization in the context of the twenty-first century. Tools for control do not equal social engineering. What they are advocating is appropriate use of tools of the old paradigm, incorporated in a new management repertoire. Social engineering as a paradigm/systems story is obsolete—period.

17. Ibid., 40.

This is a critical dimension of the mDNA of Apostolic Environment, because an essential part of apostolic leadership is to cultivate adaptability and responsiveness in order to ensure the survival, as well as the extension, of Christianity. As such, a core function of the apostolic vocation is to keep the church moving, adapting, and incarnating the gospel into new contexts.

After exploring the nature of operational versus adaptive leadership, *Surfing the Edge of Chaos* suggests four working principles of living systems theory that form the basic substance of their book.

Principle #1: Equilibrium Is Death

Tautology Most churches start from dynamic and exciting adventures in evangelism and church planting, and at the end of their organizational life cycle they are usually miserable, static, institutions.[18] And it appears that an essential part of the process is the movement from the early, more unstable, disequilibrium to that of a stable environment of equilibrium. The early days of most churches or parachurches are experienced as unpredictable and wild but at the same time seem to be filled with a kind of spiritual energy. Why is this the case? What is it about disequilibrium that seems to stimulate life and energy? And what is it about stability that seems to stifle it? (Remember the story of SMRC.) Is it because life itself is unpredictable and chaotic and that when we establish organizations that seek to control and minimize the dangers of life, these organizations in the end stifle it? The history of missions is quite clear about this: Christianity is at its very best when it is on the more chaotic fringes. It is when church settles down, and moves away from the edge of chaos, that things go awry.

The assertion that "equilibrium is death" is a derivative of an obscure but important law of cybernetics called the Law of Requisite Variety. This law states that "the survival of any organism depends on its capacity to *cultivate* (not just tolerate) variety in its internal structure. Failure to do so results in an inability to cope successfully with 'variety' when it is introduced from an external source."[19] The authors give us a great example as to how this law works in reality. They note that

> Fish in a bowl can swim, breed, get food with minimal effort, and remain safe from predators. But, as aquarium owners know, such fish are excruciatingly sensitive to even the slightest disturbances in the fishbowl. On the other hand, fish in the sea have to work much harder to sustain themselves and they are

18. Material in this section is drawn from ibid., ch. 2.
19. Ibid., 20.

subjected to many threats. But because they cope with more variation, they are more robust when faced with a challenge.[20]

We know from nature that "survival favors heightened adrenaline levels, wariness, and experimentation."[21] We can recognize the same sentiment in the more popular phrase "history favors the brave."

So what is the role of leadership in all this? "Leaders are to a social system what a properly shaped lens is to light."[22] They serve to focus the capacities of the organization, and they do this for better or worse. If adaptive *intention* and capacity are required, the organization must be disturbed in an intense and extended fashion if leaders are to break the stifling equilibrium that has overwhelmed it. But this is not achieved quickly or without significant wisdom as to human motivations and as to how human communities are activated in a new search for answers. Adaptive leaders must resist the urge to move too quickly or reach for quick fixes or packaged solutions. Rather, they must activate a corporate search from deep within the ranks of the organization in order to help plot a way forward. This adaptive activation is achieved by

1. Communicating the urgency of the adaptive challenge (i.e., the threat of death or the promise of opportunity);
2. Establishing a broad understanding of the circumstances creating the problem, to clarify why traditional solutions won't work, and;
3. Holding the stress in play until "guerrilla" leaders come forward with innovative solutions.[23]

This sequence of activities will obviously generate significant anxiety and tension in the organization, but we had better get used to it if we are to adapt to the rapidly changing environment of the twenty-first century. One of the skills of adaptive church leadership will be to manage the stress and make it a stimulus for innovation in church and mission. The Christian church ought to be highly responsive to its missional contexts. I call this missional fitness.[24] It is in the constant pursuit of this fitness, or innate adaptability, that mission must become the organizing principle of church. When we are truly *missional*, the whole church becomes highly sensitive to its environment and also has a natural, inbuilt, and theologically funded

20. Ibid.

21. Ibid., 21. Or as Alfred North Whitehead once commented; "Without adventure [which we might define here as disequilibrium caused by breaks with convention], civilization is in full decay."

22. Ibid., 40.

23. Ibid.

24. I have developed a way to assess missional fitness in a community on the basis of the six elements of mDNA (see www.theforgottenways.org).

mechanism for triggering adaptive responses. A genuine missional church is therefore a genuine learning organization. It was by being missionally fit that the church in the apostolic and postapostolic periods (and in China) not only survived but thrived. It was forced by external conditions to live by its message and adapt to threats as they came along. This made these Christians far more vigorous than their more stable brothers and sisters in more static periods. They did not live in an artificial environment of a churchy fishbowl but were the *ecclesia* in all the dangerous spheres of life. And, as with our own immune system, what didn't kill them served to make them stronger.

Brian McLaren, a key voice for what is called the emerging church in the United States, recommends that the churches adopt a core value of valuing adaptability itself. He says, "Change your church's attitude towards change and everything else will change as it should."[25] Tom Peters, in his book *Thriving on Chaos*, insists that this is an indispensable element of successful enterprise in a chaos situation. He has a useful model for developing the "love of change" at every level of business practice.[26] In this book however, this is called *missional fitness*—the ability to embed in the church's working philosophy a willingness to be highly agile and missionally responsive.

Principle #2: Surfing the Edge of Chaos

It is remarkable to me that the theologically most fertile parts of the Bible are all, yes all, set in the context of the people of God facing significant danger and chaos. This features strongly in the mDNA of *communitas*, but whether it is an Abraham called to leave home and journey, or in the harrowing experiences of the Exodus and Exile, whether it is David's adventures, Jeremiah's struggles, Jesus's ministry, or the book of Acts, none of these were stable situations. They were dynamic and even life-threatening.

But *communitas*, or at least the questing adventure that is contained therein, is not limited to the Bible or human situation; it is part of the very structure of life itself.[27] The study of living systems teaches us that

> nature is at its innovative best near the edge of chaos. The edge of chaos is a condition, not a location. It is a permeable, intermediate state through which order and disorder flow, not a finite line of demarcation. Moving to the edge

25. Brian McLaren, *The Church on the Other Side: Doing Ministry in the Postmodern Matrix* (Grand Rapids: Zondervan, 2000).

26. Tom Peters, *Thriving on Chaos: Handbook for a Management Revolution* (London: Pan, 1987), section 5, 388ff.

27. Much of the following is based on Pascale, Millemann, and Gioja, *Surfing the Edge of Chaos*, chapter 4.

of chaos creates upheaval but not dissolution; that's why being on the edge is so important. The *edge* is not the abyss. It's the sweet spot for productive change. And when productive agitation runs high, innovation often thrives and startling breakthroughs can come about. This elusive, much sought after, sweet spot is sometimes called "a burning platform." The living sciences call it the edge of chaos.[28]

The role of leaders in the equation? Well, once again this goes back to Heifetz's understanding of the nature of adaptive leadership. Adaptive leadership moves the system to the edge of chaos, not *over* it, but to the *edge* of it. As was said before, the leader's role is to ensure that the system is directly facing up to the issues that confront it, issues that if left unattended will eventually destroy it. If people in the organization never seriously face the problem and stay with it for a reasonable time, they will never feel the need to move to find a genuine and more lasting solution—hence, the idea of a burning platform. We teach the Forge interns this simple formula. It is the role of transformative leadership to "sell the problem before you try evoking a solution," because it is at this "edge of chaos" where real innovation takes place.

When I reflect on the early days of SMRC, I can see all the signs of living systems as proposed in this chapter. Those days were chaotic, fluid, dynamic, and highly missional. And in my time there the church went through at least three adaptive leaps as described in the first chapter. The point is that we were at our very best when we were on the fringes. It is when we settled down and moved away from the edge of chaos that things went awry.

By and large, churches are very conservative organizations, and after they have been around just a few years they can quickly become institutional, largely because of the Christendom mode and assumptions underlying it, but also because of leadership style and influence. On the whole, churches seek to conserve the past, and particularly in the historical denominations (e.g., Anglicanism and Presbyterianism) their primary orientation is often backward to an idealized past rather than forward to a new vision of the future. As such they are classic, often inflexible, institutions that enshrine an inherited tradition. Hence, the historical churches are leading the decline of the church in the West. For instance, in some areas, the Uniting Church of Australia is losing members at 20 percent exponentially per annum! This would be similar for many liberal mainline denominations and is due almost entirely to the fact that they are closed systems built squarely on institutional systems story with a liberal theological base—a classic sign of institutionalism (see the chapter on organic systems).

Theological liberalism is an indicator of institutional decline not only because it tries to minimize the necessary tension between gospel and cul-

28. Ibid., 61.

ture by eliminating the culturally offending bits, but because it is basically a *parasitical* ideology. I don't mean this to be offensive to my liberal bothers and sisters; I wish merely to point out that theological liberalism rarely creates new forms of church or extends Christianity in any significant way, but rather exists and "feeds off" what the more orthodox missional movements started. Theological liberalism *always* comes later in the history of a movement, and it is normally associated with its decline. It is therefore a highly institutional manifestation of Christendom. As such it is *deadly* to apostolic forms of missional movement. But most established denominations, including the more evangelical ones, are also built squarely on Christendom assumptions of church and therefore, like all institutions, are facing significant threat and need to be led to the edge of chaos. It is there, by living in the tension that it brings, they *will* find more authentic and missional ways of being God's people. So leaders, turn the heat up, but manage it.

Principle #3: Self-organization and Emergence

The third principle of nature, self-organization and emergence, captures two sides of the same coin of life. [29] "Self-organization is the tendency of certain (but not all) systems operating on the edge of chaos to shift to a new state when their constituent elements generate unlikely combinations. When systems become sufficiently populated and properly interconnected, the interactions assemble themselves into a new order: proteins into cells, cells into organs, organs into organisms, organisms into societies. Simple parts networked together can undergo a metamorphosis."[30] A single fire ant can't possibly drive off an attacking wasp, but a whole nest of them are deadly to organisms much larger than themselves. But this can be demonstrated right under your hat: a single brain cell is useless by itself, but millions of them together can perform analytic miracles the likes of which we have yet to fathom.[31]

Most change in complex systems is emergent; that is to say, it comes about as a result of the free (and often informal) interactions among the various "agents" in the system. In an organization the agents are people—themselves complex systems. Complexity theory suggests that when there is enough connectivity between them and the complexity reaches a critical point, emergence is likely to occur spontaneously.[32]

29. Material for this section is drawn from ibid., chs. 7 and 8. On this subject, however, there is a fascinating book by Steven Johnson called *Emergence: The Connected Lives of Ants, Brains, Cities, and Software* (London; Penguin, 2001). If this discussion tickles your fancy, this is a relatively easy book to read.

30. Pascale, Millemann, and Gioja, *Surfing the Edge of Chaos*, 113.

31. Ibid.

32. This is the principle of emergence, and it one of the most remarkable attributes of complex systems. It is both mysterious and commonplace, as well as very hard to define. Kevin

Just so that we can get this concept nailed down, let me quote Roxburgh and Romanuk again:

> The principle of emergence was developed to explain the ways organisms develop and adapt in differing environments. Contrary to popular notions that they develop through some top-down, predetermined, well-planned strategy, emergence theory shows that complex systems develop from the bottom up. Relatively simple clusters of cells, or groups of individuals, who individually don't know how to address a complex challenge, when they come together will form, out of relatively simple interactions, an organizational culture of a higher complexity that can address these challenges. In other words the answers to the challenges faced by organisms and organizations in changing environments tend to emerge from the bottom up rather than get planned before hand from the top down. This is why we describe missional leadership as the cultivation of environments within which the missional imagination of the people of God might emerge.[33]

To my mind, it is not just "missional imagination" that must be cultivated, but rather Apostolic Genius, which is latent in the people of God. Keep this in mind, because it is a vital concept of leadership that is delved into in the chapter on Apostolic Environment.

Emergence is the outcome of all this: a new state or condition. At the end of this chapter I will present the case history of the emerging missional church, but this phenomenon can appear just about anywhere that a system allows the free flow of information and relationships and creates the conditions of bottom-up learning. The classic example of our time is that of the Internet. A few hundred, or even a few thousand, computers linked together do not together make an emergent phenomenon. But a few million computers interconnected around the sharing of information, in many ways like the structure of a human brain, creates an emergent entity with a distinct life of its own. A colony of fire ants has very effective emergent capabilities and constitutes an organism weighing twenty kilograms, with twenty million mouths and stings. And a group of them on the march is just about impossible to stop. A jazz ensemble creates an emergent sound that no one could imagine from listening to the individual instruments. Two hundred years ago, Adam Smith was on the scent of these insights. As one of the pioneers of the new discipline of economics, he called our attention

---

Mihata does as well as any when he says that emergence is the process by which patterns or higher levels of organization arise from interactive processes on the micro level. He notes that the resultant structure or pattern of organization cannot be understood or predicted from the behavior or properties of the component units alone. (See Kevin Mihata, "The Persistence of 'Emergence,'" in Raymond A. Eve, Sara Horsfall, and Mary E. Lee, eds., *Chaos, Complexity & Sociology: Myths, Models & Theories* (Thousand Oaks, CA: Sage, 1997), 30–38.

33. Quote taken from Roxburgh and Romanuk, "Christendom Thinking," 28.

to the "invisible hand" of the market economy and its aggregate effects as a commercial force. Smith recognized that individual choice did not explain everything, since individuals, as members of communities, constantly generate relationships and dependencies that suit them. All of this, he noted, added up to a more complex *emergent* phenomenon called "an economy." It is a powerful "social force," or an emergent structure, that seems to have a life of its own. And none of us could doubt the influence of the economy on our daily lives.

Principle #4: Disturbing Complexity

The fourth principle of a living systems approach to organization teaches us that merely enhancing the effectiveness of an existing organization seldom yields radical innovation. At best, it only optimizes the existing organization.[34] In many ways, this is what church growth theory did for the institutional church in the sixties and beyond. It maximized the prevailing model but did not fundamentally alter it—it remains trapped within the prevailing paradigm or systems story. Therefore, "optimization founders because efforts to direct living systems, beyond very general goals, are counterproductive. Like herding the proverbial butterfly, living things can be ushered forth with reasonable expectation of progress but they do this in their own unique way. This seldom conforms to the linear path that we have in mind."[35] At SMRC we found trying to lead our twenty-something community was akin to herding cats; it was very hard to direct, control, and predict, and we had to adjust our approach to organization and leadership. This adjustment led to some amazing creativity and innovation as we surfed the edge of chaos.

"In fitness landscape terms,[36] it is impossible to get to a distant and higher fitness peak (discover radical breakthroughs) by climbing still higher on the peak one is already on (optimizing)." Or, as previously stated in *The Shaping of Things to Come*, if one wants to dig a hole in another place, it is no good digging the same hole deeper and better.[37] Rather, if we wish to activate genuine innovation in the organizations we serve, we need "to descend into

---

34. Material for this section is based on Pascale, Millemann, and Gioja, *Surfing the Edge*, chs. 9 and 10.

35. Ibid., 154.

36. The concept of fitness landscapes has been used by biologists since the 1930s to characterize the developmental evolution of a species as a search across a landscape of fitness points Adaptation is usually thought to be a process similar to "hill climbing," where minor variations of the species (from one generation to the next) result in a move toward a peak of high fitness on a fitness landscape. The innate impulses for survival and development will push a population of species toward such peaks. See http://en.wikipedia.org/wiki/Fitness_landscape.

37. Frost and Hirsch, *Shaping of Things to Come*, 196.

the unknown, disregard the proven cause-and-effect formulas, and defy the odds. We need to embark on a journey of sequential disturbances and adjustments, not a lock-step march along a predetermined path. We may only be able to see as far as our headlights, but proceeding in this fashion can still bring us to our journey's destination."[38]

After defining the four principles of the living systems approach, the authors advise us about how we sustain adaptive learning organizations—how we remain fit and agile . . . *adaptive.*

The Disciplines of Agility

"Having breathed new life into organizations, how do we sustain it? Paradoxically, the answer lies in disciplines."[39] This is what we called "practices" at SMRC. "The disciplines help organizations sustain disequilibrium, thrive in near-chaos conditions, and foster self-organization. If taken to heart, they can also foster changes at the individual level. Indeed, they must be internalized if their far-reaching benefits are to be fully realized."[40]

According to Pascale et al., there are seven critical disciplines.

1. Infuse an intricate understanding of what drives organizational success.
2. Insist on uncompromising straight talk.
3. Manage from the future.
4. Reward inventive accountability.
5. Harness adversity by learning from prior mistakes.
6. Foster relentless discomfort.
7. Cultivate reciprocity between the individual and the organization.[41]

Each of the seven disciplines can stand alone, but enormous power exists in the relationship among them.

How, Then, Shall We Live?

By now, for many of you, either your head is spinning or, if I have failed to be clear enough, much of this has gone over your head. I do apologize for the somewhat technical description of what for many will be a new paradigm of organic leadership and living systems. But I think that you will

38. Pascale, Millemann, and Gioja, *Surfing the Edge of Chaos,* 229.
39. Ibid. They explore these ideas fully in chapters 11 and 12.
40. Ibid.
41. Ibid. I have not attempted a summary here because it is not essential to my task. Once again, I refer the reader to the book itself. It is a multicourse meal.

agree with me that at the very least, it is a fruitful area for research, study, and new ways of looking at old tasks. For me, delving into this material has been like striking gold, because it has helped me see the role of leadership in an entirely different light. I feel much freer to pursue what I had over the years come to believe, that the church was much too machinelike, with its programs and management of people, and that it needed to move closer to the feel of the NT church, with its organic movement ethos. I am not alone in this. Recall David Barrett's statistics in chapter 2. It's also liberating to realize that God never intended his leaders to be people with all the answers and all the vision. Rather, our role is to help God's people discover the answers for themselves through the activity of leaders who awaken their imagination and stimulate a search. Our task is not to control, but under the guidance of the Holy Spirit try to both harness and direct the flow. We move from being managers to being servants or, even more specifically, cultivators of fields or environments wherein certain behaviors or actions take place (see the chapter on *apostolic environment*).

Let's ground this in something of a case study involving you, me, and Western Christianity.

Come Forth! A Case Study in Emergent Structures

It is significant that the universe itself was formed by the Spirit of God brooding over a situation of primal chaos (Genesis 1). The "let there be . . ." of the creation story calls forth life and existence out of the chaos and constructs something out of nothing. But in some sense the basic elements of life must have been made by God prior to the creation of life as we know it. Life emerges from lower forms of complexity to higher forms of intelligence and complexity—the highest life form being the human, the bearer of the very image of God. In a real way, the creation is the archetypal story of emergence.

We have already explored the flourishing of new forms of Christian community that form part of the emerging missional church. The question that anyone with a sense of history might ask is this: is this just another trend that will come and then go? I do not think so. It is not just a trend, but in actuality a new form (imagination) of church. This statement is built on the understanding of emergence as previously explained. But a bit of background first:

Moving out of equilibrium: the adaptive challenge

As previously noted, while Christendom as a cultural, religious, and political force operating from the center of society was basically eliminated in the modern period, our current imagination of church nonetheless remains fundamentally the same. In the late twentieth century the best missional thinkers and strategists are beginning to recognize that the game is up. This recognition has been partly due to the fact that Christianity is in massive, trended decline in the West but paradoxically is on the increase in the developing world. There is a sense of dread that somehow the church in its current and predominant mode is not going to cut it. As a result, in the last few decades there has been a sense of unease and a roaming of the collective mind in search of new answers.

In terms of living systems, we are in a classic situation of *adapt or die*. We are facing a profound adaptive challenge, and there are signs that segments of the church are beginning to move. The movement is still marginal, mind you, and it is mostly on the fringes of the church, but that's exactly where all movements of mission start.

It's not all danger and threat: much of what is going on around us is a great opportunity—this is one reason for organizational adaptation, remember? There is a massive spiritual quest going on in our day and under our noses. People are wide open to the issues of God, faith, meaning, spirituality, New Age religions, etc. This kind of spiritual openness has not existed in broader society and culture for hundreds of years. The problem is that, by and large, the church is not featuring. People are not lining up at our doors, are they? To make matters worse, it is probable that we likely have only a limited window of opportunity. Because of the consumptive nature of Western culture, the window will close as society gluts on faddish spiritualities.

But make no mistake, as well as providing profound new opportunities for mission, the issues above present to many churches all too real challenges to actual survival, because all too commonly churches, and the pietist forms of Christianity we have fostered in them, tend to shy away from the public sphere and are not very responsive to the issues "out there." When you combine the above scenario with the massive cultural shifts in our day—whether you call it hypermodernism or postmodernism—we find ourselves in a strange land where the cultural maps developed in previous eras when things were more stable simply don't work anymore. The sheer immensity of the task feels overwhelming, *and it should*—we are peering into the edge of chaos. But it does us no good to simply deny reality. This is our mission field, and unless we begin to recalibrate the church taking these into account, many congregations and believers will be swept away.

Here is the deal: the basic Christendom mode of church is simply unable to respond, because it was not made for this kind of fluidity. Most churches are too institutional, and therefore too clumsy in their inherited form, to be able to adapt and respond adequately to this missional environment. A useful comparison is between a supertanker and a speedboat. The tanker takes many miles just to stop or turn, but the speedboat maximizes on responsiveness. Our situation requires agility and adaptation and not solidity and fixedness. It's the age of the speedboat-style church. And it is happening . . . a new species of Christian community is being born, and to use the technical phrase of this chapter, it is *emergent* as well as adaptive. Interestingly, the same process is happening in the corporate world. Tom Peters notes that excessive, unwieldy structure is "management's time bomb" in a rapidly changing, global environment. The smaller, more responsive organizations are the ones that will thrive in the new millennium.[42]

Moving to the Edge of Chaos

There are signs of real movement going on. One of the more obvious signs is the sense of holy discontent among Christians of all ages and classes— it's not just the younger generations that are asking questions. Even the boomers are asking, "Has it all come down to this? Attending church services, singing songs to God, and attending cell groups? Is this really what Christianity is all about?" But more disquieting perhaps is that there is a mass exodus from the church: remember the research of David Barrett and Todd Johnson that there are 111 million Christians without a local church in the world today. These people claim to take Jesus seriously but feel alienated from current expressions of church. We all know them, don't we? My own experience tells me that there are more Christians aged twenty-something outside the church than inside the church at any given time. The statistics and premonitions must say something to us, and they are not unnecessarily gloomy. What they tell us is that there is a search going on. This search for alternatives is a sign that the system is responding, and it has led to significant experimentation, and eventually to some genuine innovation.[43]

But there's more: as mentioned, Christians are beginning to come together to study scripture and follow Jesus together in some strange places. Many of them don't even recognize themselves as a church, per se, but they have all the marks of authentic Christian community in biblical terms. The flourishing of new ecclesial experiments on the fringes of the church is causing the established church to begin to take notice. There is a whole new public discourse taking place on blogs (web logs, a kind of e-journal)[44] and in a whole new genre of

---

42. Peters, *Thriving on Chaos*, 355.

43. I refer you to my book (with Michael Frost) for a thorough survey of these trends. Also significant in this area is Eddie Gibbs and Ian Coffey, *Church Next: Quantum Changes in Christian Ministry* (Downers Grove, IL: InterVarsity, 2000).

44. See, for instance, http://tallskinnykiwi.com/, http://www.livingroom.org.au/blog/, http://backyardmissionary.typepad.com/, or http://jonnybaker.blogs.com/jonnybaker/. You can just follow the links on these sites to discover a whole new world of conversation about the emerging church.

books on the emerging church,[45] and seminaries are beginning to host whole courses around the issues of the so-called emerging church. Most noteworthy are the previously mentioned statistics by David Barrett in his *World Christian Encyclopedia* and George Barna's disturbing book *Revolution*.[46]

There is no question that something fundamental, even elemental, is going in our day. But as previously noted, you have to have the "eyes to see it," or else you can miss it entirely.

Emergence and Self-organization

Remember that emergence happens when systems become sufficiently populated and properly interrelated; then the interactions assemble themselves into a new order. Complexity theory suggests that when there is enough connectivity between the different aspects of the system, emergence is likely to occur spontaneously. This is precisely what has happened in the EMC. The end result is a species of organization different from the previous elements.

Note the following diagram:

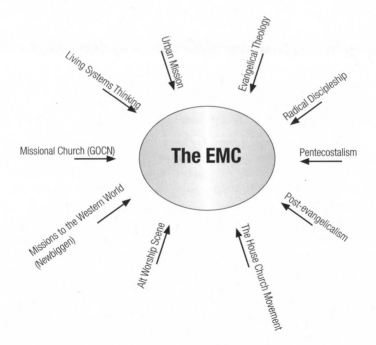

45. See books by Brian McLaren, Eddie Gibbs, and Gerard Kelly in the bibliography.
46. http://www.globalchristianity.org/; and George Barna, *Revolution* (Carol Stream, IL: Tyndale House, 2005).

The emerging expression of church has come about through precisely this process of "increasing population and interrelationships" of people and ideas. It has come about from the above movements within the church beginning to compare notes and cross-fertilize each other.

- From *urban mission* among the poor we learned about incarnating the gospel, and it reminded us of the power of incarnation in any context.
- From *evangelical theology* we learned to value the gospel, the *evangel,* as the central organizing principle of theology.
- *Pentecostalism and the charismatic movement* taught us the real value of apostolic, evangelistic, and prophetic ministries and radical reliance on the Spirit of God.
- From the *radical discipleship movement* of the seventies (including movements like Jesus People USA, God's Squad, Sojourners, etc.) we learned that seriously following Jesus involves a radical change in lifestyle.
- From the *postevangelical* movement and *emergent,* as controversial as it is, we learned that rejecting the popular cultural expressions of evangelicalism didn't amount to heresy.
- From the *alternative worship movement* we learned to resymbolize and contextualize the gospel in ways that made sense to postmodern people.
- From Lesslie Newbigin and his writings we began to take seriously the stance of missions-to-the-Western-world.
- This was extended through the vital, but somewhat theoretical, work of the *Gospel and Our Culture Network,* based mainly in North America.
- And from *living systems theory* (as in this chapter), we rediscovered the organic nature of faith and community and our innate ability to adapt and respond to our environment though our participation in God's redemptive mission to the world.
- From the *house church movement* we learned that ecclesial units can be small but missionally effective. Witness much of the neo-apostolic phenomenon.

Each of these in itself was not emergent and was unequal to the total adaptive challenge that was facing us. Each was only part of the picture. But when they began to inform each other in the context of the demise of Christendom and the edge of chaos, the EMC was born. And it's good breeding. It is a new phenomenon but in some sense is ancient insofar as it mirrors the elemental and powerful apostolic mode of church that was so profoundly used by God to change the course of history and bring millions of people to faith in Jesus.

What is still largely missing from this emergent phenomenon is any sustained and explicit Pentecostal presence, with all its passion and fire. While it is true that Pentecostalism taught us the true value of apostolic ministry, the Pentecostals have not been a noteworthy part of any real expression of EMC, as far as I am aware. This is probably because Pentecostalism is still basking in the relative success that church growth praxis has brought them.[47] In Australia, we are beginning to attract the attention of some really innovative postfundamentalist Pentecostal leaders from the Christian Revival Crusade, and they bring something really special with them. They have a wonderful openness to God and the kind of immediacy that when they hear something that seems true to them, they are remarkably willing to give it a go. As an undercover "Pentecostal on assignment" myself, I pray for this constantly, as I believe that this is possibly the final missing link that will catalyze this movement into being a true *phenomenon* in the West.

Thus ends this more technical addendum. When dealing with issues of complexity and organizational change, it is very useful to remember the old adage that it is better to light one candle than to curse the darkness, and to note that in the history of God's people, the fire of the movements of God begin with little flames like you and me. Come, Holy Spirit.

47. In fact, I would argue that the Pentecostal emphasis on apostolic, as well as evangelistic and prophetic, ministry alone accounts for continued growth through the lifecycle. Though much of the Pentecostal ecclesiology remains basically Constantinian, they have maintained a vigorous apostolic leadership vision that keeps the movement growing and prevents normal organizational degeneration.

glossary of key terms

In order to assist the reader with some of the more technical words and phrases, I have constructed this glossary, in alphabetical order. Essentially, it is a set of definitions that are key to understanding the book.

Adaptive Challenge

A concept deriving from chaos theory. Adaptive challenges are situations in which a living system faces the challenge to find a new reality. Adaptive challenges come from two possible sources: a situation of (1) significant threat or (2) compelling opportunity. The threat poses an "adapt or die" scenario on the organism or organization. The compelling opportunity might simply come as "the food is better in the next valley . . . lets move!" type scenario. Adaptive challenges set the context for innovation and adaptation.

Adaptive Leadership

An adaptive leader is the type of leader who develops learning organizations and manages to help the organization transition into different forms of expression where agility, responsiveness, innovation, and entrepreneurship are needed. Adaptive leaders are needed in times of significant threat

273

or considerable new opportunity, or both. This has direct relevance to our situation at the dawn of the twenty-first century. Compare to *operational leadership* below.

APEPT

The term I use to describe the fivefold ministry formula in Ephesians 4. APEPT is an acronym for Apostle, Prophet, Evangelist, Pastor, Teacher.

Early Church

The period of the history of the church spanning the New Testament church as well as that up to the time of Constantine in AD 312. The way I use the term implies a certain type or mode of the church: that of a radical, grassroots network of churches and people, organized as a movement, largely in the context of persecution.

Apostolic

I use the term very specifically to describe not so much the theology of the church but the mode of the New Testament church—to describe something of its energy, impulse, and genius as well as its leadership structures.

Apostolic Genius

Apostolic Genius is the phrase I developed to try to conceive and articulate that unique energy and force that imbues phenomenal Jesus movements in history. My own conclusions are that Apostolic Genius is made up of six components (perhaps more, never less). Five are what I call mDNA, and the other has to do with its spirituality and theology. For the most part, I focus on the six elements of mDNA when I use the term. The five elements are missional-incarnational impulse, apostolic environment, disciple making, organic systems, and *communitas*. Loaded into the term *Apostolic Genius* is the full combination of all the elements of mDNA that together form a constellation, as it were, each shedding light on the others. I also believe it is latent, or embedded, into the very nature of God's gospel people. I suggest that when all the elements of mDNA are present and are in dynamic relationship with the other elements, and an adaptive challenge acts as a catalyst, then Apostolic Genius is activated.

Diagrammatically it will look something like this . . .

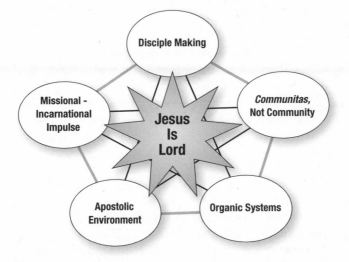

I see this book as an attempt to explore Apostolic Genius and try to assist the Western church to recover and implement it in order to find a new yet ancient way of engaging the twenty-first century.

See the introduction to section 1 for a full explanation.

Attractional Church

Essentially, attractional church operates from the assumption that to bring people to Jesus we need to first bring them to church. It also describes the type or mode of engagement that was birthed during the Christendom period of history, when the church was perceived as a central institution of society and therefore expected people to "come and hear the gospel" rather than taking a "go-to-them" type of mentality. Not to be confused with being culturally attractive.

Biblical Hebraic

Describes the worldview that basically formed, framed, and sustains the biblical revelation. Refers to the Hebraic worldview specifically found in the scriptures. *Hebraic* on its own can encompass the insights of later Judaism as well.

Chaos and Chaos Theory

Chaos theory is a new scientific discipline that seeks to explore the nature of living systems and how they respond to their environment. Thus, it applies not only to organisms but also to human organizations, which are considered living systems that operate in a very similar way to organic life. In the light of living systems, chaos is not necessarily a negative thing but can be the context for significant innovation. However, it does pose a threat to living systems that fail to respond appropriately to the conditions of chaos. See chapters 3 and 7 for explorations into these ideas.

Christendom

Describes the standardized form and expression of the church and mission formed in the post-Constantine period (AD 312 to present). It is important to note that it was not the original form in which the church expressed itself. The Christendom church is fundamentally different from the NT church, which is made up of a network of grassroots missional communities organized as a movement. Christendom is marked by the following characteristics:

1. Its mode of engagement is attractional as opposed to missional/sending. It assumes a certain centrality of the church in relation to its surrounding culture. (The missional church is a "going/sending one" and operates in the incarnational mode.)
2. A shift of focus to dedicated, sacred buildings/places of worship. The association of buildings with *church* fundamentally altered the way the church perceived itself. It became more static and institutional in form. (The early church had no recognized dedicated buildings other than houses and shops, etc.)
3. The emergence of an institutionally recognized, professional clergy class acting primarily in a pastor-teacher mode. (In the NT church, people were commissioned into leadership by local churches or by an apostolic leader. But this was basically different from a denominational or institutional ordination we know in Christendom, which had the effect of breaking up the people of God into the professional Christian and the lay Christian. The idea of a separated clergy, I maintain, is alien to an NT church, as it is in the Jesus movements of the early church and China.)
4. The paradigm is also characterized by the institutionalization of grace in the form of sacraments administered by an institutionally authorized priesthood. (The NT church's form of communion was an actual

[daily?] meal dedicated to Jesus in the context of everyday life and the home.)

Christocentric

Simply that Christ is center. If something is Christocentric, then its organizing principle is the person and work of Christ.

Christology/Christological

Essentially, Christology comprises the biblical teaching of and about Jesus the Messiah. For instance, when I say that Christology must inform all aspects of the church's life and work, it means that Jesus must be first and foremost in our life and self-definition as church and disciple. The adjectival form simply means that the element being described must be referenced primarily by our understanding and experience of Jesus the Messiah.

Church Planting

The initiation and development of new, organic, missional-incarnational communities of faith in multiple contexts. I would affirm that all true mission aims at the development of communities of faith. Thus, church planting is an essential part of any authentic missional strategy.

Communitas

Adopted from the work of anthropologist Victor Turner, who used the term to describe the experiences that were part of initiation ceremonies of young African boys (see *liminality*). As key elements of mDNA, the related ideas of liminality and *communitas* describe the dynamics of the Christian community inspired to overcome their instincts to "huddle and cuddle," and to instead form themselves around a common mission that calls them onto a dangerous journey to unknown places, a mission that calls the church to shake off its collective securities and to plunge into the world of action. There they will experience disorientation and marginalization but also will encounter God and one another in a new way. *Communitas* is therefore always linked with the experience of liminality. It involves adventure and movement, and it describes that unique experience of *togetherness* that really happens only among a group of people inspired by the vision of a better world actually attempting to do something about it.

Complexity

Complexity is related to a situation of chaos. In essence, living systems theory maintains that living organisms tend to organize themselves in greater degrees of complexity. Complexity also acknowledges that when we are dealing with living systems that they are indeed complex. Because of complexity relatively small actions can have significant consequences in the system.

Constantinianism

This is another word for Christendom, because Christendom was basically initiated by Constantine's actions in bringing the church into official relationship with the state. Constantinianism is the type of all modes of church that resulted from the merger between church and state and has dominated our mind-sets for the last seventeen centuries.

Cultural Distance

A concept that helps us try and assess just how far a people group is from a *meaningful* engagement with the gospel. To do this we have to construct a continuum that looks like this:

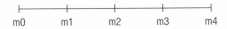

Each numeral with the prefix *m* indicates *one significant cultural barrier to the meaningful communication of the gospel.* An obvious example of such a barrier would be language. If you have to reach across a language barrier, you have a problem. But others could be race, history, religion/worldview, culture, etc. For instance, in Islamic contexts, the gospel has struggled to make any significant inroads because religion, race, and history make a meaningful engagement with the gospel very difficult indeed. Because of the Crusades, the Christendom church badly damaged the capacity for Muslim people to apprehend Christ, and Semitic peoples have long memories. So we might put mission to Islamic people in a m3 to m4 situation (religion, history, language, race, and culture). The same is true for the Jewish people in the West. It is very hard to "speak meaningfully" in either of these situations.

Dualism (Particularly Platonic Dualism)

The view that spirit is good and that anything that resists spirit is necessarily bad. Matter resists spirit and is therefore evil. The form that really impacted the church came from Plato. Plato believed that the *real* world was in fact the world of eternal ideas and essences located in an invisible spiritual reality, and that the world of matter and things is but its shadow and therefore has no essential reality. A shadow is only a reflection of the real and not the real itself. The real was to be found in its essence of an object, in the Idea of it, and not in the way it appears to us in our world. This has also been called dualism, and by the fifth century AD it had become the predominant worldview in the Western church. Dualism thus naturally leans toward *essence* over *function*. The reality of a thing abides in its idea or essence and not in its appearance or in what it does. The net effect of this doctrine was to divide the world between the sacred or the essential, and the secular or the functional/physical. This has massive ramifications for the way we do church and structure our spirituality.

Ecclesia

The predominant biblical word translated as "church" in English. The way I use it in this book will highlight something of the pristine idea of the church as God intended it.

Ecclesiology

Classically, this refers to the biblical teaching about the church.

Emergence

"The principle of *emergence* was developed to explain the ways organisms develop and adapt in differing environments. Contrary to popular notions that they develop through some top-down, pre-determined, well planned strategy, *emergence theory* shows that complex systems develop from the bottom up. Relatively simple clusters of cells, or groups of individuals, who individually don't know how to address a complex challenge, when they come together will form, out of relatively simple interactions, an organizational culture of a higher complexity that can address these challenges. In other words, the answers to the challenges faced by organisms and organizations in changing environments tend to emerge from the bottom up rather than get planned beforehand from the top down. This is why we describe missional leadership as *the cultivation of environments within which the missional imagination of the people of God might emerge.*"[1]

Emerging Missional Church (EMC)

Essentially I developed the term to identify and describe the new form of *ecclesia* forming in our day. In the way that it is used in this book, it will be viewed as an emergent structure, a new form of *ecclesia* in our day. As such it is not just emerging or missional, but it is the combination of these two factors that has created a new form of church. I also use it to describe the phenomenal movement that is going on in our day. This is not to deny the continuity of the EMC with the people of God in all ages, but to distinguish it in form alone.

Evangelistic-attractional

This describes the missional impulse of the Christendom church and that of the church growth movement. Essentially, it involves the assumption that all outreach and evangelism must bring people back to church in order to facilitate the numerical growth of that church. Another way to say it is "outreach and in-drag." The way I use it is to pose it as the opposite of the missional-incarnational impulse.

Environments/Fields

The universe in which we live is filled with unseen fields. Though invisible, fields assert a definite influence on objects within their orbit. There are gravitational fields, electromagnetic fields, quantum fields, etc., which form part of the very structure of reality. These unseen influences affect the behavior of atoms, objects, and people. But fields don't just exist in nature and physics; they exist in social systems as well. For example, think about the power of ideas in human affairs—a powerful idea has no substance, but one cannot doubt its influence. Note too the power of good and evil on people and societies. I use this idea to try to communicate that leadership itself creates an invisible field wherein certain behaviors take place. To try to conceptualize leadership as influence, think of a magnet and its effect on iron filings scattered on a sheet of paper. When the filings come into

---

1. A. Roxburgh and F. Romanuk, "Christendom Thinking ," 28.

the orbit of influence of the magnet, they form a certain pattern that we all recognize from our school days. I think leadership does exactly the same thing—it creates a *field*, which in turn influences people in a certain way, just as the magnet "influences" the iron filings

Fitness Landscape

Essentially, a context that tests the fitness of a living system, be it an organism or an organization.

Hebraic

Refer to *Biblical Hebraic*, above. Essentially, the worldview nurtured primarily by the Bible. *Hebraic* in the broader sense can also mean the worldview of the Jewish people as a racial group, deeply influenced as it is by Judaism.

Hellenism

The way it is used in this book is as a contrast to Hebraic thinking. Hellenism is the ideologies that shaped and informed the Greek worldview. Together with Roman ideas it formed the basis of the worldview of the Roman Empire, and as the church moved further away from its Hebraic roots, Hellenism became the predominant worldview of the Christendom church.

Incarnational

The Incarnation refers to the act of God in entering into the created universe and realm of human affairs as the man Jesus of Nazareth. When we talk of *incarnational* in relation to mission it means similarly embodying the culture and life of a target group in order to meaningfully reach that group of people from within their culture. I also use the term to describe the missionary act of *going* to a target people group as opposed to the invitation to come to our cultural group in order to hear the gospel.

Institution and Institutionalism

Institutions are organizations initially set up in order to fill a necessary religious and social function and to provide some sort of structural support for whatever that function needs. In many ways this is the very purpose of structure, as organizations are needed if we seek to act collectively for common cause, for example, the original purpose of denominations. The problem happens when institutions move beyond being mere structural support and become a governing body of sorts. My working definition of institutionalization is that it occurs *when we outsource an essentially grassroots/local function to a centralized structure/organization. Over time the centralized structure tends to become depersonalized and becomes restrictive of deviating behavior and freedom.* In other words, it occurs when in the name of some convenience we get others to do what we must do ourselves. When this happens there is a transfer of responsibility and power/authority to the governing body. In this situation it inevitably becomes a locus of power that uses some of that power to sanction behaviors of its members who are out of keeping with the institution. It becomes a power to itself and begins to assert a kind of restrictive authority on nonconforming behaviors. The problem exaggerates when over time power is entrenched in the institution and it creates a culture of restraint. No one intends this in the first place; it seems to be of our fallen human condition in relation to power. When institutions get to this point, they are extremely hard to change. Seen in this light, all great innovators and thinkers are rebels against institutionalism. We often see portrayals of the institution of the Roman Catholic Church on TV and in movies that highlight how oppressive religious institutionalism can get. And while these are sometimes caricature, make no mistake: there is real historical substance to this portrayal. Most non-Christian people in the West view most churches as repressive institutions, with some justification.

Seen in this light, all great innovators and thinkers are rebels against institutionalism.

Jesus Movements

When I refer to Jesus movements (or substitute this term with "phenomenal Christian or apostolic movements"), I am primarily referring to the two test cases I have adopted, namely those of the early church and the Chinese underground church. But the phrase also refers to those other amazing movements in history where exponential growth and impact occurred, for example Wesley's revival, or Third World Pentecostalism today.

Leadership Matrix

The term for apostolic, prophetic, evangelistic, pastoral, and didactic (teaching) leadership as it is drawn from the *ministry matrix* (see below; also APEPT). Viewed as such, leadership is a *calling within a calling.*

Liminality

Liminality comes from the word *liminal,* which describes a boundary or threshold situation. In the way that it is used in this book, it describes the contexts or condition from which *communitas* can emerge. Situations of liminality can be extreme, where the participant is literally cast out of the normal structures of life, is humbled, disoriented, and subjected to various rites of passage, which together constitute a form of test as to whether the participant will be allowed back into society and to transition to the next level in the prevailing social structure. *Liminality* therefore applies to that situation where people find themselves in an in-between, marginal state in relation to the surrounding society, a place of danger and disorientation

mDNA

I have appended the *m* to the letters *DNA* purely to differentiate it from the biological version—it simply means *missional*DNA. What DNA does for biological systems, mDNA does for ecclesial ones. DNA in biological life

- is found in all living cells,
- codes genetic information for the transmission of inherited traits beyond that of the initiating organism,
- is self-replicating, and
- carries vital information for healthy reproduction.

mDNA therefore does the same for the church as God has designed it. And with this concept/metaphor I hope to explain why the presence of a simple, intrinsic, reproducible, central guiding mechanism is necessary for the reproduction and sustainability of genuine missional movements. As an organism holds together, and each cell understands its function in relation to its DNA, so the church in given contexts finds its reference point in its built-in mDNA.

Memes and Memeplex

Essentially, a meme is to the world of ideas what genes are to the world of biology—they encode ideas in easily reproducible form. In this theory, a memeplex is a complex of memes (ideas) that constitute the inner structure of an ideology or a belief system. And like DNA, it seeks to replicate itself by mutation into evolving forms of ideas by adding, developing, or shedding memes as the situation requires. Sounds strange, doesn't it? Why this idea is so valuable is that the memeplex has the capacity to reproduce itself by embedding itself in the receiver's brain and passing itself on from there to other brains via human communication. We all know the feeling of being captivated by an idea, don't we? We get caught up into its life. In some way that is exactly the way we all got caught up into the gospel and so adopted a biblical worldview.

Ministry Matrix

This term is used to describe the ministry callings of the church in terms of the teaching of Ephesians 4:7ff., namely, that the whole church is comprised of people who are apostolic, prophetic, evangelistic, pastoral, and didactic (teaching). Ephesians 4:7 indicates that "to *each one* is given," and 4:11 says, "It was he who gave *some* to be apostles, *some* to be prophets, *some* to be evangelists, and *some* to be pastors and teachers." Therefore, the term *ministry matrix* applies the APEPT model to the *whole* church and not just its leadership, as per the more common interpretation (cf. *leadership matrix*).

Missiology/Missiological

Missiology is the study of missions. As a discipline, it seeks to identify the primal impulses in the scriptures that compel God's people into engagement with the world. Such impulses involve, for example, the *missio Dei* (the mission of God), the Incarnation, and the kingdom of God. It also describes the authentic church's commitment to social justice, relational righteousness, and evangelism. As such missiology seeks to define the church's purposes in light of God's will for the world. It also seeks to study the methods of achieving these ends, both from scripture and from history. The term *missiological* is simply the adjectival form of these meanings.

Missional

A favorite term I use to describe a certain type or mode of church, leadership, Christianity, etc. For example, a *missional church* is one whose primary commitment is to the missionary calling of the people of God. *Missional leadership* is that form of leadership that emphasizes the primacy of the missionary calling of God's people, etc.

Missional Church

A missional church is a church that defines itself, and organizes its life around, its real purpose as an agent of God's mission to the world. In other words, the church's true and authentic organizing principle is mission. When the church is in mission, it is the true church. The church itself is not only a product of that mission but is obligated and destined to extend it by whatever means possible. The mission of God flows directly through every believer and every community of faith that adheres to Jesus. To obstruct this is to block God's purposes in and through his people.

Missional Ecclesiology

Similar to missiology (see above), the area of study that explores the nature of the Christian movements, and therefore the church, as they are shaped by Jesus and his mission. The attention is chiefly on how the church organizes and expresses itself when mission is the central focus.

Missional-Incarnational

A phrase I have coined to try to describe the impetus that is part of significant Jesus movements in history. In putting the two words together, I hope to link the two practices that in essence form one and the same action. Namely, *missional* . . . the outgoing thrust of the Jesus movements, like the scattering of seeds or of the dispersion of bacteria in a sneeze. It is an essential aspect of Christianity's capacity to spread itself and cross cultural boundaries. It is linked to the theology of the *missio Dei* (the mission of God), where God *sends* his Son and we ourselves become a *sent* people.

The incarnational side of the equation relates to the embedding and deepening of the gospel and church into host cultures. It means that to relate to and influence the host group, it will need to do it from within its cultural forms and expressions. This is linked directly to the Incarnation of God in Jesus. See chapter 5.

Mode

Another favorite word; it simply describes the method, style, manner of that which it refers to. The online Encarta dictionary defines *mode* as "a way, manner, or form, for example, a way of doing something, or the form in which something exists." Thus, the mode of the early church describes its methodology, its stance, its approach to the world, etc.

Movement

In this book I use the term sociologically to describe the organizational structures and ethos of the missional church. I believe that the NT church was itself a movement and not an institution (cf. *institution/institutionalism*, above). I believe that to be genuinely missional, a church must always strive to maintain a movement style and ethos.

Operational Leadership

Essentially, operational leadership is that type suited for organizations that are in relatively stable environments where maintenance and development of current programming constitute the core tasks of leadership. This form of leadership is built on the assumptions of social engineering and is thus built squarely on a mechanistic view of the world. It works, and is appropriate for *some* organizations: those who find themselves in situations of stability. Operational leadership works best when the problems faced can be dealt with by drawing upon a preexisting repertoire and are exploited with more speed, quality, or scale. It is usually a top-down form of leadership, where a solution is devised from above and rolled out through the ranks. If an organization requires downsizing, restructuring, or reducing costs, if sharpened execution is the key to success, then operational leadership *is* probably the best bet.

Strange Attractors

In living systems theory there exists a phenomenon called the "strange attractor." Essentially, strange attractors are that force, analogous to a compass, or an animal's deep instinct, which orients a living system in one particular direction and provides organisms with the impetus to migrate out of their comfort zone.[2] They are found in all living systems, including human organizations. As has been discussed in the chapter on chaos theory, a system that is in equilibrium is inevitably in decline and to become adaptive needs to move toward the edge of chaos to initiate its latent capacity to adapt and therefore survive. As in biological systems, the role of the strange attractor in organizations as living systems is therefore critical to the ability of the organization to survive an adaptive challenge.

2. Pascale, Millemann, and Gioja, *Surfing the Edge of Chaos*, 69.

bibliography

Addison, S. B. "A Basis for the Continuing Ministry of the Apostle in the Church's Mission," D.Min. diss., Fuller Theological Seminary, 1995.

———. "Movement Dynamics, Keys to the Expansion and Renewal of the Church in Mission" (unpublished manuscript, 2003).

Adeney, D. H. *China: The Church's Long March* (Ventura, CA: Regal, 1985).

Arquilla J., and D. Ronfeldt. *Networks and Netwars: The Future of Terror, Crime, and Militancy* (downloadable online resource, available at www.rand .org/publications/MR/MR1382/).

Barker, A., and J. Hayes. *Sub-Merge: Living Deep in a Shallow World* (Springvale, VIC, Aus.: GO Alliance, 2002).

Barrett, C. K. *The Signs of an Apostle* (Carlisle: Paternoster, 1996).

Borden, P. D. *Hit the Bullseye: How Denominations Can Aim the Congregation at the Mission Field* (Nashville: Convergence, 2003).

Bosch, D. *Transforming Mission: Paradigm Shifts in the Theology of Mission* (Maryknoll, NY: Orbis, 1991).

Breen, M., and W. Kallestad. *The Passionate Church: The Art of Life-Changing Discipleship* (Colorado Springs: Nexgen, 2004).

Brewin, K. *The Complex Christ: The Signs of Emergence in the Urban Church* (London: SPCK, 2004).

Cahill, T. *How the Irish Saved Civilization: The Untold Story of Ireland's Heroic Role from the Fall of Rome to the Rise of Medieval Europe* (New York: Anchor, 1995).

Capra, F. *The Hidden Connections: A Science for Sustainable Living* (London: HarperCollins, 2002).

————. *The Turning Point: Science, Society, and the Rising Culture* (London: Flamingo, 1982).

————.*The Web of Life* (New York: Anchor, 1996).

Carnell, Corbin. *Bright Shadow of Reality* (Grand Rapids: Eerdmans, 1974).

Castells, M., *The Rise of the Network Society,* 2nd ed. (Oxford: Blackwell, 2000).

Christensen, C. M. *Seeing What's Next: Using the Theories of Innovation to Predict Industry Change* (Boston: Harvard Business, 2004).

Cole, N. *Cultivating a Life for God: Multiplying Disciples through Life Transformation Groups* (Elgin, IL: Brethren Press, 1999).

————. *"Organic Church: Growing Faith Where Life Happens* (San Francisco: Jossey-Bass, 2005).).

Collins, Jim. *Good to Great: Why Some Companies Make the Leap, and Others Don't* (New York: HarperBusiness, 2001).

Dale, T. and F. *Simply Church* (Manchaca, TX: Karis, 2002).

Daniel-Rops, H. *The Church of Apostles and Martyrs* (New York: Image, 1962).

de Bono, Edward. *New Thinking for a New Millennium* (St. Ives, NSW, Aus.: Viking, 1999), ix.

Easum, B. *Unfreezing Moves: Following Jesus into the Mission Field* (Nashville: Abingdon, 2001).

Friedman, Maurice. *Martin Buber: The Life of Dialogue* (New York: Harper & Row, 1960).

Frost, Michael, and Alan Hirsch. *The Shaping of Things to Come: Innovation and Mission for the 21ˢᵗ-Century Church* (Peabody, MA: Hendrickson, 2003

Garrison, D. *Church Planting Movements: How God Is Redeeming a Lost World* (Midlothian, VA: WIGTake Resources, 2004).

Gehring, R. W., *House Church and Mission: The Importance of Household Structures in Early Christianity* (Peabody, MA: Hendrickson, 2004).

Gerlach, L. P., and V. H. Hine. *People, Power, Change: Movements of Social Transformation* (Indianapolis: Bobbs-Merrill, 1970).

Gibbs, E., and R. K. Bolger. *Emerging Churches: Creating Christian Communities in Postmodern Cultures* (Grand Rapids: Baker Academic, 2006).

Gibbs, E., and I. Coffey. *Church Next: Quantum Changes in Christian Ministry* (Downers Grove, IL: InterVarsity, 2000).

Godin, S. *Survival Is Not Enough: Zooming, Evolution, and the Future of Your Company* (New York: Free Press, 2002).

————. *Unleashing the Ideavirus* (Dobbs Ferry, NY: Do You Zoom, 2000).

Guder, D. *The Incarnation and the Church's Witness* (Harrisburg, PA: Trinity, 1999).

——— (ed.). *Missional Church: A Vision for the Sending of the Church in North America* (Grand Rapids: Eerdmans, 1998).

Hall, D. J., *The End of Christendom and the Future of Christianity* (Harrisburg, PA: Trinity, 1997).

Hamilton, C., and R. Denniss. *Affluenza: When Too Much Is Never Enough* (Crows Nest, NSW, Aus.: Allen & Unwin, 2005).

Hollenwager, Walter J. "From Azusa Street to the Toronto Phenomena: Historical Roots of the Pentecostal Movement, *Concilium 3*, ed. Juergen Moltmann and Karl-Josef Kuschel (1996), 3, quoted in Veli-Matti Karkkainen, "Pentecostal Missiology in Ecumenical Perspective: Contributions, Challenges, Controversies," in *International Review of Mission* 88 (July 1999), 207 (whole article 207–25).

Hunter, George G. III. *To Spread the Power: Church Growth in the Wesleyan Spirit* (Nashville: Abingdon, 1987).

Hurst, David K. *Crisis and Renewal* (Cambridge: Harvard Business School Press, 2002).

Inchausti, Robert. *Subversive Orthodoxy: Rebels, Revolutionaries, and Other Christians in Disguise* (Grand Rapids: Brazos Press, 2005).

Johnson, S. *Emergence: The Connected Lives of Ants, Brains, Cities, and Software* (London: Penguin, 2001).

Kelly, G. *RetroFuture: Rediscovering Our Roots, Recharting Our Routes* (Downers Grove, IL: InterVarsity, 1999).

Kelly, Julie. *Consumerism* (Cambridge: Grove Books, 2003).

Kreider, A. *The Change of Conversion and the Origin of Christendom* (Harrisburg, PA: Trinity, 1999).

Kuhn, T. *The Structure of Scientific Revolutions,* 3rd ed. (Chicago: University of Chicago Press, 1996).

Lambert, T. *China's Christian Missions: The Costly Revival* (London: Monarch, 1999).

———. *The Resurrection of the Chinese Church* (London: Hodder & Stoughton, 1991).

Langmead, R. *The Word Made Flesh: Towards an Incarnational Missiology* (Lanham, MD: University Press of America, 2004).

Lewis, C. S. "Tolkien's Lord of the Rings," in *Essay Collection and Other Short Pieces* (London: HarperCollins, 2000).

Lyall, L. *The Phoenix Rises: The Phenomenal Growth of Eight Chinese Churches* (Singapore: OMF Books, 1992).

McGavran, Donald. *The Bridges of God: A Study in the Strategy of Missions* (London: World Dominion Press, 1955).

McLaren, B., *The Church on the Other Side: Doing Ministry in the Postmodern Matrix* (Grand Rapids: Zondervan, 2000).

McQuarrie, J., *Principles of Christian Theology* (London: SCM, 1966).

Mihata, K. "The Persistence of 'Emergence,'" in R. A. Eve, S. Horsfall, and M. E. Lee (eds.), *Chaos, Complexity, and Sociology: Myths, Models, and Theories* (Thousand Oaks, CA: Sage, 1997).

Miller, V. J. *Consuming Religion: Christian Faith and Practice in a Consumer Culture* (New York: Continuum, 2004).

Murray, S. *Church Planting: Laying Foundations* (Carlisle: Paternoster,1998)

———. *Post-Christendom: Church and Mission in a Strange New World* (Carlisle: Paternoster, 2004) .

Nacpil, E. P. *Jesus' Strategy for Social Transformation* (Nashville: Abingdon, 1998).

Niebuhr, H. R. *Radical Monotheism and Western Culture* (online e-text available from www.religion-online.org/).

Pascale, R. T. *Managing on the Edge: How Successful Companies Use Conflict to Stay Ahead* (London: Viking, 1990).

Pascale, R. T., M. Millemann, L. Gioja. *Surfing the Edge of Chaos: The Laws of Nature and the New Laws of Business* (New York: Three Rivers Press, 2000).

Patzia, A. G. *The Emergence of the Church: Context, Growth, Leadership & Worship* (Downers Grove, IL: InterVarsity, 2001).

Peters, T. *Thriving on Chaos: Handbook for a Management Revolution* (London: Pan, 1987).

Peterson, J. *Church without Walls: Moving beyond Traditional Boundaries* (Colorado Springs: Navpress, 1992).

Peterson, J., and M. Shamy. *The Insider: Bringing the Kingdom of God into Your Everyday World* (Colorado Springs: Navpress, 2003).

Popper, K. *The Open Society and Its Enemies.* Vol. 1, *Plato* (London: Routledge, 1966).

Robinson, M., and Q. Smith. *Invading Secular Space: Strategies for Tomorrow's Church* (Grand Rapids: Kregel, 2003).

Roxburgh, A. J., *The Missionary Congregation, Leadership, & Liminality* (Harrisburg, PA: Trinity, 1997).

Roxburgh, A. J., and F. Romanuk. "Christendom Thinking to Missional Imagination: Leading the Cultivation of Missional Congregations" (unpublished manuscript, 2004).

Rushkoff, D. *Children of Chaos: Surviving the End of the World as We Know It* (London: Flamingo, 1997).

Rutba House (ed.). *Schools for Conversion: 12 Marks of a New Monasticism* (Eugene, OR: Cascade, 2005).

Snyder, H. A. *The Community of the King* (Downers Grove, IL: InterVarsity, 1977).

———. *Decoding the Church: Mapping the DNA of Christ's Body* (Grand Rapids: Baker, 2002).

———. New Wineskins: *Changing the Man-Made Structures of the Church* (London: Marshall, Morgan and Scott, 1978).

Stark, R., *The Rise of Christianity: How the Obscure, Marginal Jesus Movement Became the Dominant Religious Force in the Western World in a Few Centuries* (San Francisco: HarperCollins: 1996).

Stern, J. *Terror in the Name of God: Why Religious Militants Kill* (New York: HarperCollins, 2003).

Taylor, J. V. *The Christlike God* (London: SCM, 1992).

Turner, V. "Passages, Margins, and Poverty: Religious Symbols of *Communitas,*" part 1. *Worship* 46 (1972): 390–412.

———. *The Ritual Process* (Ithaca, NY: Cornell University Press, 1969).

Vaus, W. *Mere Theology, A Guide to the Thought of C. S. Lewis* (Downers Grove, IL: InterVarsity, 2004).

Wallis, A. *The Radical Christian* (Columbia, MO: Cityhill, 1987).

Ward, P. *Liquid Church* (Peabody, MA: Hendrickson, 2002).

Webber, R. E. *The Younger Evangelicals: Facing the Challenges of the New World* (Grand Rapids: Baker, 2002).

Wheatley, M. *Leadership and the New Science: Discovering Order in a Chaotic World* (San Francisco: Berrett-Koehler, 1999).

Winter, R., and S. Hawthorne (eds.). *Perspectives on the World Christian Movement: A Reader* (Pasadena, CA: William Carey Library, 1999).

Yancey, Philip. "Discreet and Dynamic: Why, With No Apparent Resources, Chinese Churches Thrive," *Christianity Today,* July 2004, vol. 48, no. 7, 72.

index

adaptive challenge 16, 20, 77–78, 100, 120, 151, 157, 164, 183–84, 207, 210–11, 214, 222, 229, 232, 247, 256, 259, 266–67, 270, 273–74, 286

adaptive leadership 164, 254–58, 261, 273

APEPT 79, 149, 158–59, 169–72, 174–77, 243, 274, 282, 284

Apostolic Genius 11, 18–22, 24–25, 56, 62–63, 66–67, 71, 73, 76–82, 84–88, 90, 92, 94, 96, 98–100, 102, 104–6, 108, 110, 112–14, 116, 118, 120, 122, 124–25, 128–30, 132, 134, 136–38, 140, 142, 144, 146–47, 150, 152–54, 156, 158, 160, 162, 164–66, 168–70, 172, 174, 176–77, 180, 182–86, 188–94, 196, 198–200, 202–4, 206, 208–12, 214, 216, 218, 220, 222–24, 226, 228, 230, 232, 234, 236, 238, 240–41, 243–44, 256, 263, 274–75

apostolic 20, 22, 25–26, 29, 32, 47, 54, 64, 67, 75, 77–80, 105–6, 113, 116, 118–19, 128–29, 138–39, 149–71, 173–77, 186, 199–200, 202, 206, 214, 224, 243, 253, 258, 260, 262–63, 266, 270–71, 274–76, 282, 284

attractional 34, 37, 39, 62, 64–65, 79, 110, 128–31, 136, 142, 147, 215–16, 275–76, 280

Biblical Hebraic 275, 281

chaos and chaos theory 22, 28–30, 54, 71, 75, 78, 174, 181–82, 184, 191, 229, 231–32, 234, 247–71, 276

China/Chinese 15, 19–20, 22, 26, 75, 77, 81, 85–86, 92, 100, 103, 106, 119, 139, 150, 154, 156, 177, 185–86, 188–89, 192, 195–96, 204–8, 210, 214, 216, 218, 222, 244, 248

Christendom 16–17, 34, 42, 50–52, 57–66, 68–72, 89, 95, 104, 108, 110, 118, 122, 130, 147, 151, 157, 169, 190, 122, 231, 237–38, 248, 252, 254, 256, 261–63, 26–67, 270, 275–76, 278, 280–81, 289–90

Christology 68, 85, 94, 99, 142–43, 154, 277

communitas 12, 25, 79, 81, 105, 217–29, 231, 233–37, 239, 241, 243, 260, 274–75, 277, 283, 291

community 12, 15, 22–23, 25–26, 28–33, 39–42, 44–48, 55, 57, 64, 67–68, 75–76, 78–79, 81–82, 99–102, 104, 107–12, 115, 127, 129, 133, 135–36, 140–41, 144–46, 152, 158, 167–68, 170–71, 174, 176, 180, 182–85, 187, 190–91, 193, 199, 202, 205–6, 208,

213, 217–41, 243–44, 247, 259, 264, 266, 268, 270, 275, 277, 285
complexity 54, 71, 247, 250, 252, 254, 262–64, 266, 269, 271, 278–79, 290
Constantinian 66, 104, 151, 213, 244, 271,
cultural distance 35, 56, 58, 60–62, 278

discipleship 21, 39, 41–42, 45–47, 68, 88, 94, 97, 102–6, 110, 113, 115, 119–22, 124, 136, 146, 159, 161, 170, 208, 216, 228, 269–70
dualism 95–97, 237–240, 279

early Christian movement 19–20, 22, 62, 85, 100, 104, 191, 218, 222
early church 185, 193, 195–96, 204–05, 207–8, 214, 237, 241, 245, 253, 274, 276, 282, 286
ecclesiology 17, 79, 111, 128, 142–43, 171, 198, 271, 285
emergence 67, 71, 162, 177, 182–83, 194, 232–33, 254, 262–63, 266, 269, 276, 279, 287, 289, 290
emerging missional church (EMC) 12, 26, 66–67, 69, 71, 151, 209, 263, 266, 280
evangelistic-attractional 34, 128–29, 131, 147, 280

fields 87–88, 161–62, 200, 266, 280
Forge Mission Training Network 5, 34, 67, 105, 118, 124, 132, 142–43, 152, 166, 240, 249, 261

gospel 21–22, 25–26, 30, 32–33, 35, 37, 50–51, 56–58, 62, 65, 78, 80, 82, 85–86, 94, 98–99, 103, 105–7, 114–16, 120, 128–30, 132–38, 140–43, 147, 151–58, 161, 164, 168, 170, 188, 197, 210–12, 214, 216, 219, 224, 236, 245, 258, 261, 270, 274–75, 278, 281, 284–85

Hebraic 84, 87, 89, 91, 122, 237, 275, 281
Hellenism 281

house church 18–20, 29, 33, 39, 67–69, 80, 119, 150, 189, 194, 199, 204–5, 269–70, 276

incarnational 12, 21, 23, 25, 34, 37, 62, 64, 76, 79–80, 98, 105, 127–29, 131, 133–45, 147, 170, 205, 207, 209, 239–40, 243, 274–77, 280–81, 285, 289
institutionalism 23, 55, 187–88, 190, 195, 203, 261, 281–82, 286

Jesus movement(s) 15, 18, 21–26, 30, 60, 64, 67, 71, 76–77, 79, 82, 84–87, 99, 102, 106, 118, 120, 125, 128, 131, 137–38, 142, 147, 150, 152, 158, 188–90, 195, 218, 222, 224, 241, 244, 248, 254, 274, 276, 282, 285, 291

leadership matrix 171, 282, 284
liminality 151–52, 220–27, 229, 231, 233, 241, 277, 283, 290
living systems 22, 79, 81, 151, 163, 172, 174, 179–80, 182–86, 195, 213, 216, 229–32, 234, 247, 250–51, 253–61, 264–65, 267, 269–70, 273, 276, 278, 281, 286

mDNA 11, 18, 20, 24–25, 33, 45–46, 48, 62, 67, 75–81, 85, 97, 100, 102, 104, 106, 113, 125, 128, 131, 139, 142, 147, 151, 153–56, 158–59, 165, 168, 177, 180, 183, 196, 206, 213, 216, 218, 243–44, 258–60, 274, 277, 283
memes 208–10, 212, 283–84
Methodist(s) 20, 103
ministry matrix 171, 282, 284
missional church 12, 18, 22, 26, 32, 37, 48, 50, 63, 65–67, 69, 71, 76, 81–82, 84, 129, 142, 144, 151–52, 158, 162, 166, 168–69, 174, 185, 190, 200, 209, 218–19, 223, 232, 234, 237, 254, 260, 263, 266, 269, 276, 280, 284–86, 289
missional ecclesiology 17, 79, 111, 128, 142, 285
missional-incarnational 23, 25, 34, 62, 76, 80, 105, 127–29, 131, 133, 135,

137–41, 143–45, 147, 207, 209, 239, 243, 274, 277, 280, 285

operational leadership 254–55, 274, 286

paradigm/paradigmatic 16–17, 24, 26, 53–54, 60, 63, 66, 69, 71, 95, 123, 131, 180, 190, 198, 232, 244, 248, 250–54, 256–57, 264–65, 276
Pentecostal(s) 20, 56, 136, 191, 205, 269–71, 282
potency/potencies 15, 22, 86, 180, 205, 214, 226, 240
pray(er) 21, 34, 47, 68, 86, 96, 105, 145–46, 170, 175, 189, 235, 237, 271

sneeze 130–31, 211, 214, 285
South Melbourne Restoration Community (SMRC) 5, 28–32, 37, 42, 48, 174, 218
strange attractor(s) 164, 234, 286

TEMPT model 47

worship 19, 39, 41–42, 44–47, 58, 68, 70, 88, 90–91, 95–98, 100, 109–10, 136–38, 143, 146, 170, 175, 185, 199, 214–15, 219, 222, 235, 237–40, 250, 269–70, 276

theforgottenways.org

Visit **www.theforgottenways.org** to engage with Alan
Hirsch on the ideas he presents in this book. You will also
find significant resources that will help you implement
some of the book's insights. One such resource is an online
assessment of ministry related to the APEPT model as
articulated by Alan in chapter 5. This is a unique test that
involves something of a 360-degree assessment on each
applicant—an invaluable tool in trying to understand how
God has shaped your ministry and leadership.

Those who are convinced of the Apostolic Genius concept as
articulated in section two of this book and who wish to use
this as a strategic assessment on their own church or agency
can undertake the "missional fitness" test that is available
online. Other resources are also available.